MW00617314

I

The Glory Page

To

Our Lord and Savior Jesus Christ

All honor and glory belongs to Him

Psalm 24:8 Who is this King of glory? The Lord strong and mighty, the Lord mighty in battle. Psalm 29:2 Give unto the Lord the glory due unto his name; worship the Lord in the beauty of holiness. Psalm 104:31 The glory of the Lord shall endure for ever: the Lord shall rejoice in his works. Psalm 145:11 They shall speak of the glory of thy kingdom, and talk of thy power; Philippians 4:20 Now unto God and our Father be glory for ever and ever. Amen. Psalm 24:8 Who is this King of glory? The Lord strong and mighty, the Lord mighty in battle. Psalm 29:2 Give unto the Lord the glory due unto his name; worship the Lord in the beauty of holiness. Psalm 104:31 The glory of the Lord shall endure for ever: the Lord shall rejoice in his works. Psalm 145:11 They shall speak of the glory of thy kingdom, and talk of thy power; Philippians 4:20 Now unto God and our Father be glory for ever and ever. Amen. Psalm 24:8 Who is this King of glory? The Lord strong and mighty, the Lord mighty in battle. Psalm 29:2 Give unto the Lord the glory due unto his name; worship the Lord in the beauty of holiness. Psalm 104:31 The glory of the Lord shall endure for ever: the Lord shall rejoice in his works. Psalm 145:11 They shall speak of the glory of thy kingdom, and talk of thy power; Philippians 4:20 Now unto God and our Father be glory for ever and ever. Amen. Psalm 24:8 Who is this King of glory? The Lord strong and mighty, the Lord mighty in battle. Psalm 29:2 Give unto the Lord the glory due unto his name; worship the Lord in the beauty of holiness. Psalm 104:31 The glory of the Lord shall endure for ever: the Lord shall rejoice in his works. Psalm 145:11 They shall speak of the glory of thy kingdom, and talk of thy power; Philippians 4:20 Now unto God and our Father be glory for ever and ever. Amen. Psalm 24:8 Who is this King of glory? The Lord strong and mighty, the Lord mighty in battle. Psalm 29:2 Give unto the Lord the glory due unto his name; worship the Lord in the beauty of holiness. Psalm 104:31 The glory of the Lord shall endure for ever: the Lord shall

III

I BELIEVE BIGGER BETTER BOLDER BLESSINGS

LEGAL PAGE
ISBN 978-0-9679816-1-1
Copyright © 2022 by Abiding Life Publisher, Ron Warren
Abiding Life Publishing
1730 West 3rd Street
Hobart. IN 46342
email: abidinglifepub@aol.com
Printed in the United States of America.
Ist Printing. Unless otherwise indicated.
All scripture quotations an:
taken from the King James Version,
Permission to use by Merrim Webster INC.
Stephanie Wright Permission Editor
Webster's American Dictionary of the English Language,
1828 Edition.

About Us: Abiding Life Publishers is a non-denominational
publisher of the Good News of Jesus Christ. Dedicated to
providing you with truth and tools for your spiritual
well-being. Our mission is to point you to God through the
knowledge of His Word. With more than 33 years of service
in the Christian marketplace

www.ibelievebigger.com

Table of Content

Table of Content

Table of Contents

Table of Contents

Alphabetical Order

Alphabetical Order

Alphabetical Order

Noah Webster Dictionary
1828 Edition - May Be View in the Back of the Book

ACKNOWLEDGMENTS

This book would not be possible without the influence of the following:

Candee Sweet Warren

Doug Glassford

Doug Koch

Liz Cruz

Diana Rozich

Miguel Conde

Tina Granstrom

Mike & Sheila Erway

Manuel & Lori Corazzari

Thank you for your contribution, Lord Bless you for your services.

First off, let me say, "Welcome" and "Thank You" for purchasing this book. Now, if you will indulge us, let us share with you how it came about. We love the Word of God and have spent many hours devouring its text. Fascinated by the heroes of the Old Testament we discovered that three of our favorites, King David, Daniel and Elijah, used a similar pattern in their approach to seeking God's favor and getting their prayers answered. We do not seek formulas as a means of manipulating God into doing my will, but we noticed the similarities in their actions and approach to seeking God. While implementing what we've learned and experiencing a greater level of intimacy with God and success in our personal walk, we felt inspired to compile this book it so that everyone who will accept this challenge and faithfully follow this plan of action will see their lives changed for the better, and their prayers answered. Our hope is for you to experience **"BIGGER, BETTER, BOLDER BLESSINGS"** in your life too.

Our vision for this book, is that it will answer a question that has troubled the Body of Christ for who knows how long... "Why is it that many believers seem to have such a hard time struggling with their walk with God?" In the Gospel of John 21:14-17, three times Jesus said to Peter, "feed my sheep." That is the preaching and teaching of His Word, and the Word is where we will find our answers for our Christian walk. Through God's Word, He will give you a better way to reach your potential in Christ Jesus. As we did, you will discover what King David, Daniel and Elijah did to get their prayers answered from God.

To make a change in one's life, you need to do something different than what you have done in the past. When a farmer plants a seed. The seed needs water, light and soil to grow. You are the soil, and the Word of God is both water and light. (Psalm 119:20 says, "the entrance of His Word gives light, and Ephesians 5:26, "the washing of the water of the Word.)

Jesus gave us insight into the power of the Word as illustrated in the following scriptures:

Mark 4:14-20
"14. The sower soweth the word.

15. And these are they by the way side, where the word is sown; but when they have heard, Satan cometh immediately, and taketh away the word that was sown in their hearts.

16. And these are they likewise which are sown on stony ground; who, when they have heard the word, immediately receive it with gladness;

17. And have no root in themselves, and so endure but for a time: afterward, when affliction or persecution ariseth for the word's sake, immediately they are offended.

18. And these are they which are sown among thorns; such as hear the word,

19. And the cares of this world, and the deceitfulness of riches, and the lusts of other things entering in, choke the word, and it becometh unfruitful.

20. And these are they which are sown on good ground; such as hear the word, and receive it, and bring forth fruit, some thirtyfold, some sixty, and some an hundred."

Let me break this down as I understand this passage to mean:

I. Sowed the Word - Wayside (did not get imbedded in the soil deeply enough to take root).
A. Satan came immediately - to take the word from their heart.

II. Sown on Stony Ground- heard the word with gladness (rocks indicate seed laying on open ground - unprotected, easily blown away).

Having no root, endure but a time. Then affliction or persecution arise because the words sake. Immediately they are offended.

III. Sown Among Thorns - cares of this world (weeds not removed from soil - undisciplined farmer). Deceitfulness of riches, lust of other things entering in. Choke the Word, unfruitful.

IV. Good Ground - hear the Word and receive it. 30 fold, 60 fold, 100 fold. Also remember, weeds grow faster than good seed. But, given proper care and diligent farming will overtake and starve out the weed.

One of the best ways to be good ground is to meditate upon the Word of God, this is where the light and watering work best. What is meditation you might ask?

MEDITATION
Meditation is giving yourself totally to one subject at a time, to ponder on a word or thought. **Meditation** is your chance to really get to know what a word or thought means to you and how you can apply it to your life. **Meditation** will help build thoughts of confidence in God's Word. Through **meditation** you will lose all your anxiety, fear, worry and doubt. **Meditation** builds knowledge of God's Word which is a higher truth that we can believe in. Gives you a deeper understanding of the Word of God and places it in your heart. Jesus spent much time in **mediation** by prayer communing with His Father. He understood the need for power through **meditation** and disciplined himself to do it daily. See it for yourself in the Gospels, Jesus was always going off to a quiet place to spend time with God. Should we do less? This is how he was able to share this principle to his disciples and all who would listen. Remember what he said would happen if you were too casual with the Word of God:

- Satan comes immediately to steal the Word out of your heart.
- Stony Ground, someone who hears with gladness, but has no root in their heart.
- Affliction or persecution rises up for the words sake, immediately offended.
- Sown among thorns, hear the Word, cares of this world and
- Deceitfulness of Riches- lust of other things enter in and choke the Word, and became unfruitful...

Meditation is like, marinating your favorite meat, giving it time to absorb the juices, herbs and spices into the meat, so that it changes the flavor of the meat. Likewise with the Word of God, if you marinate the Word of God you will change the flavor of your heart and the words that you speak will be sweet to the hearer.

The practice of **meditation** needs to be established in our daily lives - and this is how you do it: Take a scripture and repeat it over and over in your mind until it becomes a part of you.

Allow yourself time to marinate in God's Word to create a new you. Your words by **meditation** or marinating will be sweet to the one who hears your words spoken.

Discover what King David prayed in the Psalms,

Psalms 19:14
*"Let the words of my mouth, and the **meditation** of my heart, be acceptable in thy sight, O Lord, my strength, and my redeemer."*

God spoke this to Joshua who wrote:
Joshua 1:8 *"This book of the law shall not depart out of thy mouth; but thou shalt **meditate** therein day and night, that thou mayest observe to do according to all that is written therein: for then thou shalt make thy way prosperous, and then thou shalt have good success."*

Psalm 49:3
*"My mouth shall speak of wisdom; and the **meditation** of my heart shall be of understanding."*

Psalm 104:39
*"My **meditation** of him shall be sweet: I will be glad in the Lord."*

Psalm 119:99
*"I have more understanding than all my teachers: for thy testimonies are my **meditation**."*
[For more on meditation... read page 42]

The real truth about **'the great deceiver'** the Bible calls Satan is revealed by Jesus in:

John 10:10.
"The thief cometh not, but for to steal, and to kill, and to destroy: I am come that they might have life, and that they might have it more abundantly."

Jesus said in verse 11, **"I am the good Shepherd."** He was telling us that like a good shepherd guards his sheep from

wolves and other dangers, He, as the Living Word made flesh, will guard us in all we allow Him to. Everything in the Kingdom of God and the workings of this Universe created by God works by the Words that God spoke. Because we have been given free will by God we can choose to follow God or be drawn away by the temptations of the enemy. Jesus said so Himself in:

John 14:23-24.
"23 Jesus answered and said unto him, If a man love me, he will keep my words: and my Father will love him, and we will come unto him, and make our abode with him.

24 He that loveth me not keepeth not my sayings: and the word which ye hear is not mine, but the Father's which sent me."

Satan will try to steal God's Word out of your heart. Don't let him and do not be ignorant of his devices of deception.

Stand in faith and let the Word of God fight your battles while you stand and see the salvation of your God.

Even though we have heard this all before and know it to be truth, for many of us the reality of living in Christ, in the Word of God, somehow manages to allude us. Our busy 21st Century life in Western society pushes us onto thorny or stony ground and our faith wavers or fails. This ought not be so. I believe that I have discovered a secret behind the success of three of the most pivotal men of God in the Old Testament and I would like to share it with you not simply as an 'AHA' moment but as another tool or means for you to overcome and grow strong in Christ.

THREE TIMES

So what did King David, Daniel and Elijah have in common? They all cried out loud to the Lord in the same manner, **three times a day**. In reading their stories we see that they got their much needed breakthroughs via diligent and persistent prayer. This is the cornerstone process of this book. It is working in my life and if you apply this process with diligence and persistence you will achieve similar results and manifest the glory of God in your own life.

Note the specific actions recorded of each of these three men in their approach to seeking God in their most urgent times of need.

King David
Psalm 55:16,17
"As for me, I will call upon God; and the Lord shall save me.
Evening, and morning, and at noon, *will I pray, and cry aloud: and he shall hear my voice."*

Daniel
Daniel 6:10,13
*Now when Daniel knew that the writing was signed, he went into his house; and his windows being open in his chamber toward Jerusalem, he kneeled upon his knees **three times a***

day, and prayed, and gave thanks before his God, as he did aforetime. 13.Then answered they and said before the king, "That Daniel, which is of the children of the captivity of Judah, regardeth not thee, O king, nor the decree that thou hast signed, **but maketh his petition three times a day.**"

Elijah
1 Kings 17:20, 21
*And he cried unto the Lord, and said, "O Lord my God, hast thou also brought evil upon the widow with whom I sojourn, by slaying her son?" **And he stretched himself upon the child three times, and cried unto the Lord,** and said, "O Lord my God, I pray thee, let this child's soul come into him again."*

There is something about the number three and what it represents to mankind, something we need to understand and tap into. Let us continue to examine the power of three through its frequent use in the Word of God:

Joshua 1:11
*Pass through the host, and command the people, saying, "Prepare you victuals; for within **three days** ye shall pass over this Jordan, to go in to possess the land, which the Lord your God giveth you to possess it."*

Ecclesiastes 4:12
"And if one prevail against him, two shall withstand him; and a threefold cord is not quickly broken."

Jonah 1:17
*So Jonah arose, and went unto Nineveh, according to the word of the Lord. Now Nineveh was an exceeding great city of three days' journey. Jonah 3:3 Now the Lord had prepared a great fish to swallow up Jonah. And Jonah was in the belly of the fish **three days and three nights**.*

Matthew 15:32
*Three times, Jesus said to Peter, "**feed my sheep**." Then Jesus called his disciples unto him, and said, "I have compassion on the multitude, because they continue with me now three days, and have nothing to eat: and I will not send them away fasting, lest they faint in the way."*

Matthew 27:63
*Saying, "Sir, we remember that that deceiver said, while he was yet alive, 'after **three days** I will rise again'."*

John 2:19
*Jesus answered and said unto them, "Destroy this temple, and in **three days** I will raise it up."*

Mark 15:25
And it was the third hour, and they crucified him.

John 21:14
This is now the third time that Jesus shewed himself to his disciples, after that he was risen from the dead. There were three crosses at Calvary.

2 Corinthians 11:25
*Paul said, "**Three times** I was beaten with rods; once I was stoned; three times I was shipwrecked; a night and a day I have been in the deep;"*

2 Corinthians 12:8
*"Concerning this thing I pleaded with the Lord **three times** that it might depart from me."*

The significance of the power of three is confirmed in the life of Jesus. Before He started His earthly ministry He was tested and tempted by Satan **three times and three times** He overcame Satan by saying "It is written" and quoting the written Word of God. (Mark 4:4, 7, 10)

Most importantly we serve a triune God - Father, Son, and Holy Ghost:

1 John 5:7-8
"For there are three that bear record in heaven, the Father, the Word, and the Holy Ghost: and these three are one. And there are three that bear witness in earth, the Spirit, and the water, and the blood: and these three agree in one."

We are created in God's image and likeness, like God we are a triune being:

- Spirit - where God resides
- Soul - our mind and intellect
- Body - our physical senses

This brings us to a word, a concept that makes many folks, even Christians uncomfortable:

SIN

Sin literally means, "to miss the mark". This implies that if you err and fall short you have the opportunity to try again. Ignorance of sin and how to deal with it causes many to misfire or quit trying. God knew that mankind could not overcome sin and the sin nature on our own. This is why He sent Jesus to offer us His grace. God extended the olive branch of peace first and He continues to extend it through His Word and through we who are in Christ to the lost and dying world that surrounds us. We overcome by the Blood of the Lamb and the word of our testimony (Revelation 12:11).

If you are having trouble with sin (any sin) in your life... First, one must repent (turn away from) sin and ask God to forgive you. Secondly, you must fill yourself the Word of God so you can overcome and stay free.

Psalm 119:11
"Thy word have I hid in mine heart, that I might not sin against thee."

Your troubles are because you need more Word sown in your heart... and again we are told in

Psalm 119:130
" The entrance of thy words giveth light; it giveth understanding unto the simple."

or 'the receiving of the Word of God opens our eyes dispelling the darkness of ignorance giving us insight and understanding into all the affairs of life'.

So take the **90 Day Challenge**. Sow more seed into the garden of your heart. Gain understanding as you acknowledge Him in all your ways and He shall direct your paths

We're told to 'seek first' His Kingdom to gain right standing with Him, and when we do all of the things that pertain to life and godliness will be made available to us as we need them.

Matthew 6:33
"But seek ye first the kingdom of God, and his righteousness; and all these things shall be added unto you."

Like bookends, the preceding scripture and the one that follows encapsulate the 'Good News' of the Gospel and the fullness of God's love and provision for us who will dare to believe. Everything in between points to or reiterates the bounty of God's grace towards us... while we were yet sinners, He loved us.

3 John 2
*"Beloved, I wish above all things that thou mayest prosper and be in health, **even as thy soul prospereth.**"*

Our spirits prosper by feeding upon the Word of God. We all need more **nutrition in our spirits**.

Even if we have failed to realize it before now, we hunger and thirst for more seed - a deeper relationship with God and for more faith.

It is our belief that, as you read, faithfully applying the principles of this challenge, while feeding upon the Word of God in these pages, **three times a day** as did King David, Daniel, and Elijah, that you will rise to a greater level of understanding of these critical topics as presented within these scripture verses making you a **Bigger**, **Better**, **Bolder** follower of Jesus.

- An overcomer, a bright light, and a strong Christian.

- It is all about His written Word.

- It is His Word that will change us completely **from the inside out.**

- His Word will not return void . . . ever.

- So guard your heart and allow His Word to grow in you.

- And when your heart gets full . . . out of the abundance of your heart, your mouth will speak His Word.

- It will flow out and to creation around you it will sound like God Himself spoke.

When you are reading these verses it will be helpful to have your bible handy so you could read other verses around the scriptures in the book to gain better understanding.

- Read out loud.
- Meditate on his word.
- The box is for you to mark your favorite scripture.☐
- Guard your heart.
- Read three times a day.
- 90 Day challenge.
- Take the time to do it.

DRAW NEAR
INFORMATION ENCOURAGEMENT IN THE WHITE LETTERING SIGNS

WORDS IN BLUE ARE BONUS KEYWORDS
FOR ADDITIONAL SCRIPTURES ON OUR WEBSITE

✱ ASTRAL ARE WORDS FROM THE NOAH WEBSTER DICTIONARY

WORDS IN BLUE ARE
BONUS KEYWORDS
FOR ADDITIONAL
SCRIPTURES ON OUR
WEBSITE

INFORMATION
ENCOURAGEMENT
IN THE WHITE
LETTERING SIGNS

It only takes . . .

IT ONLY TAKES a spark to start a fire.

IT ONLY TAKES a raindrop to start a shower.

IT ONLY TAKES a seed to have a harvest.

IT ONLY TAKES a step to start your journey.

IT ONLY TAKES a small stream in Minnesota to make a large river in New Orleans, the mighty Mississippi River.

IT ONLY TAKES a DECISION OF action to live a dream and what will it take for you to do what God has for you?

"MORE Seed, More Faith"
the Word of God.

VISIT OUR WEB SITE
www.ibelievebigger.com

Isaiah 55:11, So shall my word be that goeth forth out of my mouth: it shall not return unto me void, but it shall accomplish that which I **please**, and it shall prosper in the thing whereto I sent it. □

Proverbs 16:7, When a man's ways **please** the Lord, he maketh even his enemies to be at peace with him. □

Romans 8:8, So then they that are in the flesh cannot **please** God. □

Romans 15:1, We then that are strong ought to bear the infirmities of the weak, and not to **please** ourselves. □

1 Corinthians 7: 32 - 33, But I would have you without carefulness. He that is unmarried careth for the things that belong to the Lord, how he may **please** the Lord: 33 But he that is married careth for the things that are of the world, how he may **please** his wife. □

Colossians 1:10, That ye might walk worthy of the Lord unto all **pleasing**, being fruitful in every good work, and increasing in the knowledge of God; □

1 Thessalonians 4:1, Furthermore then we beseech you, brethren, and exhort you by the Lord Jesus, that as ye have received of us how ye ought to walk and to **please** God, so ye would abound more and more. □

Hebrews 11:6, But without faith it is impossible to **please** him: for he that cometh to God must believe that he is, and that he is a rewarder of them that diligently seek him. □

1 John 3:22, And whatsoever we ask, we receive of him, because we keep his commandments, and do those things that are **pleasing** in his sight. □

LEARN THE VALUE OF GOD'S WORD

In God We Trust

1

Daniel 6:27, He delivereth and rescueth, and he worketh signs and wonders in heaven and in earth, who hath delivered Daniel from the **power** of the lions. ☐

Matthew 6:13, And lead us not into temptation, but deliver us from evil: For thine is the kingdom, and the **power**, and the glory, forever. Amen. ☐

Matthew 9:6, But that ye may know that the Son of man hath **power** on earth to forgive sins, Arise, take up thy bed, and go unto thine house. ☐

Matthew 28:18, And Jesus came and spake unto them, saying, All **power** is given unto me in heaven and in earth. ☐

Mark 3:15, And to have **power** to heal sicknesses, and to cast out devils. ☐

Luke 10:19, Behold, I give unto you **power** to tread on serpents and scorpions, and over all the **power** of the enemy: and nothing shall by any means hurt you. ☐

Luke 12:5, But I will forewarn you whom ye shall fear: Fear him, which after he hath killed hath **power** to cast into hell; yea, I say unto you, Fear him. ☐

Luke 21:27, And then shall they see the Son of man coming in a cloud with **power** and great glory. ☐

Luke 22:69, Hereafter shall the Son of man sit on the right hand of the **power** of God. ☐

Acts 6:8, And Stephen, full of faith and **power**, did great wonders and miracles among the people. ☐

Romans 13:1, Let every soul be subject unto the higher **powers**. For there is no **power** but of God: the **powers** that be are ordained of God. ☐

Romans 13:2, Whosoever therefore resisteth the **power**, resisteth the ordinance of God: and they that resist shall receive to themselves damnation. ☐

In God We Trust

I BELIEVE
BIGGER
BETTER
BOLDER
BLESSINGS

SEASON *
SEASONS

1 DAY
EVENING
90 DAY CHALLENGE

Deuteronomy 28:12, The LORD shall open unto thee his good treasure, the heaven to give the rain unto thy land in his **season**, and to bless all the work of thine hand: and thou shalt lend unto many nations, and thou shalt not borrow. ☐

Psalms 1:3, And he shall be like a tree planted by the rivers of water, that bringeth forth his fruit in his **season**; his leaf also shall not wither; and whatsoever he doeth shall prosper. ☐

Psalms 16:7, I will bless the LORD, who hath given me counsel: my reins also instruct me in the night **seasons**. ☐

Psalms 104:19, He appointed the moon for **seasons**: the sun knoweth his going down. ☐

Psalms 104:27, These wait all upon thee; that thou mayest give them their meat in due **season**. ☐

Proverbs 15:23, A man hath joy by the answer of his mouth: and a word spoken in due **season**, how good is it! ☐

Ecclesiastes 3:1, To every thing there is a **season**, and a time to every purpose under the heaven: ☐

Isaiah 50:4, The Lord GOD hath given me the tongue of the learned, that I should know how to speak a word in **season** to him that is weary: he wakeneth morning by morning, he wakeneth mine ear to hear as the learned. ☐

Matthew 24:45, Who then is a faithful and wise servant, whom his lord hath made ruler over his household, to give them meat in due **season**? ☐

Mark 9:50, Salt is good: but if the salt have lost his saltness, wherewith will ye **season** it? Have salt in yourselves, and have peace one with another. ☐

Galatians 6:9, And let us not be weary in well doing: for in due **season** we shall reap, if we faint not. ☐

In God We Trust

Psalms 119:59, I thought on my ways, and turned my feet unto thy **testimonies**.☐

Psalms 119:79, Let those that fear thee turn unto me, and those that have known thy **testimonie**s. ☐

Psalms 119:95, The wicked have waited for me to destroy me: but I will consider thy **testimonies**.☐

Psalms 119:99, I have more understanding than all my teachers: for thy **testimonies** are my meditation. ☐

Psalms 119:111, Thy **testimonies** have I taken as an heritage for ever: for they are the rejoicing of my heart. ☐

Psalms 119:119, Thou puttest away all the wicked of the earth like dross: therefore I love thy **testimonies**.☐

Psalms 119:125, I am thy servant; give me understanding, that I may know thy **testimonies**. ☐

Psalms 119:129, Thy **testimonies** are wonderful: therefore doth my soul keep them.☐

Psalms 119:138, Thy **testimonies** that thou hast commanded are righteous and very faithful. ☐

Psalms 119:144, The righteousness of thy **testimonies** is everlasting: give me understanding, and I shall live. ☐

Psalms 119:146, I cried unto thee; save me, and I shall keep thy **testimonies**. ☐

Psalms 119:152, Concerning thy **testimonies**, I have known of old that thou hast founded them forever. ☐

In God We Trust

Psalms 119:114, Thou art my hiding place and my shield: I **hope** in thy word. ☐

Psalms 119:116, Uphold me according unto thy word, that I may live: and let me not be ashamed of my **hope.** ☐

Psalms 130:5, I wait for the LORD, my soul doth wait, and in his word do I **hope.** ☐

Psalms 130:7, Let Israel **hope** in the LORD: for with the LORD there is mercy, and with him is plenteous redemption. ☐

Psalms 131:3, Let Israel **hope** in the LORD from henceforth and forever. ☐

Psalms 146:5, Happy is he that hath the God of Jacob for his help, whose **hope** is in the LORD his God. ☐

Psalms 147:11, The LORD taketh pleasure in them that fear him, in those that **hope** in his mercy. ☐

Proverbs 10:28, The **Hope** of the righteous shall be gladness: but the expectation of the wicked shall perish. ☐

Proverbs 11:7, When a wicked man dieth, his expectation shall perish: and the **hope** of unjust men perisheth. ☐

Proverbs 13:12, **Hope** deferred maketh the heart sick: but when the desire cometh, it is a tree of life. ☐

Proverbs 14:32, The wicked is driven away in his wickedness: but the righteous hath **hope** in his death. ☐

Proverbs 19:18, Chasten thy son while there is **hope**, and let not thy soul spare for his crying. ☐

Proverbs 26:12, Seest thou a man wise in his own conceit? there is more **hope** of a fool than of him. ☐

Psalms 33:5, He loveth **righteousness** and judgment: the earth is full of the goodness of the LORD. ☐

Psalms 35:28, And my tongue shall speak of thy **righteousness** and of thy praise all the day long. ☐

Psalms 36:6, Thy **righteousness** is like the great mountains; thy judgments are a great deep: O LORD, thou preservest man and beast. ☐

Psalms 36:10, O continue thy lovingkindness unto them that know thee; and thy **righteousness** to the upright in heart. ☐

Psalms 37:6, And he shall bring forth thy **righteousness** as the light, and thy judgment as the noonday. ☐

Psalms 40:9. I have preached **righteousness** in the great congregation: lo, I have not refrained my lips, O LORD, thou knowest. ☐

Psalms 40:10, I have not hid thy **righteousness** within my heart; I have declared thy faithfulness and thy salvation: I have not concealed thy lovingkindness and thy truth from the great congregation. ☐

Psalms 45:4, And in thy majesty ride prosperously because of truth and meekness and **righteousness**; and thy right hand shall teach thee terrible things. ☐

Psalms 45:7, Thou lovest **righteousness**, and hatest wickedness: therefore God, thy God, hath anointed thee with the oil of gladness above thy fellows. ☐

Psalms 48:10, According to thy name, O God, so is thy praise unto the ends of the earth: thy right hand is full of **righteousness**. ☐

Psalms 50:6, And the heavens shall declare his **righteousness**: for God is judge himself. Selah. ☐

Psalms 52:3, Thou lovest evil more than good; and lying rather than to speak **righteousness**. Selah. ☐

In God We Trust

Psalms 3:16, A little that a righteous man hath is **better** than the riches of many wicked.☐

Psalms 63:3, Because thy lovingkindness is **better** than life, my lips shall praise thee.☐

Psalms 84:10, For a day in thy courts is **better** than a thousand. I had rather be a doorkeeper in the house of my God, than to dwell in the tents of wickedness.☐

Psalms 118:8, It is **better** to trust in the LORD than to put confidence in man.☐

Psalms 118:9, It is **better** to trust in the LORD than to put confidence in princes.☐

Psalms 119:72, The law of thy mouth is **better** unto me than thousands of gold and silver. ☐

Proverbs 3:14, For the merchandise of it is **better** than the merchandise of silver, and the gain thereof than fine gold.☐

Proverbs 8:11, For wisdom is **better** than rubies; and all the things that may be desired are not to be compared to it.☐

Proverbs 8:19, My fruit is **better** than gold, yea, than fine gold; and my revenue than choice silver. ☐

Proverbs 12:9, He that is despised, and hath a servant, is **better** than he that honoureth himself, and lacketh bread. ☐

Proverbs 15:16, **Better** is little with the fear of the LORD than great treasure and trouble therewith. ☐

In God We Trust

7

Psalms 18:43, Thou hast delivered me from the strivings of the people; and thou hast made me the head of the heathen: a people whom I have not known shall **serve** me. ☐

Psalms 22:30, A seed shall **serve** him; it shall be accounted to the Lord for a generation. ☐

Psalms 101:6, Mine eyes shall be upon the faithful of the land, that they may dwell with me: he that walketh in a perfect way, he shall **serve** me. ☐

John 12:26, If any man **serve** me, let him follow me; and where I am, there shall also my servant be: if any man **serve** me, him will my Father honour. ☐

Romans 1:9, For God is my witness, whom I **serve** with my spirit in the gospel of his Son, that without ceasing I make mention of you always in my prayers. ☐

Romans 6:6, Knowing this, that our old man is crucified with him, that the body of sin might be destroyed, that henceforth we should not **serve** sin. ☐

Romans 7:6, But now we are delivered from the law, that being dead wherein we were held; that we should **serve** in newness of spirit, and not in the oldness of the letter. ☐

Galatians 5:13, For, brethren, ye have been called unto liberty; only use not liberty for an occasion to the flesh, but by love **serve** one another. ☐

Hebrews 9:14, How much more shall the blood of Christ, who through the eternal Spirit offered himself without spot to God, purge your conscience from dead works to **serve** the living God? ☐

Hebrews 12:28, Wherefore we receiving a kingdom which cannot be moved, let us have grace, whereby we may **serve** God acceptably with reverence and godly fear. ☐

In God We Trust

1 Samuel 23:21, And Saul said, Blessed be ye of the LORD; for ye have **compassion** on me. ☐

2 Kings 13:23, And the LORD was gracious unto them, and had **compassion** on them, and had respect unto them, because of his covenant with Abraham, Isaac, and Jacob, and would not destroy them, neither cast he them from his presence as yet. ☐

Psalms 78:38, But he, being full of **compassion**, forgave their iniquity, and destroyed them not: yea, many a time turned he his anger away, and did not stir up all his wrath. ☐

Psalms 86:15, But thou, O Lord, art a God full of **compassion**, and gracious, longsuffering, and plenteous in mercy and truth. ☐

Psalms 111:4, He hath made his wonderful works to be remembered: the LORD is gracious and full of **compassion**. ☐

Psalms 112:4, Unto the upright there ariseth light in the darkness: he is gracious, and full of **compassion**, and righteous. ☐

Psalms 145:8, The LORD is gracious, and full of **compassion**; slow to anger, and of great mercy. ☐

Lamentations 3:22, It is of the LORD'S mercies that we are not consumed, because his **compassions** fail not. ☐

Micah 7:19, He will turn again, he will have **compassion** upon us; he will subdue our iniquities; and thou wilt cast all their sins into the depths of the sea. ☐

Matthew 9:36, But when he saw the multitudes, he was moved with **compassion** on them, because they fainted, and were scattered abroad, as sheep having no shepherd. ☐

Matthew 18:27, Then the lord of that servant was moved with **compassion**, and loosed him, and forgave him the debt. ☐

In God We Trust

FORGIVEN
FORGIVE *
FORGIVING

DAY
MORNING
90 DAY CHALLENGE

Mark 2:9, Whether is it easier to say to the sick of the palsy, Thy sins be **forgiven** thee; or to say, Arise, and take up thy bed, and walk? ☐

Mark 3:28, Verily I say unto you, All sins shall be **forgiven** unto the sons of men, and blasphemies wherewith soever they shall blaspheme. ☐

Mark 4:12, That seeing they may see, and not perceive; and hearing they may hear, and not understand; lest at any time they should be converted, and their sins should be **forgiven** them. ☐

Luke 5:20, And when he saw their faith, he said unto him, Man, thy sins are **forgiven** thee. ☐

Luke 5:23, Whether is easier, to say, Thy sins be **forgiven** thee; or to say, Rise up and walk? ☐

Luke 6:37, Judge not, and ye shall not be judged: condemn not, and ye shall not be condemned: **forgive**, and ye shall be **forgiven**. ☐

Luke 7:47, Wherefore I say unto thee, Her sins, which are many, are **forgiven**; for she loved much: but to whom little is **forgiven**, the same loveth little. ☐

Luke 7:48, And he said unto her, Thy sins are **forgiven**. ☐

Luke 12:10, And whosoever shall speak a word against the Son of man, it shall be **forgiven** him: but unto him that blasphemeth against the Holy Ghost it shall not be **forgiven**. ☐

Acts 8:22, Repent therefore of this thy wickedness, and pray God, if perhaps the thought of thine heart may be **forgiven** thee. ☐

Romans 4:7, Saying, Blessed are they whose iniquities are **forgiven**, and whose sins are covered. ☐

Ephesians 4:32, And be ye kind one to another, tenderhearted, **forgiving** one another, even as God for Christ's sake hath **forgiven** you. ☐

Psalms 31:3, For thou art my **rock** and my fortress; therefore for thy name's sake lead me, and guide me.☐

Psalms 40:2, He brought me up also out of a horrible pit, out of the miry clay, and set my feet upon a **rock**, and established my goings.☐

Psalms 42:9, I will say unto God my **rock**, Why hast thou forgotten me? why go I mourning because of the oppression of the enemy?☐

Psalms 61:2, From the end of the earth will I cry unto thee, when my heart is overwhelmed: lead me to the **rock** that is higher than I.☐

Psalms 62:2, He only is my **rock** and my salvation; he is my defence; I shall not be greatly moved. ☐

Psalms 62:6, He only is my **rock** and my salvation: he is my defence; I shall not be moved.☐

Psalms 62:7, In God is my salvation and my glory: the **rock** of my strength, and my refuge, is in God. ☐

Psalms 71:3, Be thou my strong habitation, whereunto I may continually resort: thou hast given commandment to save me; for thou art my **rock** and my fortress. ☐

Psalms 78:16, He brought streams also out of the **rock**, and caused waters to run down like rivers.☐

Psalms 78:20, Behold, he smote the **rock**, that the waters gushed out, and the streams overflowed; can he give bread also? can he provide flesh for his people? ☐

Psalms 78:35, And they remembered that God was their **rock**, and the high God their redeemer. ☐

Psalms 81:16, He should have fed them also with the finest of the wheat: and with honey out of the **rock** should I have satisfied thee. ☐

In God We Trust

11

Proverbs 3:3, Let not **mercy** and truth forsake thee: bind them about thy neck; write them upon the table of thine heart. ☐

Proverbs 14:21, He that despiseth his neighbour sinneth: but he that hath **mercy** on the poor, happy is he. ☐

Proverbs 14:22, Do they not err that devise evil? but **mercy** and truth shall be to them that devise good. ☐

Proverbs 14:31, He that oppresseth the poor reproacheth his Maker: but he that honoureth him hath **mercy** on the poor. ☐

Proverbs 16:6, By **mercy** and truth iniquity is purged: and by the fear of the LORD men depart from evil. ☐

Proverbs 20:28, **Mercy** and truth preserve the king: and his throne is upholden by **mercy**. ☐

Proverbs 21:21, He that followeth after righteousness and **mercy** findeth life, righteousness, and honour. ☐

Proverbs 28:13, He that covereth his sins shall not prosper: but whoso confesseth and forsaketh them shall have **mercy**. ☐

1 Timothy 1:13, Who was before a blasphemer, and a persecutor, and injurious: but I obtained **mercy**, because I did it ignorantly in unbelief. ☐

1 Timothy 1:16, Howbeit for this cause I obtained **mercy**, that in me first Jesus Christ might shew forth all longsuffering, for a pattern to them which should hereafter believe on him to life everlasting. ☐

2 Timothy 1:2, To Timothy, my dearly beloved son: Grace, **mercy**, and peace, from God the Father and Christ Jesus our Lord. ☐

Titus 1:4, To Titus, mine own son after the common faith: Grace, **mercy**, and peace, from God the Father and the Lord Jesus Christ our Saviour. ☐

Matthew 26:10, When Jesus understood it, he said unto them, Why trouble ye the woman? for she hath wrought a **good work** upon me. □

Acts 9:36, Now there was at Joppa a certain disciple named Tabitha, which by interpretation is called Dorcas: this woman was full of **good works** and almsdeeds which she did. □

1 Timothy 2:21, If a man therefore purge himself from these, he shall be a vessel unto honour, sanctified, and meet for the master's use, and prepared unto every **good work**. □

1 Timothy 3:1, This is a true saying, If a man desire the office of a bishop, he desireth a **good work**. □

1 Timothy 5:10, Well reported of for **good works**; if she have brought up children, if she have lodged strangers, if she have washed the saints' feet, if she have relieved the afflicted, if she have diligently followed every **good work**. □

2 Timothy 3:17, That the man of God may be perfect, throughly furnished unto all **good works**. □

Titus 2:7, In all things shewing thyself a pattern of **good works**: in doctrine shewing uncorruptness, gravity, sincerity. □

Titus 2:14, Who gave himself for us, that he might redeem us from all iniquity, and purify unto himself a peculiar people, zealous of **good works**. □

Titus 3:1, Put them in mind to be subject to principalities and powers, to obey magistrates, to be ready to every **good work**. □

Hebrews 13:21, Make you perfect in every **good work** to do his will, working in you that which is wellpleasing in his sight, through Jesus Christ; to whom be glory for ever and ever. Amen. □

1 Peter 2:12, Having your conversation honest among the Gentiles: that, whereas they speak against you as evildoers, they may by your **good works**, which they shall behold, glorify God in the day of visitation. □

In God We Trust

Job 38:7, When the morning stars sang together, and all the sons of God shouted for **joy**? □

Psalms 5:11, But let all those that put their trust in thee rejoice: let them ever shout for **joy**, because thou defendest them: let them also that love thy name be joyful in thee. □

Psalms 16:11, Thou wilt shew me the path of life: in thy presence is fulness of **joy**; at thy right hand there are pleasures for evermore. □

Psalms 30:5, For his anger endureth but a moment; in his favour is life: weeping may endure for a night, but **joy** cometh in the morning. □

Psalms 32:11, Be glad in the LORD, and rejoice, ye righteous: and shout for **joy**, all ye that are upright in heart. □

Psalms 35:27, Let them shout for **joy**, and be glad, that favour my righteous cause: yea, let them say continually, Let the LORD be magnified, which hath pleasure in the prosperity of his servant. □

Psalms 43:4, Then will I go unto the altar of God, unto God my exceeding **joy**: yea, upon the harp will I praise thee, O God my God. □

Psalms 48:2, Beautiful for situation, the **joy** of the whole earth, is mount Zion, on the sides of the north, the city of the great King. □

Psalms 51:8, Make me to hear **joy** and gladness; that the bones which thou hast broken may rejoice. □

Psalms 51:12, Restore unto me the **joy** of thy salvation; and uphold me with thy free spirit. □

Psalms 126:5, They that sow in tears shall reap in **joy**. □

Psalms 132:9, Let thy priests be clothed with righteousness; and let thy saints shout for **joy**. □

Psalms 105:43, And he brought forth his people with **joy**, and his chosen with gladness. □

TAKE TIME TO MEDITATE ON GOD'S WORD

In God We Trust

14

Luke 18:5, Yet because this widow troubleth me, **I will** avenge her, lest by her continual coming she weary me. ☐

Luke 21:15, For **I will** give you a mouth and wisdom, which all your adversaries shall not be able to gainsay nor resist. ☐

John 2:19, Jesus answered and said unto them, Destroy this temple, and in three days **I will** raise it up. ☐

John 6:37, All that the Father giveth me shall come to me; and him that cometh to me **I will** in no wise cast out. ☐

John 6:40, And this is the will of him that sent me, that every one which seeth the Son, and believeth on him, may have everlasting life: and **I will** raise him up at the last day. ☐

John 6:44, No man can come to me, except the Father which hath sent me draw him: and **I will** raise him up at the last day. ☐

John 6:51, I am the living bread which came down from heaven: if any man eat of this bread, he shall live forever: and the bread that **I will** give is my flesh, which **I will** give for the life of the world. ☐

John 6:54, Whoso eateth my flesh, and drinketh my blood, hath eternal life; and **I will** raise him up at the last day. ☐

John 14:3, And if I go and prepare a place for you, **I will** come again, and receive you unto myself; that where I am, there ye may be also. ☐

John 14:14, If ye shall ask any thing in my name, **I will** do it. ☐

John 14:16, And **I will** pray the Father, and he shall give you another Comforter, that he may abide with you forever. ☐

John 14:18, I will not leave you comfortless: **I will** come to you. ☐

John 14:21, He that hath my commandments, and keepeth them, he it is that loveth me: and he that loveth me shall be loved of my Father, and **I will** love him, and will manifest myself to him. ☐

In God We Trust

15

FOOL *
FOOLISH *
FOOLISHNESS *

6 DAY
MORNING
90 DAY CHALLENGE

I BELIEVE **BIGGER** BETTER **BOLDER BLESSINGS**

Proverbs 26:1, As snow in summer, and as rain in harvest, so honour is not seemly for a **fool**. ☐

Proverbs 26:4, Answer not a **fool** according to his folly, lest thou also be like unto him. ☐

Proverbs 26:5, Answer a **fool** according to his folly, lest he be wise in his own conceit. ☐

Proverbs 26:6, He that sendeth a message by the hand of a **fool** cutteth off the feet, and drinketh damage. ☐

Proverbs 26:10, The great God that formed all things both rewardeth the **fool**, and rewardeth transgressors. ☐

Proverbs 26:11, As a dog returneth to his vomit, so a **fool** returneth to his folly. ☐

Proverbs 26:12, Seest thou a man wise in his own conceit? there is more hope of a **fool** than of him. ☐

Proverbs 28:26, He that trusteth in his own heart is a **fool**: but whoso walketh wisely, he shall be delivered. ☐

Proverbs 29:9, If a wise man contendeth with a **foolish** man, whether he rage or laugh, there is no rest. ☐

Proverbs 29:11, A **fool** uttereth all his mind: but a wise man keepeth it in till afterwards. ☐

Proverbs 29:20, Seest thou a man that is hasty in his words? there is more hope of a **fool** than of him. ☐

Ecclesiastes 7:17, Be not over much wicked, neither be thou **foolish**: why shouldest thou die before thy time? ☐

Ecclesiastes 7:25, I applied mine heart to know, and to search, and to seek out wisdom, and the reason of things, and to know the wickedness of folly, even of **foolishness** and madness. ☐

In God We Trust

John 15:5, I am the vine, ye are the branches: He that abideth in me, and I **in him**, the same bringeth forth much fruit: for without me ye can do nothing.☐

Acts 10:43, To him give all the prophets witness, that through his name whosoever believeth **in him** shall receive remission of sins. ☐

Acts 20:10, And Paul went down, and fell on him, and embracing him said, Trouble not yourselves; for his life is **in him**.☐

Romans 10:14, How then shall they call on him in whom they have not believed? and how shall they believe **in him** of whom they have not heard? and how shall they hear without a preacher? ☐

2 Corinthians 1:20, For all the promises of God **in him** are yea, and **in him** Amen, unto the glory of God by us.☐

2 Corinthians 5:21, For he hath made him to be sin for us, who knew no sin; that we might be made the righteousness of God **in him**.☐

2 Corinthians 13:4, For though he was crucified through weakness, yet he liveth by the power of God. For we also are weak **in him**, but we shall live with him by the power of God toward you. ☐

Ephesians 1:4, According as he hath chosen us **in him** before the foundation of the world, that we should be holy and without blame before him in love. ☐

Ephesians 1:10, That in the dispensation of the fulness of times he might gather together in one all things in Christ, both which are in heaven, and which are on earth; even **in him**.☐

Philippians 3:9, And be found **in him**, not having mine own righteousness, which is of the law, but that which is through the faith of Christ, the righteousness which is of God by faith. ☐

LEARN TO FORGIVE OTHERS ALWAYS

Colossians 1:19, For it pleased the Father that **in him** should all fulness dwell. ☐

In God We Trust

Genesis 3:8, And they heard the **voice of the LORD** God walking in the garden in the cool of the day: and Adam and his wife hid themselves from the presence of the LORD God amongst the trees of the garden. ☐

Deuteronomy 8:20, As the nations which the LORD destroyeth before your face, so shall ye perish; because ye would not be obedient unto the **voice of the LORD** your God. ☐

Deuteronomy 13:18, When thou shalt hearken to the **voice of the LORD** thy God, to keep all his commandments which I command thee this day, to do that which is right in the eyes of the LORD thy God. ☐

Deuteronomy 28:1, And it shall come to pass, if thou shalt hearken diligently unto the **voice of the LORD** thy God, to observe and to do all his commandments which I command thee this day, that the LORD thy God will set thee on high above all nations of the earth. ☐

Deuteronomy 28:2, And all these blessings shall come on thee, and overtake thee, if thou shalt hearken unto the **voice of the LORD** thy God. ☐

Psalms 29:3, The **voice of the LORD** is upon the waters: the God of glory thundereth: the LORD is upon many waters. ☐

Psalms 29:4, The **voice of the LORD** is powerful; the **voice of the LORD** is full of majesty. ☐

Psalms 29:5, The **voice of the LORD** breaketh the cedars; yea, the LORD breaketh the cedars of Lebanon. ☐

Psalms 29:7, The **voice of the LORD** divideth the flames of fire. ☐

Psalms 29:8, The **voice of the LORD** shaketh the wilderness; the LORD shaketh the wilderness of Kadesh. ☐

Psalms 29:9, The **voice of the LORD** maketh the hinds to calve, and discovereth the forests: and in his temple doth every one speak of his glory. ☐

CHEERFULNESS *
CHEERFUL *
CHEER

7 DAY
MORNING
90 DAY CHALLENGE

Proverbs 15:13, A merry heart maketh a **cheerful** countenance: but by sorrow of the heart the spirit is broken. ☐

Matthew 9:2, And, behold, they brought to him a man sick of the palsy, lying on a bed: and Jesus seeing their faith said unto the sick of the palsy; Son, be of good **cheer** thy sins be forgiven thee. ☐

Matthew 14:27, But straightway Jesus spake unto them, saying, Be of good **cheer**; it is I; be not afraid. ☐

Mark 6:50, For they all saw him, and were troubled. And immediately he talked with them, and saith unto them, Be of good **cheer**: it is I; be not afraid. ☐

John 16:33, These things I have spoken unto you, that in me ye might have peace. In the world ye shall have tribulation: but be of good **cheer**; I have overcome the world. ☐

Acts 23:11, And the night following the Lord stood by him, and said, Be of good **cheer**, Paul: for as thou hast testified of me in Jerusalem, so must thou bear witness also at Rome. ☐

Acts 27:22, And now I exhort you to be of good **cheer**: for there shall be no loss of any man's life among you, but of the ship. ☐

Acts 27:25, Wherefore, sirs, be of good **cheer**: for I believe God, that it shall be even as it was told me. ☐

Acts 27:36, Then were they all of good **cheer**, and they also took some meat. ☐

Romans 12:8, Or he that exhorteth, on exhortation: he that giveth, let him do it with simplicity; he that ruleth, with diligence; he that sheweth mercy, with **cheerfulness**. ☐

In God We Trust
19

Genesis 15:6, And he believed in the LORD; and he counted it to him for **righteousness**. ☐

Psalms 4:1, Hear me when I call, O God of my **righteousness**: thou hast enlarged me when I was in distress; have mercy upon me, and hear my prayer. ☐

Psalms 4:5, Offer the sacrifices of **righteousness**, and put your trust in the LORD. ☐

Psalms 7:8, The LORD shall judge the people: judge me, O LORD, according to my **righteousness**, and according to mine integrity that is in me. ☐

Psalms 7:17, I will praise the LORD according to his **righteousness**: and will sing praise to the name of the LORD most high. ☐

Psalms 11:7, For the righteous LORD loveth **righteousness**; his countenance doth behold the upright. ☐

Psalms 15:2, He that walketh uprightly, and worketh **righteousness**, and speaketh the truth in his heart. ☐

Psalms 17:15, As for me, I will behold thy face in **righteousness**: I shall be satisfied, when I awake, with thy likeness. ☐

Psalms 18:20, The LORD rewarded me according to my **righteousness**; according to the cleanness of my hands hath he recompensed me. ☐

Psalms 18:24, Therefore hath the LORD recompensed me according to my **righteousness**, according to the cleanness of my hands in his eyesight. ☐

Psalms 23:3, He restoreth my soul: he leadeth me in the paths of **righteousness** for his name's sake. ☐

Psalms 31:1, In thee, O LORD, do I put my trust; let me never be ashamed: deliver me in thy **righteousness**. ☐

In God We Trust

Psalms 27:14, Wait on the LORD: be of good courage, and he shall strengthen thine heart: wait, **I say**, on the LORD.☐

Psalms 139:11, If **I say**, Surely the darkness shall cover me; even the night shall be light about me.☐

Isaiah 36:5, **I say**, sayest thou, (but they are but vain words) I have counsel and strength for war: now on whom dost thou trust, that thou rebellest against me? ☐

Ezekiel 12:25, For I am the LORD: I will speak, and the word that I shall speak shall come to pass; it shall be no more prolonged: for in your days, O rebellious house, will **I say** the word, and will perform it, saith the Lord GOD. ☐

Ezekiel 33:14, Again, when **I say** unto the wicked, Thou shalt surely die; if he turn from his sin, and do that which is lawful and right. ☐

Matthew 5:18, For verily **I say** unto you, Till heaven and earth pass, one jot or one tittle shall in no wise pass from the law, till all be fulfilled.☐

Matthew 5:20, For **I say** unto you, That except your righteousness shall exceed the righteousness of the scribes and Pharisees, ye shall in no case enter into the kingdom of heaven. ☐

Matthew 5:26, Verily **I say** unto thee, Thou shalt by no means come out thence, till thou hast paid the uttermost farthing. ☐

Matthew 6:16, Moreover when ye fast, be not, as the hypocrites, of a sad countenance: for they disfigure their faces, that they may appear unto men to fast. Verily **I say** unto you, They have their reward. ☐

Matthew 6:25, Therefore **I say** unto you, Take no thought for your life, what ye shall eat, or what ye shall drink; nor yet for your body, what ye shall put on. Is not the life more than meat, and the body than raiment? ☐

Matthew 6:29, And yet **I say** unto you, That even Solomon in all his glory was not arrayed like one of these. ☐

Proverbs 10:23, It is as sport to a fool to do mischief: but a man of **understanding** hath wisdom. ☐

Proverbs 11:12, He that is void of wisdom despiseth his neighbour: but a man of **understanding** holdeth his peace. ☐

Proverbs 12:11, He that tilleth his land shall be satisfied with bread: but he that followeth vain persons is void of **understanding**. ☐

Proverbs 13:15, Good understanding giveth favour: but the way, He that is slow to wrath is of great **understanding**: but he that is hasty of spirit exalteth folly. ☐

Proverbs 14:33, Wisdom resteth in the heart of him that hath **understanding**: but that which is in the midst of fools is made known. ☐

Proverbs 15:14, The heart of him that hath **understanding** seeketh knowledge: but the mouth of fools feedeth on foolishness. ☐

Proverbs 15:21, Folly is joy to him that is destitute of wisdom: but a man of **understanding** walketh uprightly. ☐

Proverbs 15:32, He that refuseth instruction despiseth his own soul: but he that heareth reproof getteth **understanding**. ☐

Proverbs 16:16, How much better is it to get wisdom than gold! and to get **understanding** rather to be chosen than silver! ☐

Proverbs 16:22, **Understanding** is a wellspring of life unto him that hath it: but the instruction of fools is folly. ☐

Proverbs 17:18, A man void of **understanding** striketh hands, and becometh surety in the presence of his friend. ☐

Proverbs 17:24, Wisdom is before him that hath **understanding**; but the eyes of a fool are in the ends of the earth. ☐

Joel 2:11, And the LORD shall utter his voice before his army: for his camp is very great: for **he is** strong that executeth his word: for the day of the LORD is great and very terrible; and who can abide it?☐

Luke 6:47, Whosoever cometh to me, and heareth my sayings, and doeth them, I will shew you to whom **he is** like.☐

John 8:54, Jesus answered, If I honour myself, my honour is nothing: it is my Father that honoureth me; of whom ye say, that **he is** your God. ☐

Acts 10:36, The word which God sent unto the children of Israel, preaching peace by Jesus Christ: **he is** Lord of all.☐

Acts 17:24, God that made the world and all things therein, seeing that **he is** Lord of heaven and earth, dwelleth not in temples made with hands.☐

1 Corinthians 7:24, Brethren, let every man, wherein **he is** called, therein abide with God.☐

2 Corinthians 5:17, Therefore if any man be in Christ, **he is** a new creature: old things are passed away; behold, all things are become new.☐

2 Corinthians 10:7, Do ye look on things after the outward appearance? If any man trust to himself that **he is** Christ's, let him of himself think this again, that, as **he is** Christ's, even so are we Christ's. ☐

Galatians 6:3, For if a man think himself to be something, when **he is** nothing, he deceiveth himself. ☐

2 Timothy 1:12, For the which cause I also suffer these things: nevertheless I am not ashamed: for I know whom I have believed, and am persuaded that **he is** able to keep that which I have committed unto him against that day.☐

Hebrews 7:25, Wherefore **he is** able also to save them to the uttermost that come unto God by him, seeing he ever liveth to make intercession for them.☐

In God We Trust

Hebrews 11:1, Now **faith** is the substance of things hoped for, the evidence of things not seen.□

Hebrews 11:3, Through **faith** we understand that the worlds were framed by the word of God, so that things which are seen were not made of things which do appear. □

Hebrews 11:39, And these all, having obtained a good report through **faith**, received not the promise.□

Hebrews 12:2, Looking unto Jesus the author and finisher of our **faith**; who for the joy that was set before him endured the cross, despising the shame, and is set down at the right hand of the throne of God.□

James 1:3, Knowing this, that the trying of your **faith** worketh patience.□

James 1:6, But let him ask in **faith**, nothing wavering. For he that wavereth is like a wave of the sea driven with the wind and tossed. □

James 2:1, My brethren, have not the **faith** of our Lord Jesus Christ, the Lord of glory, with respect of persons.□

James 2:5, Hearken, my beloved brethren, Hath not God chosen the poor of this world rich in **faith**, and heirs of the kingdom which he hath promised to them that love him? □

James 2:17, Even so **faith**, if it hath not works, is dead, being alone.□

James 2:18, Yea, a man may say, Thou hast **faith**, and I have works: shew me thy **faith** without thy works, and I will shew thee my **faith** by my works. □

James 2:20, But wilt thou know, O vain man, that **faith** without works is dead? □

James 2:22, Seest thou how **faith** wrought with his works, and by works was **faith** made perfect? □

James 2:26, For as the body without the spirit is dead, so **faith** without works is dead also.□

In God We Trust

PROSPER *
PROSPERED
PROSPERITY *

9 DAY

MORNING
90 DAY CHALLENGE

Genesis 24:56, And he said unto them, Hinder me not, seeing the LORD hath **prospered** my way; send me away that I may go to my master. ☐

2 Kings 18:7, And the LORD was with him; and he **prospered** whithersoever he went forth: and he rebelled against the king of Assyria, and served him not. ☐

1 Chronicles 29:23, Then Solomon sat on the throne of the LORD as king instead of David his father, and **prospered**; and all Israel obeyed him. ☐

2 Chronicles 26:5, And he sought God in the days of Zechariah, who had understanding in the visions of God: and as long as he sought the LORD, God made him to **prosper.** ☐

2 Chronicles 31:21, And in every work that he began in the service of the house of God, and in the law, and in the commandments, to seek his God, he did it with all his heart, and **prospered.** ☐

Nehemiah 1:11, O Lord, I beseech thee, let now thine ear be attentive to the prayer of thy servant, and to the prayer of thy servants, who desire to fear thy name: and **prosper**, I pray thee, thy servant this day, and grant him mercy in the sight of this man. For I was the king's cupbearer. ☐

Nehemiah 2:20, Then answered I them, and said unto them, The God of heaven, he will **prosper** us; therefore we his servants will arise and build: but ye have no portion, nor right, nor memorial, in Jerusalem. ☐

Job 36:11, If they obey and serve him, they shall spend their days in **prosperity**, and their years in pleasures. ☐

Psalms 1:3, And he shall be like a tree planted by the rivers of water, that bringeth forth his fruit in his season; his leaf also shall not wither; and whatsoever he doeth shall **prosper.** ☐

Psalms 37:7, Rest in the LORD, and wait patiently for him: fret not thyself because of him who **prospereth** in his way, because of the man who bringeth wicked devices to pass. ☐

In God We Trust

GIVE THANKS
GIVING THANKS
THANKS *

9 DAY
AFTERNOON
90 DAY CHALLENGE

Psalms 18:49, Therefore will I **give thanks** unto thee, O LORD, among the heathen, and sing praises unto thy name. ☐

Romans 16:4, Who have for my life laid down their own necks: unto whom not only I **give thanks**, but also all the churches of the Gentiles. ☐

Ephesians 5:20, **Giving thanks** always for all things unto God and the Father in the name of our Lord Jesus Christ. ☐

Ephesians 1:16, Cease not to **give thanks** for you, making mention of you in my prayers. ☐

Colossians 1:3, We **give thanks** to God and the Father of our Lord Jesus Christ, praying always for you. ☐

Colossians 1:12, **Giving thanks** unto the Father, which hath made us meet to be partakers of the inheritance of the saints in light. ☐

Colossians 3:17, And whatsoever ye do in word or deed, do all in the name of the Lord Jesus, **giving thanks** to God and the Father by him. ☐

1 Thessalonians 1:2, We **give thanks** to God always for you all, making mention of you in our prayers. ☐

1 Thessalonians 5:18, In everything **give thanks**: for this is the will of God in Christ Jesus concerning you. ☐

2 Thessalonians 2:13, But we are bound to **give thanks** always to God for you, brethren beloved of the Lord, because God hath from the beginning chosen you to salvation through sanctification of the Spirit and belief of the truth. ☐

1 Timothy 2:1, I exhort therefore, that, first of all, supplications, prayers, intercessions, and giving of **thanks**, be made for all men. ☐

In God We Trust

Psalms 98:3, He hath remembered his **mercy** and his truth toward the house of Israel: all the ends of the earth have seen the salvation of our God. ☐

Psalms 101:1, I will sing of **mercy** and judgment: unto thee, O LORD, will I sing. ☐

Psalms 102:13, Thou shalt arise, and have **mercy** upon Zion: for the time to favour her, yea, the set time, is come. ☐

Psalms 103:8, The LORD is merciful and gracious, slow to anger, and plenteous in **mercy**. ☐

Psalms 103:11, For as the heaven is high above the earth, so great is his **mercy** toward them that fear him. ☐

Psalms 103:17, But the **mercy** of the LORD is from everlasting to everlasting upon them that fear him, and his righteousness unto children's children. ☐

Psalms 108:4, For thy **mercy** is great above the heavens: and thy truth reacheth unto the clouds. ☐

Psalms 109:26, Help me, O LORD my God: O save me according to thy **mercy**. ☐

Psalms 115:1, Not unto us, O LORD, not unto us, but unto thy name give glory, for thy **mercy**, and for thy truth's sake. ☐

Psalms 119:64, The earth, O LORD, is full of thy **mercy**: teach me thy statutes. ☐

Psalms 119:124, Deal with thy servant according unto thy **mercy**, and teach me thy statutes. ☐

Psalms 123:3, Have **mercy** upon us, O LORD, have **mercy** upon us: for we are exceedingly filled with contempt. ☐

Psalms 130:7, Let Israel hope in the LORD: for with the LORD there is **mercy**, and with him is plenteous redemption. ☐

I BELIEVE
BIGGER
BETTER
BOLDER
BLESSINGS

I SAY

10 DAY
MORNING
90 DAY CHALLENGE

Luke 11:8, **I say** unto you, Though he will not rise and give him, because he is his friend, yet because of his importunity he will rise and give him as many as he needeth.☐

Luke 12:44, Of a truth **I say** unto you, that he will make him ruler over all that he hath.☐

Luke 15:7, **I say** unto you, that likewise joy shall be in heaven over one sinner that repenteth, more than over ninety and nine just persons, which need no repentance.☐

Luke 15:10, Likewise, **I say** unto you, there is joy in the presence of the angels of God over one sinner that repenteth.☐

Luke 18:17, Verily **I say** unto you, Whosoever shall not receive the kingdom of God as a little child shall in no wise enter therein.☐

Luke 21:3, And he said, Of a truth **I say** unto you, that this poor widow hath cast in more than they all.☐

Romans 9:1, **I say** the truth in Christ, I lie not, my conscience also bearing me witness in the Holy Ghost.☐

Romans 12:3, For **I say**, through the grace given unto me, to every man that is among you, not to think of himself more highly than he ought to think; but to think soberly, according as God hath dealt to every man the measure of faith.☐

2 Corinthians 5:8, We are confident, **I say**, and willing rather to be absent from the body, and to be present with the Lord.☐

2 Corinthians 9:6, But this **I say**, He which soweth sparingly shall reap also sparingly; and he which soweth bountifully shall reap also bountifully.☐

Galatians 5:16, This **I say** then, Walk in the Spirit, and ye shall not fulfil the lust of the flesh.☐

Philippians 4:4, Rejoice in the Lord alway: and again **I say**, Rejoice.☐

Romans 1:31, Without **understanding**, covenantbreakers, without natural affection, implacable, unmerciful. ☐

Ephesians 1:18, The eyes of your **understanding** being enlightened; that ye may know what is the hope of his calling, and what the riches of the glory of his inheritance in the saints. ☐

Ephesians 4:18, Having the **understanding** darkened, being alienated from the life of God through the ignorance that is in them, because of the blindness of their heart. ☐

Ephesians 5:17, Wherefore be ye not unwise, but **understanding** what the will of the Lord is. ☐

Philippians 4:7, And the peace of God, which passeth all **understanding**, shall keep your hearts and minds through Christ Jesus. ☐

Colossians 1:9, For this cause we also, since the day we heard it, do not cease to pray for you, and to desire that ye might be filled with the knowledge of his will in all wisdom and spiritual **understanding**. ☐

Colossians 2:2, That their hearts might be comforted, being knit together in love, and unto all riches of the full assurance of **understanding**, to the acknowledgement of the mystery of God, and of the Father, and of Christ. ☐

2 Timothy 2:7, Consider what I say; and the Lord give thee **understanding** in all things. ☐

1 John 5:20, And we know that the Son of God is come, and hath given us an **understanding**, that we may know him that is true, and we are in him that is true, even in his Son Jesus Christ. This is the true God, and eternal life. ☐

INCREASE *
INCREASED
INCREASETH

10 DAY
EVENING
90 DAY CHALLENGE

Leviticus 25:12, For it is the jubilee; it shall be holy unto you: ye shall eat the **increase** thereof out of the field. ☐

Leviticus 26:4, Then I will give you rain in due season, and the land shall yield her **increase**, and the trees of the field shall yield their fruit. ☐

Proverbs 11:24, There is that scattereth, and yet **increaseth**; and there is that withholdeth more than is meet, but it tendeth to poverty. ☐

Proverbs 16:21, The wise in heart shall be called prudent: and the sweetness of the lips **increaseth** learning. ☐

Proverbs 23:28, She also lieth in wait as for a prey, and **increaseth** the transgressors among men. ☐

Proverbs 24:5, A wise man is strong; yea, a man of knowledge **increaseth** strength. ☐

Ecclesiastes 1:18, For in much wisdom is much grief: and he that **increaseth** knowledge **increaseth** sorrow. ☐

Ecclesiastes 5:10, He that loveth silver shall not be satisfied with silver; nor he that loveth abundance with **increase**: this is also vanity. ☐

Ecclesiastes 5:11, When goods **increase**, they are **increased** that eat them: and what good is there to the owners thereof, saving the beholding of them with their eyes? ☐

Isaiah 29:19, The meek also shall **increase** their joy in the LORD, and the poor among men shall rejoice in the Holy One of Israel. ☐

Zechariah 10:8, I will hiss for them, and gather them; for I have redeemed them: and they shall **increase** as they have **increased**. ☐

In God We Trust

RECEIVE *
RECEIVETH
RECEIVED

_11_ DAY
MORNING
90 DAY CHALLENGE

Mark 4:16, And these are they likewise which are sown on stony ground; who, when they have heard the word, immediately **receive** it with gladness. ☐

Mark 9:37, Whosoever shall **receive** one of such children in my name, **receiveth** me: and whosoever shall **receive** me, **receiveth** not me, but him that sent me. ☐

John 14:17, Even the Spirit of truth; whom the world cannot **receive**, because it seeth him not, neither knoweth him: but ye know him; for he dwelleth with you, and shall be in you. ☐

John 16:24, Hitherto have ye asked nothing in my name: ask, and ye shall **receive**, that your joy may be full. ☐

John 20:22, And when he had said this, he breathed on them, and saith unto them, **Receive** ye the Holy Ghost. ☐

Acts 9:17, And Ananias went his way, and entered into the house; and putting his hands on him said, Brother Saul, the Lord, even Jesus, that appeared unto thee in the way as thou camest, hath sent me, that thou mightest **receive** thy sight, and be filled with the Holy Ghost. ☐

Acts 20:35, I have shewed you all things, how that so labouring ye ought to support the weak, and to remember the words of the Lord Jesus, how he said, It is more blessed to give than to **receive**. ☐

Acts 26:18, To open their eyes, and to turn them from darkness to light, and from the power of Satan unto God, that they may **receive** forgiveness of sins, and inheritance among them which are sanctified by faith that is in me. ☐

Romans 5:17, For if by one man's offence death reigned by one; much more they which **receive** abundance of grace and of the gift of righteousness shall reign in life by one, Jesus Christ. ☐

Romans 15:7, Wherefore **receive** ye one another, as Christ also **received** us to the glory of God. ☐

In God We Trust

UNBELIEF *
BELIEVE *
BELIEVETH

11 DAY

AFTERNOON
90 DAY CHALLENGE

Matthew 9:28, And when he was come into the house, the blind men came to him: and Jesus saith unto them, **Believe** ye that I am able to do this? They said unto him, Yea, Lord. ☐

Mark 1:15, And saying, The time is fulfilled, and the kingdom of God is at hand: repent ye, and **believe** the gospel. ☐

Mark 5:36, As soon as Jesus heard the word that was spoken, he saith unto the ruler of the synagogue, Be not afraid, only **believe**. ☐

Mark 9:23, Jesus said unto him, If thou canst **believe**, all things are possible to him that **believeth**. ☐

Mark 9:24, And straightway the father of the child cried out, and said with tears, Lord, I **believe**; help thou mine **unbelief**. ☐

Mark 11:23, For verily I say unto you, That whosoever shall say unto this mountain, Be thou removed, and be thou cast into the sea; and shall not doubt in his heart, but shall **believe** that those things which he saith shall come to pass; he shall have whatsoever he saith. ☐

Mark 11:24, Therefore I say unto you, What things soever ye desire, when ye pray, **believe** that ye receive them, and ye shall have them. ☐

Mark 15:32, Let Christ the King of Israel descend now from the cross, that we may see and **believe**. And they that were crucified with him reviled him. ☐

1 Timothy 1:13, Who was before a blasphemer, and a persecutor, and injurious: but I obtained mercy, because I did it ignorantly in **unbelief**. ☐

Hebrews 3:12, Take heed, brethren, lest there be in any of you an evil heart of **unbelief**, in departing from the living God. ☐

Hebrews 3:19, So we see that they could not enter in because of **unbelief**. ☐

Hebrews 4:11, Let us labour therefore to enter into that rest, lest any man fall after the same example of **unbelief**. ☐

Jeremiah 17:7, Blessed is the man that trusteth in the LORD, and whose **hope** the LORD is. ☐

Jeremiah 17:17, Be not a terror unto me: thou art my **hope** in the day of evil. ☐

Lamentations 3:21, This I recall to my mind, therefore have I **hope**. ☐

Lamentations 3:24, The LORD is my portion, saith my soul; therefore will I **hope** in him. ☐

Lamentations 3:26, It is good that a man should both **hope** and quietly wait for the salvation of the LORD. ☐

Acts 2:26, Therefore did my heart rejoice, and my tongue was glad; moreover also my flesh shall rest in **hope**. ☐

Acts 24:15, And have **hope** toward God, which they themselves also allow, that there shall be a resurrection of the dead, both of the just and unjust. ☐

Acts 26:6, And now I stand and am judged for the **hope** of the promise made of God unto our fathers. ☐

Romans 4:18, Who against **hope** believed in **hope**, that he might become the father of many nations, according to that which was spoken, So shall thy seed be. ☐

Romans 5:2, By whom also we have access by faith into this grace wherein we stand, and rejoice in **hope** of the glory of God. ☐

Romans 5:4, And patience, experience; and experience, **hope**. ☐

Romans 5:5, And **hope** maketh not ashamed; because the love of God is shed abroad in our hearts by the Holy Ghost which is given unto us. ☐

Romans 8:24, For we are saved by **hope**: but **hope** that is seen is not **hope**: for what a man seeth, why doth he yet **hope** for? ☐

In God We Trust

Deuteronomy 11:27, A blessing, if ye **obey** the commandments of the LORD your God, which I command you this day. □

Deuteronomy 13:4, Ye shall walk after the LORD your God, and fear him, and keep his commandments, and **obey** his voice, and ye shall serve him, and cleave unto him. □

Deuteronomy 21:18, If a man have a stubborn and rebellious son, which will not **obey** the voice of his father, or the voice of his mother, and that, when they have chastened him, will not hearken unto them. □

Deuteronomy 21:20, And they shall say unto the elders of his city, This our son is stubborn and rebellious, he will not **obey** our voice; he is a glutton, and a drunkard. □

Matthew 8:27, But the men marvelled, saying, What manner of man is this, that even the winds and the sea **obey** him! □

Mark 4:41, And they feared exceedingly, and said one to another, What manner of man is this, that even the wind and the sea **obey** him? □

Acts 5:29, Then Peter and the other apostles answered and said, We ought to **obey** God rather than men. □

Romans 2:8, But unto them that are contentious, and do not **obey** the truth, but **obey** unrighteousness, indignation and wrath. □

Romans 6:12, Let not sin therefore reign in your mortal body, that ye should **obey** it in the lusts thereof. □

Romans 6:16, Know ye not, that to whom ye yield yourselves servants to **obey**, his servants ye are to whom ye **obey**; whether of sin unto death, or of obedience unto righteousness? □

Ephesians 6:1, Children, **obey** your parents in the Lord: for this is right. □

In God We Trust

RIGHTEOUSNESS *

Psalms 119:142, Thy **righteousness** is an everlasting **righteousness**, and thy law is the truth. ☐

Psalms 119:144, The **righteousness** of thy testimonies is everlasting: give me understanding, and I shall live. ☐

Psalms 119:172, My tongue shall speak of thy word: for all thy commandments are **righteousness**. ☐

Psalms 132:9, Let thy priests be clothed with **righteousness**; and let thy saints shout for joy. ☐

Psalms 143:1, Hear my prayer, O LORD, give ear to my supplications: in thy faithfulness answer me, and in thy **righteousness**. ☐

Psalms 143:11, Quicken me, O LORD, for thy name's sake: for thy **righteousness** sake bring my soul out of trouble. ☐

Psalms 145:7, They shall abundantly utter the memory of thy great goodness, and shall sing of thy **righteousness**. ☐

Proverbs 2:9, Then shalt thou understand **righteousness**, and judgment, and equity; yea, every good path. ☐

Proverbs 8:8, All the words of my mouth are in **righteousness**; there is nothing forward or perverse in them. ☐

Proverbs 8:18, Riches and honour are with me; yea, durable riches and **righteousness**. ☐

Proverbs 8:20, I lead in the way of **righteousness**, in the midst of the paths of judgment. ☐

Proverbs 10:2, Treasures of wickedness profit nothing: but **righteousness** delivereth from death. ☐

Proverbs 11:4, Riches profit not in the day of wrath: but **righteousness** delivereth from death. ☐

IN CHRIST - IN CHRIST JESUS
THE CHRIST - JESUS CHRIST
 12 DAY
EVENING
90 DAY CHALLENGE

I BELIEVE BIGGER BETTER BOLDER BLESSINGS

Matthew 16:16, And Simon Peter answered and said, Thou art **the Christ**, the Son of the living God. ☐

Mark 14:61, But he held his peace, and answered nothing. Again the high priest asked him, and said unto him, Art thou **the Christ**, the Son of the Blessed? ☐

John 1:17, For the law was given by Moses, but grace and truth came by **Jesus Christ**. ☐

John 4:42, And said unto the woman, Now we believe, not because of thy saying: for we have heard him ourselves, and know that this is indeed **the Christ**, the Saviour of the world. ☐

John 11:27, She saith unto him, Yea, Lord: I believe that thou art **the Christ**, the Son of God, which should come into the world. ☐

John 17:3, And this is life eternal, that they might know thee the only true God, and **Jesus Christ**, whom thou hast sent. ☐

John 20:31, But these are written, that ye might believe that Jesus is **the Christ**, the Son of God; and that believing ye might have life through his name. ☐

Acts 8:12, But when they believed Philip preaching the things concerning the kingdom of God, and the name of **Jesus Christ**, they were baptized, both men and women. ☐

Philemon 1:6, That the communication of thy faith may become effectual by the acknowledging of every good thing which is in you **in Christ Jesus.** ☐

Philemon 1:8, Wherefore, though I might be much bold **in Christ** to enjoin thee that which is convenient. ☐

1 Peter 3:16, Having a good conscience; that, whereas they speak evil of you, as of evildoers, they may be ashamed that falsely accuse your good conversation **in Christ**. ☐

Psalms 18:3, I will call upon the LORD, who is worthy to be praised: so shall I be saved from mine **enemies**. □

Psalms 18:37, I have pursued mine **enemies**, and overtaken them: neither did I turn again till they were consumed. □

Psalms 18:48, He delivereth me from mine **enemies**: yea, thou liftest me up above those that rise up against me: thou hast delivered me from the violent man.□

Psalms 23:5, Thou preparest a table before me in the presence of mine **enemies**: thou anointest my head with oil; my cup runneth over. □

Psalms 25:2, O my God, I trust in thee: let me not be ashamed, let not mine **enemies** triumph over me.□

Psalms 25:19, Consider mine **enemies**; for they are many; and they hate me with cruel hatred. □

Psalms 27:11, Teach me thy way, O LORD, and lead me in a plain path, because of mine **enemies**.□

Psalms 31:15, My times are in thy hand: deliver me from the hand of mine **enemies**, and from them that persecute me. □

Psalms 35:19, Let not them that are mine **enemies** wrongfully rejoice over me: neither let them wink with the eye that hate me without a cause. □

Psalms 42:10, As with a sword in my bones, mine **enemies** reproach me; while they say daily unto me, Where is thy God?□

Psalms 59:1, Deliver me from mine **enemies**, O my God: defend me from them that rise up against me. □

Psalms 59:10, The God of my mercy shall prevent me: God shall let me see my desire upon mine **enemies**.□

Matthew 4:19, And he saith unto them, Follow me, and **I will** make you fishers of men. ☐

Matthew 8:3, And Jesus put forth his hand, and touched him, saying, **I will**; be thou clean. And immediately his leprosy was cleansed. ☐

Matthew 8:7, And Jesus saith unto him, **I will** come and heal him. ☐

Matthew 8:19, And a certain scribe came, and said unto him, Master, **I will** follow thee whithersoever thou goest. ☐

Matthew 9:13, But go ye and learn what that meaneth, **I will** have mercy, and not sacrifice: for I am not come to call the righteous, but sinners to repentance. ☐

Matthew 11:28, Come unto me, all ye that labour and are heavy laden, and **I will** give you rest. ☐

Matthew 12:7, But if ye had known what this meaneth, **I will** have mercy, and not sacrifice, ye would not have condemned the guiltless. ☐

Matthew 12:44, Then he saith, **I will** return into my house from whence I came out; and when he is come, he findeth it empty, swept, and garnished. ☐

Matthew 13:30, Let both grow together until the harvest: and in the time of harvest **I will** say to the reapers, Gather ye together first the tares, and bind them in bundles to burn them: but gather the wheat into my barn. ☐

Matthew 13:35, That it might be fulfilled which was spoken by the prophet, saying, **I will** open my mouth in parables; **I will** utter things which have been kept secret from the foundation of the world. ☐

Matthew 15:32, Then Jesus called his disciples unto him, and said, I have compassion on the multitude, because they continue with me now three days, and have nothing to eat: and **I will** not send them away fasting, lest they faint in the way. ☐

In God We Trust

HEAL *
HEALING
HEALED

*13*DAY
EVENING
90 DAY CHALLENGE

Matthew 4:23, And Jesus went about all Galilee, teaching in their synagogues, and preaching the gospel of the kingdom, and **healing** all manner of sickness and all manner of disease among the people.☐

Matthew 8:7, And Jesus saith unto him, I will come and **heal** him. ☐

Matthew 9:35, And Jesus went about all the cities and villages, teaching in their synagogues, and preaching the gospel of the kingdom, and **healing** every sickness and every disease among the people. ☐

Matthew 10:1, And when he had called unto him his twelve disciples, he gave them power against unclean spirits, to cast them out, and to **heal** all manner of sickness and all manner of disease. ☐

Matthew 10:8, **Heal** the sick, cleanse the lepers, raise the dead, cast out devils: freely ye have received, freely give. ☐

Luke 9:2, And he sent them to preach the kingdom of God, and to **heal** the sick. ☐

Luke 9:6, And they departed, and went through the towns, preaching the gospel, and **healing** everywhere. ☐

Luke 9:11, And the people, when they knew it, followed him: and he received them, and spake unto them of the kingdom of God, and **healed** them that had need of **healing**. ☐

Luke 10:9, And **heal** the sick that are therein, and say unto them, The kingdom of God is come nigh unto you.☐

Acts 10:38, How God anointed Jesus of Nazareth with the Holy Ghost and with power: who went about doing good, and **healing** all that were oppressed of the devil; for God was with him. ☐

Acts 4:30, By stretching forth thine hand to **heal**; and that signs and wonders may be done by the name of thy holy child Jesus. ☐

In God We Trust
39

Proverbs 14:10, The heart knoweth his own bitterness; and a stranger doth not intermeddle with his **joy**.☐

Proverbs 15:21, Folly is **joy** to him that is destitute of wisdom: but a man of understanding walketh uprightly.☐

Proverbs 15:23, A man hath **joy** by the answer of his mouth: and a word spoken in due season, how good is it!☐

Proverbs 17:21, He that begetteth a fool doeth it to his sorrow: and the father of a fool hath no **joy**.☐

Proverbs 23:24, The father of the righteous shall greatly rejoice: and he that begetteth a wise child shall have **joy** of him.☐

Ecclesiastes 2:10, And whatsoever mine eyes desired I kept not from them, I withheld not my heart from any **joy**; for my heart rejoiced in all my labour: and this was my portion of all my labour. ☐

Ecclesiastes 2:26, For God giveth to a man that is good in his sight wisdom, and knowledge, and **joy**: but to the sinner he giveth travail, to gather and to heap up, that he may give to him that is good before God. This also is vanity and vexation of spirit.☐

Ecclesiastes 5:20, For he shall not much remember the days of his life; because God answereth him in the **joy** of his heart.☐

Ecclesiastes 9:7, Go thy way, eat thy bread with **joy**, and drink thy wine with a merry heart; for God now accepteth thy works.☐

Isaiah 29:19, The meek also shall increase their **joy** in the LORD, and the poor among men shall rejoice in the Holy One of Israel.☐

Isaiah 51:11, Therefore the redeemed of the LORD shall return, and come with singing unto Zion; and everlasting **joy** shall be upon their head: they shall obtain gladness and **joy**; and sorrow and mourning shall flee away.☐

In God We Trust

Psalms 9:12, When he maketh inquisition for blood, he remembereth them: he forgetteth not the **cry** of the humble. ☐

Psalms 17:1, Hear the right, O LORD, attend unto my **cry**, give ear unto my prayer, that goeth not out of feigned lips. ☐

Psalms 22:2, O my God, I **cry** in the daytime, but thou hearest not; and in the night season, and am not silent. ☐

Psalms 27:7, Hear, O LORD, when I **cry** with my voice: have mercy also upon me, and answer me. ☐

Psalms 28:1, Unto thee will I **cry**, O LORD my rock; be not silent to me: lest, if thou be silent to me, I become like them that go down into the pit. ☐

Psalms 34:15, The eyes of the LORD are upon the righteous, and his ears are open unto their **cry**. ☐

Psalms 34:17, The righteous **cry**, and the LORD heareth, and delivereth them out of all their troubles. ☐

Psalms 40:1, I waited patiently for the LORD; and he inclined unto me, and heard my **cry**. ☐

Psalms 55:17, Evening, and morning, and at noon, will I pray, and **cry** aloud: and he shall hear my voice. ☐

Psalms 56:9, When I **cry** unto thee, then shall mine enemies turn back: this I know; for God is for me. ☐

Psalms 57:2, I will **cry** unto God most high; unto God that performeth all things for me. ☐

Psalms 86:3, Be merciful unto me, O Lord: for I **cry** unto thee daily. ☐

Psalms 89:26, He shall **cry** unto me, Thou art my father, my God, and the rock of my salvation. ☐

Psalms 1:2, But his delight is in the law of the LORD; and in his law doth he **meditate** day and night. ☐

Psalms 5:1, Give ear to my words, O LORD, consider my **meditation**. ☐

Psalms 19:14, Let the words of my mouth, and the **meditation** of my heart, be acceptable in thy sight, O LORD, my strength, and my redeemer. ☐

Psalms 49:3, My mouth shall speak of wisdom; and the **meditation** of my heart shall be of understanding. ☐

Psalms 63:6, When I remember thee upon my bed, and **meditate** on thee in the night watches. ☐

Psalms 77:12, I will **meditate** also of all thy work, and talk of thy doings. ☐

Psalms 104:34, My **meditation** of him shall be sweet: I will be glad in the LORD. ☐

Psalms 119:15, I will **meditate** in thy precepts, and have respect unto thy ways. ☐

Psalms 119:23, Princes also did sit and speak against me: but thy servant did **meditate** in thy statutes. ☐

Psalms 119:48, My hands also will I lift up unto thy commandments, which I have loved; and I will **meditate** in thy statutes. ☐

Psalms 119:78, Let the proud be ashamed; for they dealt perversely with me without a cause: but I will **meditate** in thy precepts. ☐

Psalms 119:148, Mine eyes prevent the night watches, that I might **meditate** in thy word. ☐

Psalms 143:5, I remember the days of old; I **meditate** on all thy works; I muse on the work of thy hands. ☐

I Timothy 4:15, **Meditate** upon these things; give thyself wholly to them; that thy profiting may appear to all. ☐

In God We Trust

Psalms 109:20, Let this be the reward of mine adversaries from the LORD, and of them that speak evil against **my soul.** ☐

Psalms 119:28, **My soul** melteth for heaviness: strengthen thou me according unto thy word. ☐

Psalms 119:81, **My soul** fainteth for thy salvation: but I hope in thy word. ☐

Psalms 119:129, Thy testimonies are wonderful: therefore doth **my soul** keep them. ☐

Psalms 119:175, Let **my soul** live, and it shall praise thee; and let thy judgments help me. ☐

Psalms 63:9, But those that seek **my soul**, to destroy it, shall go into the lower parts of the earth. ☐

Lamentations 3:20, **My soul** hath them still in remembrance, and is humbled in me. ☐

Lamentations 3:24, The LORD is my portion, saith **my soul**; therefore will I hope in him. ☐

Lamentations 3:58, O Lord, thou hast pleaded the causes of **my soul**; thou hast redeemed my life. ☐

Matthew 12:18, Behold my servant, whom I have chosen; my beloved, in whom **my soul** is well pleased: I will put my spirit upon him, and he shall shew judgment to the Gentiles. ☐

Luke 1:46, And Mary said, **My soul** doth magnify the Lord. ☐

Luke 12:19, And I will say to **my soul**, Soul, thou hast much goods laid up for many years; take thine ease, eat, drink, and be merry. ☐

John 12:27, Now is **my soul** troubled; and what shall I say? Father, save me from this hour: but for this cause came I unto this hour. ☐

Psalms 8:9, O LORD our Lord, how **excellent** is thy name in all the earth! □

Psalms 16:3, But to the saints that are in the earth, and to the **excellent**, in whom is all my delight. □

Psalms 36:7, How **excellent** is thy lovingkindness, O God! therefore the children of men put their trust under the shadow of thy wings. □

Psalms 76:4, Thou art more glorious and **excellent** than the mountains of prey. □

Psalms 148:13, Let them praise the name of the LORD: for his name alone is **excellent**; his glory is above the earth and heaven. □

Psalms 150:2, Praise him for his mighty acts: praise him according to his **excellent** greatness. □

Proverbs 8:6, Hear; for I will speak of **excellent** things; and the opening of my lips shall be right things. □

Proverbs 12:26, The righteous is more **excellent** than his neighbour: but the way of the wicked seduceth them. □

Proverbs 17:7, **Excellent** speech becometh not a fool: much less do lying lips a prince. □

Proverbs 17:27, He that hath knowledge spareth his words: and a man of understanding is of an **excellent** spirit. □

Proverbs 22:20, Have not I written to thee **excellent** things in counsels and knowledge. □

Isaiah 12:5, Sing unto the LORD; for he hath done **excellent** things: this is known in all the earth. □

Isaiah 28:29, This also cometh forth from the LORD of hosts, which is wonderful in counsel, and **excellent** in working. □

Psalms 45:4, And in thy majesty ride prosperously because of truth and **meekness** and righteousness; and thy right hand shall teach thee terrible things ☐

Zephaniah 2:3, Seek ye the LORD, all ye **meek** of the earth, which have wrought his judgment; seek righteousness, seek **meekness**: it may be ye shall be hid in the day of the LORD'S anger. ☐

1 Corinthians 4:21, What will ye? shall I come unto you with a rod, or in love, and in the spirit of **meekness?** ☐

2 Corinthians 10:1, Now I Paul myself beseech you by the **meekness** and gentleness of Christ, who in presence am base among you, but being absent am bold toward you. ☐

Galatians 5:23, **Meekness**, temperance: against such there is no law. ☐

Galatians 6:1, Brethren, if a man be overtaken in a fault, ye which are spiritual, restore such an one in the spirit of **meekness**; considering thyself, lest thou also be tempted. ☐

Ephesians 4:2, With all lowliness and **meekness**, with longsuffering, forbearing one another in love. ☐

Colossians 3:12, Put on therefore, as the elect of God, holy and beloved, bowels of mercies, kindness, humbleness of mind, **meekness**, longsuffering. ☐

1 Timothy 6:11, But thou, O man of God, flee these things; and follow after righteousness, godliness, faith, love, patience, **meekness**. ☐

2 Timothy 2:25, In **meekness** instructing those that oppose themselves; if God peradventure will give them repentance to the acknowledging of the truth. ☐

Titus 3:2, To speak evil of no man, to be no brawlers, but gentle, shewing all **meekness** unto all men. ☐

In God We Trust
45

Psalms 75:1, Unto thee, O God, do we give thanks, unto thee do we give thanks: for that thy name is near thy wondrous works **declare**. □

Psalms 75:9, But I will **declare** for ever; I will sing praises to the God of Jacob. □

Psalms 78:6, That the generation to come might know them, even the children which should be born; who should arise and **declare** them to their children. □

Psalms 96:3, **Declare** his glory among the heathen, his wonders among all people. □

Psalms 97:6, The heavens **declare** his righteousness, and all the people see his glory. □

Psalms 102:21, To **declare** the name of the LORD in Zion, and his praise in Jerusalem. □

Psalms 107:22, And let them sacrifice the sacrifices of thanksgiving, and **declare** his works with rejoicing. □

Psalms 118:17, I shall not die, but live, and **declare** the works of the LORD. □

Psalms 145:4, One generation shall praise thy works to another, and shall **declare** thy mighty acts. □

Psalms 145:6, And men shall speak of the might of thy terrible acts: and I will **declare** thy greatness. □

Ecclesiastes 9:1, For all this I considered in my heart even to **declare** all this, that the righteous, and the wise, and their works, are in the hand of God: no man knoweth either love or hatred by all that is before them. □

Isaiah 42:12, Let them give glory unto the LORD, and **declare** his praise in the islands. □

Psalms 16:9, Therefore my heart is glad, and my glory rejoiceth: my flesh also shall rest in **hope**. □

Psalms 22:9, But thou art he that took me out of the womb: thou didst make me **hope** when I was upon my mother's breasts. □

Psalms 31:24, Be of good courage, and he shall strengthen your heart, all ye that **hope** in the LORD. □

Psalms 33:18, Behold, the eye of the LORD is upon them that fear him, upon them that **hope** in his mercy. □

Psalms 33:22, Let thy mercy, O LORD, be upon us, according as we **hope** in thee. □

Psalms 38:15, For in thee, O LORD, do I **hope**: thou wilt hear, O Lord my God. □

Psalms 39:7, And now, Lord, what wait I for? my **hope** is in thee. □

Psalms 42:5, Why art thou cast down, O my soul? and why art thou disquieted in me? **hope** thou in God: for I shall yet praise him for the help of his countenance. □

Psalms 71:5, For thou art my **hope**, O Lord GOD: thou art my trust from my youth. □

Psalms 71:14, But I will **hope** continually, and will yet praise thee more and more. □

Psalms 78:7, That they might set their **hope** in God, and not forget the works of God, but keep his commandments. □

Psalms 119:49, Remember the word unto thy servant, upon which thou hast caused me to **hope**. □

Psalms 119:81, My soul fainteth for thy salvation: but I **hope** in thy word. □

In God We Trust

CORRECT * - CORRECTED
CORRECTION *
CORRECTETH

16 DAY

EVENING
90 DAY CHALLENGE

Proverbs 3:11, My son, despise not the chastening of the LORD; neither be weary of his **correction**. □

Proverbs 3:12, For whom the LORD loveth he **correcteth**; even as a father the son in whom he delighteth. □

Proverbs 29:17, **Correct** thy son, and he shall give thee rest; yea, he shall give delight unto thy soul. □

Proverbs 29:19, A servant will not be **corrected** by words: for though he understand he will not answer. □

Proverbs 15:10, **Correction** is grievous unto him that forsaketh the way: and he that hateth reproof shall die. □

Proverbs 22:15, Foolishness is bound in the heart of a child; but the rod of **correction** shall drive it far from him. □

Proverbs 23:13, Withhold not **correction** from the child: for if thou beatest him with the rod, he shall not die. □

Jeremiah 10:24, O LORD, **correct** me, but with judgment; not in thine anger, lest thou bring me to nothing. □

Jeremiah 7:28, But thou shalt say unto them, This is a nation that obeyeth not the voice of the LORD their God, nor receiveth **correction**: truth is perished, and is cut off from their mouth. □

Zephaniah 3:2, She obeyed not the voice; she received not **correction**; she trusted not in the LORD; she drew not near to her God. □

2 Timothy 3:16, All scripture is given by inspiration of God, and is profitable for doctrine, for reproof, for **correction**, for instruction in righteousness. □

Hebrews 12:9, Furthermore we have had fathers of our flesh which **corrected** us, and we gave them reverence: shall we not much rather be in subjection unto the Father of spirits, and live? □

In God We Trust

2 Chronicles 34:31, And the king stood in his place, and made a **covenant** before the LORD, to walk after the LORD, and to keep his commandments, and his testimonies, and his statutes, with all his heart, and with all his soul, to perform the words of the **covenant** which are written in this book. ☐

Nehemiah 1:5, And said, I beseech thee, O LORD God of heaven, the great and terrible God, that keepeth **covenant** and mercy for them that love him and observe his commandments. ☐

Psalms 25:10, All the paths of the LORD are mercy and truth unto such as keep his **covenant** and his testimonies. ☐

Psalms 25:14, The secret of the LORD is with them that fear him; and he will shew them his **covenant**. ☐

Psalms 44:17, All this is come upon us; yet have we not forgotten thee, neither have we dealt falsely in thy **covenant**. ☐

Psalms 50:5, Gather my saints together unto me; those that have made a **covenant** with me by sacrifice. ☐

Psalms 50:16, But unto the wicked God saith, What hast thou to do to declare my statutes, or that thou shouldest take my **covenant** in thy mouth? ☐

Psalms 55:20, He hath put forth his hands against such as be at peace with him: he hath broken his **covenant**. ☐

Psalms 74:20, Have respect unto the **covenant**: for the dark places of the earth are full of the habitations of cruelty. ☐

Psalms 78:10, They kept not the **covenant** of God, and refused to walk in his law. ☐

Psalms 78:37, For their heart was not right with him, neither were they stedfast in his **covenant**. ☐

In God We Trust

Romans 5:18, Therefore as by the offence of one judgment came upon all men to condemnation; even so by the **righteousness** of one the free gift came upon all men unto justification of life. □

Romans 5:21, That as sin hath reigned unto death, even so might grace reign through **righteousness** unto eternal life by Jesus Christ our Lord. □

Romans 6:18, Being then made free from sin, ye became the servants of **righteousness**. □

Isaiah 32:16, Then judgment shall dwell in the wilderness, and **righteousness** remain in the fruitful field. □

Romans 8:10, And if Christ be in you, the body is dead because of sin; but the Spirit is life because of **righteousness**. □

Romans 10:3, For they being ignorant of God's **righteousness**, and going about to establish their own **righteousness**, have not submitted themselves unto the **righteousness** of God. □

Romans 10:10, For with the heart man believeth unto **righteousness**; and with the mouth confession is made unto salvation. □

2 Corinthians 6:14, Be ye not unequally yoked together with unbelievers: for what fellowship hath **righteousness** with unrighteousness? and what communion hath light with darkness? □

Galatians 5:5, For we through the Spirit wait for the hope of **righteousness** by faith. □

Ephesians 5:9, For the fruit of the Spirit is in all goodness and **righteousness** and truth. □

In God We Trust
50

TRUST *
TRUST IN
TRUST IN THE LORD

17 DAY
EVENING
90 DAY CHALLENGE

2 Samuel 22:31, As for God, his way is perfect; the word of the LORD is tried: he is a buckler to all them that **trust in** him. ☐

Psalms 7:1, O LORD my God, in thee do I put my **trust**: save me from all them that persecute me, and deliver me. ☐

Psalms 11:1, In the LORD put I my **trust**: how say ye to my soul, Flee as a bird to your mountain? ☐

Psalms 16:1, Preserve me, O God: for in thee do I put my **trust**. ☐

Psalms 17:7, Shew thy marvellous lovingkindness, O thou that savest by thy right hand them which put their **trust in** thee from those that rise up against them. ☐

Psalms 56:4, In God I will praise his word, in God I have put my **trust**; I will not fear what flesh can do unto me. ☐

Psalms 56:11, In God have I put my **trust**: I will not be afraid what man can do unto me. ☐

Psalms 71:5, For thou art my hope, O Lord GOD: thou art my **trust** from my youth. ☐

Psalms 73:28, But it is good for me to draw near to God: I have put my **trust in the Lord** GOD, that I may declare all thy works. ☐

Psalms 118:8 It is better to **trust in the LORD** than to put confidence in man. ☐

Proverbs 3:5, **Trust in the LORD** with all thine heart; and lean not unto thine own understanding. ☐

Jeremiah 7:8, Behold, ye **trust in** lying words, that cannot profit. ☐

1 Timothy 1:11, According to the glorious gospel of the blessed God, which was committed to my **trust**. ☐

In God We Trust

Psalms 30:10, Hear, O LORD, and have **mercy** upon me: LORD, be thou my helper. ☐

Psalms 31:7, I will be glad and rejoice in thy **mercy**: for thou hast considered my trouble; thou hast known my soul in adversities. ☐

Psalms 31:9, Have **mercy** upon me, O LORD, for I am in trouble: mine eye is consumed with grief, yea, my soul and my belly. ☐

Psalms 32:10, Many sorrows shall be to the wicked: but he that trusteth in the LORD, **mercy** shall compass him about. ☐

Psalms 33:18, Behold, the eye of the LORD is upon them that fear him, upon them that hope in his **mercy**. ☐

Psalms 33:22, Let thy **mercy**, O LORD, be upon us, according as we hope in thee. ☐

Psalms 36:5, Thy **mercy**, O LORD, is in the heavens; and thy faithfulness reacheth unto the clouds. ☐

Psalms 37:21, The wicked borroweth, and payeth not again: but the righteous sheweth **mercy**, and giveth. ☐

Psalms 51:1, Have **mercy** upon me, O God, according to thy lovingkindness: according unto the multitude of thy tender mercies blot out my transgressions. ☐

Psalms 52:8, But I am like a green olive tree in the house of God: I trust in the **mercy** of God for ever and ever. ☐

Psalms 57:10, For thy **mercy** is great unto the heavens, and thy truth unto the clouds. ☐

Psalms 59:16, But I will sing of thy power; yea, I will sing aloud of thy **mercy** in the morning: for thou hast been my defence and refuge in the day of my trouble. ☐

In God We Trust

2 Chronicles 19:7, Wherefore now let the fear of the LORD be upon you; take heed and **do it**: for there is no iniquity with the LORD our God, nor respect of persons, nor taking of gifts. ☐

2 Chronicles 25:8, But if thou wilt go, **do it**, be strong for the battle: God shall make thee fall before the enemy: for God hath power to help, and to cast down. ☐

Ezra 10:4, Arise; for this matter belongeth unto thee: we also will be with thee: be of good courage, and **do it**. ☐

Jeremiah 42:20, For ye dissembled in your hearts, when ye sent me unto the LORD your God, saying, Pray for us unto the LORD our God; and according unto all that the LORD our God shall say, so declare unto us, and we will **do it**. ☐

Ezekiel 24:14, I the LORD have spoken it: it shall come to pass, and I will **do it**; I will not go back, neither will I spare, neither will I repent; according to thy ways, and according to thy doings, shall they judge thee, saith the Lord GOD. ☐

Luke 8:21, And he answered and said unto them, My mother and my brethren are these which hear the word of God, and **do it**. ☐

John 2:5, His mother saith unto the servants, Whatsoever he saith unto you, **do it**. ☐

John 14:14, If ye shall ask any thing in my name, I will **do it**. ☐

Colossians 3:23, And whatsoever ye do, **do it** heartily, as to the Lord, and not unto men.☐

1 Thessalonians 5:24, Faithful is he that calleth you, who also will **do it**.☐

James 4:17, Therefore to him that knoweth to do good, and **doeth** it not, to him it is sin. ☐

DECEITFULNESS OF RICHES

In God We Trust

Proverbs 13:7, There is that maketh himself rich, yet hath nothing: there is that maketh himself poor, yet hath **great** riches. ☐

Proverbs 14:29, He that is slow to wrath is of **great** understanding: but he that is hasty of spirit exalteth folly. ☐

Proverbs 15:16, Better is little with the fear of the LORD than **great** treasure and trouble therewith. ☐

Proverbs 16:8, Better is a little with righteousness than **great** revenues without right. ☐

Proverbs 18:9, He also that is slothful in his work is brother to him that is a **great** waster. ☐

Proverbs 18:16, A man's gift maketh room for him, and bringeth him before **great** men. ☐

Proverbs 22:1, A good name is rather to be chosen than **great** riches, and loving favour rather than silver and gold. ☐

Proverbs 28:12, When righteous men do rejoice, there is **great** glory: but when the wicked rise, a man is hidden. ☐

Ecclesiastes 1:16, I communed with mine own heart, saying, Lo, I am come to **great** estate, and have gotten more wisdom than all they that have been before me in Jerusalem: yea, my heart had **great** experience of wisdom and knowledge. ☐

Jonah 1:17, Now the LORD had prepared a **great** fish to swallow up Jonah. And Jonah was in the belly of the fish three days and three nights. ☐

Jonah 3:2, Arise, go unto Nineveh, that **great** city, and preach unto it the preaching that I bid thee. ☐

Matthew 15:28, Then Jesus answered and said unto her, O woman, **great** is thy faith: be it unto thee even as thou wilt. And her daughter was made whole from that very hour. ☐

Psalms 119:78, Let the proud be ashamed; for they dealt perversely with me without a cause: but **I will** meditate in thy precepts. □

Psalms 119:93, **I will** never forget thy precepts: for with them thou hast quickened me. □

Psalms 119:95, The wicked have waited for me to destroy me: but **I will** consider thy testimonies. □

Psalms 119:106, I have sworn, and **I will** perform it, that **I will** keep thy righteous judgments. □

Psalms 119:115, Depart from me, ye evildoers: for **I will** keep the commandments of my God. □

Psalms 119:117, Hold thou me up, and I shall be safe: and **I will** have respect unto thy statutes continually. □

Psalms 119:145, I cried with my whole heart; hear me, O LORD: **I will** keep thy statutes. □

Psalms 121:1, **I will** lift up mine eyes unto the hills, from whence cometh my help. □

Psalms 122:8, For my brethren and companions' sakes, **I will** now say, Peace be within thee. □

Psalms 122:9, Because of the house of the LORD our God **I will** seek thy good. □

Psalms 138:1, **I will** praise thee with my whole heart: before the gods will I sing praise unto thee.□

Psalms 138:2, **I will** worship toward thy holy temple, and praise thy name for thy lovingkindness and for thy truth: for thou hast magnified thy word above all thy name. □

Psalms 139:14, **I will** praise thee; for I am fearfully and wonderfully made: marvellous are thy works; and that my soul knoweth right well. □

Psalms 112:9, He hath dispersed, he hath given to the **poor**; his righteousness endureth for ever; his horn shall be exalted with honour. □

Psalms 113:7, He raiseth up the **poor** out of the dust, and lifteth the needy out of the dunghill. □

2 Corinthians 6:10, As sorrowful, yet alway rejoicing; as **poor**, yet making many **rich**; as having nothing, and yet possessing all things. □

2 Corinthians 8:9, For ye know the grace of our Lord Jesus Christ, that, though he was **rich**, yet for your sakes he became **poor**, that ye through his poverty might be **rich**. □

Ephesians 2:4, But God, who is **rich** in mercy, for his great love wherewith he loved us. □

1 Timothy 6:9, But they that will be **rich** fall into temptation and a snare, and into many foolish and hurtful lusts, which drown men in destruction and perdition. □

1 Timothy 6:17, Charge them that are **rich** in this world, that they be not highminded, nor trust in uncertain **riches**, but in the living God, who giveth us richly all things to enjoy. □

1 Timothy 6:18, That they do good, that they be **rich** in good works, ready to distribute, willing to communicate. □

James 1:10, But the **rich**, in that he is made low: because as the flower of the grass he shall pass away. □

James 1:11, For the sun is no sooner risen with a burning heat, but it withereth the grass, and the flower thereof falleth, and the grace of the fashion of it perisheth: so also shall the **rich** man fade away in his ways. □

James 2:5, Hearken, my beloved brethren, Hath not God chosen the **poor** of this world **rich** in faith, and heirs of the kingdom which he hath promised to them that love him? □

In God We Trust

Proverbs 21:22, A wise man scaleth the city of the mighty, and casteth down the **strength** of the confidence thereof. □

Proverbs 24:5, A wise man is strong; yea, a man of knowledge increaseth **strength**. □

Proverbs 24:10, If thou faint in the day of adversity, thy **strength** is small. □

Proverbs 31:25, **Strength** and honour are her clothing; and she shall rejoice in time to come. □

Ecclesiastes 9:16, Then said I, Wisdom is better than **strength**: nevertheless the poor man's wisdom is despised, and his words are not heard. □

Isaiah 12:2, Behold, God is my salvation; I will trust, and not be afraid: for the LORD JEHOVAH is my **strength** and my song; he also is become my salvation. □

Isaiah 26:4, Trust ye in the LORD for ever: for in the LORD JEHOVAH is everlasting **strength**. □

Isaiah 35:3, **Strengthen** ye the weak hands, and confirm the feeble knees. □

Isaiah 41:10, Fear thou not; for I am with thee: be not dismayed; for I am thy God: I will **strengthen** thee; yea, I will help thee; yea, I will uphold thee with the right hand of my righteousness. □

Zechariah 10:12, And I will **strengthen** them in the LORD; and they shall walk up and down in his name, saith the LORD. □

Mark 12:30, And thou shalt love the Lord thy God with all thy heart, and with all thy soul, and with all thy mind, and with all thy **strength**: this is the first commandment. □

Luke 22:32, But I have prayed for thee, that thy faith fail not: and when thou art converted, **strengthen** thy brethren. □

Ezekiel 34:26, And I will make them and the places round about my hill a **blessing**; and I will cause the shower to come down in his season; there shall be showers of **blessing**. ☐

Ezekiel 44:30, And the first of all the firstfruits of all things, and every oblation of all, of every sort of your oblations, shall be the priest's: ye shall also give unto the priest the first of your dough, that he may cause the **blessing** to rest in thine house. ☐

Daniel 2:19, Then was the secret revealed unto Daniel in a night vision. Then Daniel **blessed** the God of heaven. ☐

Daniel 2:20, Daniel answered and said, **Blessed** be the name of God for ever and ever: for wisdom and might are his. ☐

Malachi 3:10, Bring ye all the tithes into the storehouse, that there may be meat in mine house, and prove me now herewith, saith the LORD of hosts, if I will not open you the windows of heaven, and pour you out a **blessing**, that there shall not be room enough to receive it. ☐

Malachi 3:12, And all nations shall call you **blessed**: for ye shall be a delightsome land, saith the LORD of hosts. ☐

Matthew 5:3, **Blessed** are the poor in spirit: for theirs is the kingdom of heaven. ☐

Matthew 5:4, **Blessed** are they that mourn: for they shall be comforted. ☐

Matthew 5:5, **Blessed** are the meek: for they shall inherit the earth. ☐

Matthew 5:6, **Blessed** are they which do hunger and thirst after righteousness: for they shall be filled. ☐

Matthew 5:7, **Blessed** are the merciful: for they shall obtain mercy. ☐

RECEIVE HIS WORD WITH GLADNESS

Matthew 5:8, **Blessed** are the pure in heart: for they shall see God. ☐

Matthew 5:9, **Blessed** are the peacemakers: for they shall be called the children of God. ☐

In God We Trust

Psalms 4:1, Hear me when I call, O God of my righteousness: thou hast enlarged me when I was in distress; have **mercy** upon me, and hear my prayer. ☐

Psalms 5:7, But as for me, I will come into thy house in the multitude of thy **mercy**: and in thy fear will I worship toward thy holy temple. ☐

Psalms 6:2, Have **mercy** upon me, O LORD; for I am weak: O LORD, heal me; for my bones are vexed. ☐

Psalms 9:13, Have **mercy** upon me, O LORD; consider my trouble which I suffer of them that hate me, thou that liftest me up from the gates of death. ☐

Psalms 18:50, Great deliverance giveth he to his king; and sheweth **mercy** to his anointed, to David, and to his seed for evermore. ☐

Psalms 21:7, For the king trusteth in the LORD, and through the **mercy** of the most High he shall not be moved. ☐

Psalms 23:6, Surely goodness and **mercy** shall follow me all the days of my life: and I will dwell in the house of the LORD forever. ☐

Psalms 25:7, Remember not the sins of my youth, nor my transgressions: according to thy **mercy** remember thou me for thy goodness' sake, O LORD. ☐

Psalms 25:10, All the paths of the LORD are **mercy** and truth unto such as keep his covenant and his testimonies. ☐

Psalms 25:16, Turn thee unto me, and have **mercy** upon me; for I am desolate and afflicted. ☐

Psalms 27:7, Hear, O LORD, when I cry with my voice: have **mercy** also upon me, and answer me. ☐

Psalms 147:11, The LORD taketh pleasure in them that fear him, in those that hope in his **mercy**. ☐

Proverbs 10:31, The mouth of the just bringeth forth wisdom: but the froward **tongue** shall be cut out. ☐

Proverbs 12:18, There is that speaketh like the piercings of a sword: but the **tongue** of the wise is health. ☐

Proverbs 12:19, The lip of truth shall be established for ever: but a lying **tongue** is but for a moment. ☐

Proverbs 15:2, The **tongue** of the wise useth knowledge aright: but the mouth of fools poureth out foolishness. ☐

Proverbs 15:4, A wholesome **tongue** is a tree of life: but perverseness therein is a breach in the spirit. ☐

Proverbs 16:1, The preparations of the heart in man, and the answer of the **tongue**, is from the LORD. ☐

Proverbs 17:20, He that hath a froward heart findeth no good: and he that hath a perverse **tongue** falleth into mischief. ☐

Proverbs 18:21, Death and life are in the power of the **tongue**: and they that love it shall eat the fruit thereof. ☐

Proverbs 21:6, The getting of treasures by a lying **tongue** is a vanity tossed to and fro of them that seek death. ☐

Proverbs 21:23, Whoso keepeth his mouth and his **tongue** keepeth his soul from troubles. ☐

Proverbs 26:28, A lying **tongue** hateth those that are afflicted by it; and a flattering mouth worketh ruin. ☐

Proverbs 31:26, She openeth her mouth with wisdom; and in her **tongue** is the law of kindness. ☐

Isaiah 28:11, For with stammering lips and another **tongue** will he speak to this people. ☐

In God We Trust

Psalms 78:4, We will not hide them from their children, shewing to the generation to come the praises of the LORD, and his **strength**, and his wonderful works that he hath done. ☐

Psalms 81:1, Sing aloud unto God our **strength**: make a joyful noise unto the God of Jacob. ☐

Psalms 84:5, Blessed is the man whose **strength** is in thee; in whose heart are the ways of them. ☐

Psalms 84:7, They go from **strength** to **strength**, every one of them in Zion appeareth before God. ☐

Psalms 90:10, The days of our years are threescore years and ten; and if by reason of **strength** they be fourscore years, yet is their **strength** labour and sorrow; for it is soon cut off, and we fly away. ☐

Psalms 96:6, Honour and majesty are before him: **strength** and beauty are in his sanctuary. ☐

Psalms 105:4, Seek the LORD, and his **strength**: seek his face evermore.☐

Psalms 118:14, The LORD is my **strength** and song, and is become my salvation. ☐

Psalms 119:28, My soul melteth for heaviness: **strengthen** thou me according unto thy word. ☐

Psalms 132:8, Arise, O LORD, into thy rest; thou, and the ark of thy **strength**. ☐

Psalms 138:3, In the day when I cried thou answeredst me, and strengthenedst me with **strength** in my soul. ☐

Psalms 144:1, Blessed be the LORD my **strength**, which teacheth my hands to war, and my fingers to fight. ☐

Proverbs 10:29, The way of the LORD is **strength** to the upright: but destruction shall be to the workers of iniquity. ☐

In God We Trust

**I BELIEVE
BIGGER
BETTER
BOLDER
BLESSINGS**

LOVE *

21 DAY
AFTERNOON
90 DAY CHALLENGE

John 15:13, Greater **love** hath no man than this, that a man lay down his life for his friends. ☐

Romans 13:10, **Love** worketh no ill to his neighbour: therefore **love** is the fulfilling of the law. ☐

1 Corinthians 16:24, My **love** be with you all in Christ Jesus. Amen. ☐

2 Corinthians 13:11, Finally, brethren, farewell. Be perfect, be of good comfort, be of one mind, live in peace; and the God of **love** and peace shall be with you. ☐

2 Corinthians 13:14, The grace of the Lord Jesus Christ, and the **love** of God, and the communion of the Holy Ghost, be with you all. Amen. ☐

Galatians 5:22, But the fruit of the Spirit is **love**, joy, peace, longsuffering, gentleness, goodness, faith. ☐

1 Timothy 1:14, And the grace of our Lord was exceeding abundant with faith and **love** which is in Christ Jesus. ☐

1 Timothy 6:10, For the **love** of money is the root of all evil: which while some coveted after, they have erred from the faith, and pierced themselves through with many sorrows. ☐

1 Timothy 6:11, But thou, O man of God, flee these things; and follow after righteousness, godliness, faith, **love**, patience, meekness. ☐

2 Timothy 1:7, For God hath not given us the spirit of fear; but of power, and of **love**, and of a sound mind. ☐

James 2:8, If ye fulfil the royal law according to the scripture, Thou shalt **love** thy neighbour as thyself, ye do well. ☐

MORNING

1 John 2:15, **Love** not the world, neither the things that are in the world. If any man **love** the world, the **love** of the Father is not in him. ☐

In God We Trust

Psalms 65:13, The pastures are clothed with flocks; the valleys also are covered over with corn; they shout for **joy**, they also sing. ☐

Psalms 132:16, I will also clothe her priests with salvation: and her saints shall shout aloud for **joy**. ☐

Proverbs 12:20, Deceit is in the heart of them that imagine evil: but to the counsellors of peace is **joy**. ☐

Proverbs 14:10, The heart knoweth his own bitterness; and a stranger doth not intermeddle with his **joy**. ☐

Proverbs 15:21, Folly is **joy** to him that is destitute of wisdom: but a man of understanding walketh uprightly. ☐

Proverbs 15:23, A man hath **joy** by the answer of his mouth: and a word spoken in due season, how good is it! ☐

Proverbs 17:21, He that begetteth a fool doeth it to his sorrow: and the father of a fool hath no **joy**. ☐

Proverbs 21:15, It is **joy** to the just to do judgment: but destruction shall be to the workers of iniquity. ☐

Isaiah 12:3, Therefore with **joy** shall ye draw water out of the wells of salvation. ☐

Isaiah 29:19, The meek also shall increase their **joy** in the LORD, and the poor among men shall rejoice in the Holy One of Israel. ☐

Isaiah 35:10, And the ransomed of the LORD shall return, and come to Zion with songs and everlasting **joy** upon their heads: they shall obtain **joy** and gladness, and sorrow and sighing shall flee away. ☐

Isaiah 51:3, For the LORD shall comfort Zion: he will comfort all her waste places; and he will make her wilderness like Eden, and her desert like the garden of the LORD; **joy** and gladness shall be found therein, thanksgiving, and the voice of melody. ☐

Proverbs 2:4, If thou **seekest** her as silver, and searchest for her as for hid treasures. □

Proverbs 11:27, He that diligently **seeketh** good procureth favour: but he that **seeketh** mischief, it shall come unto him. □

Proverbs 14:6, A scorner **seeketh** wisdom, and findeth it not: but knowledge is easy unto him that understandeth. □

Proverbs 15:14, The heart of him that hath understanding **seeketh** knowledge: but the mouth of fools feedeth on foolishness. □

Proverbs 17:9, He that covereth a transgression **seeketh** love; but he that repeateth a matter separateth very friends. □

Proverbs 17:11, An evil man **seeketh** only rebellion: therefore a cruel messenger shall be sent against him. □

Proverbs 17:19, He loveth transgression that loveth strife: and he that exalteth his gate **seeketh** destruction. □

Proverbs 18:1, Through desire a man, having separated himself, **seeketh** and intermeddleth with all wisdom. □

Matthew 18:12, How think ye? if a man have an hundred sheep, and one of them be gone astray, doth he not leave the ninety and nine, and goeth into the mountains, and **seeketh** that which is gone astray? □

Luke 11:10, For every one that asketh receiveth; and he that **seeketh** findeth; and to him that knocketh it shall be opened. □

John 4:23, But the hour cometh, and now is, when the true worshippers shall worship the Father in spirit and in truth: for the Father **seeketh** such to worship him. □

John 7:18, He that speaketh of himself **seeketh** his own glory: but he that **seeketh** his glory that sent him, the same is true, and no unrighteousness is in him. □

Matthew 10:20, For it is not ye that speak, but the Spirit of your Father which speaketh **in you**. ☐

John 5:38, And ye have not his word abiding **in you**: for whom he hath sent, him ye believe not. ☐

John 5:42, But I know you, that ye have not the love of God **in you**. ☐

John 6:53, Then Jesus said unto them, Verily, verily, I say unto you, Except ye eat the flesh of the Son of man, and drink his blood, ye have no life **in you**. ☐

John 14:17, Even the Spirit of truth; whom the world cannot receive, because it seeth him not, neither knoweth him: but ye know him; for he dwelleth with you, and shall be **in you**. ☐

John 14:20, At that day ye shall know that I am in my Father, and ye in me, and I **in you**. ☐

John 15:4, Abide in me, and I **in you**. As the branch cannot bear fruit of itself, except it abide in the vine; no more can ye, except ye abide in me. ☐

John 15:7, If ye abide in me, and my words abide **in you**, ye shall ask what ye will, and it shall be done unto you. ☐

John 15:11, These things have I spoken unto you, that my joy might remain **in you**, and that your joy might be full. ☐

Romans 8:9, But ye are not in the flesh, but in the Spirit, if so be that the Spirit of God dwell **in you**. Now if any man have not the Spirit of Christ, he is none of his. ☐

Romans 8:10, And if Christ be **in you**, the body is dead because of sin; but the Spirit is life because of righteousness. ☐

Romans 8:11, But if the Spirit of him that raised up Jesus from the dead dwell **in you**, he that raised up Christ from the dead shall also quicken your mortal bodies by his Spirit that dwelleth **in you**. ☐

In God We Trust

FOOL * - FOOLS
FOOLISH *
FOOLISHNESS *

22 DAY
EVENING
90 DAY CHALLENGE

Ecclesiastes 9:17, The words of wise men are heard in quiet more than the cry of him that ruleth among **fools**. ☐

Ecclesiastes 10:2, A wise man's heart is at his right hand; but a **fool**'s heart at his left. ☐

Ecclesiastes 10:3, Yea also, when he that is a **fool** walketh by the way, his wisdom faileth him, and he saith to everyone that he is a **fool**. ☐

Ecclesiastes 10:12, The words of a wise man's mouth are gracious; but the lips of a **fool** will swallow up himself. ☐

Ecclesiastes 10:13, The beginning of the words of his mouth is **foolishness**: and the end of his talk is mischievous madness. ☐

Ecclesiastes 10:14, A **fool** also is full of words: a man cannot tell what shall be; and what shall be after him, who can tell him? ☐

Matthew 25:3, They that were **foolish** took their lamps, and took no oil with them. ☐

Matthew 25:8, And the **foolish** said unto the wise, Give us of your oil; for our lamps are gone out. ☐

Romans 1:21, Because that, when they knew God, they glorified him not as God, neither were thankful; but became vain in their imaginations, and their **foolish** heart was darkened. ☐

1 Corinthians 1:27, But God hath chosen the **foolish** things of the world to confound the wise; and God hath chosen the weak things of the world to confound the things which are mighty. ☐

2 Timothy 2:23, But **foolish** and unlearned questions avoid, knowing that they do engender strifes. ☐

In God We Trust

Genesis 30:13, And Leah said, **Happy** am I, for the daughters will call me blessed: and she called his name Asher. ☐

Deuteronomy 33:29, **Happy** art thou, O Israel: who is like unto thee, O people saved by the LORD, the shield of thy help, and who is the sword of thy excellency! and thine enemies shall be found liars unto thee; and thou shalt tread upon their high places. ☐

1 Kings 10:8, **Happy** are thy men, **happy** are these thy servants, which stand continually before thee, and that hear thy wisdom. ☐

Job 5:17, Behold, **happy** is the man whom God correcteth: therefore despise not thou the chastening of the Almighty. ☐

Psalms 127:5, **Happy** is the man that hath his quiver full of them: they shall not be ashamed, but they shall speak with the enemies in the gate. ☐

Psalms 128:2, For thou shalt eat the labour of thine hands: **happy** shalt thou be, and it shall be well with thee. ☐

Psalms 137:8, O daughter of Babylon, who art to be destroyed; **happy** shall he be, that rewardeth thee as thou hast served us. ☐

Psalms 144:15, **Happy** is that people, that is in such a case: yea, **happy** is that people, whose God is the LORD. ☐

Psalms 146:5, **Happy** is he that hath the God of Jacob for his help, whose hope is in the LORD his God. ☐

Proverbs 3:13, **Happy** is the man that findeth wisdom, and the man that getteth understanding. ☐

Proverbs 3:18, She is a tree of life to them that lay hold upon her: and **happy** is every one that retaineth her. ☐

Acts 26:2, I think myself **happy**, king Agrippa, because I shall answer for myself this day before thee touching all the things whereof I am accused of the Jews ☐

In God We Trust

Deuteronomy 32:4, He is the **Rock**, his work is perfect: for all his ways are judgment: a God of truth and without iniquity, just and right is he. ☐

Deuteronomy 32:31, For their **rock** is not as our **Rock**, even our enemies themselves being judges. ☐

2 Samuel 22:2, And he said, The LORD is my **rock**, and my fortress, and my deliverer. ☐

2 Samuel 22:3, The God of my **rock**; in him will I trust: he is my shield, and the horn of my salvation, my high tower, and my refuge, my saviour; thou savest me from violence. ☐

2 Samuel 22:47, The LORD liveth; and blessed be my **rock**; and exalted be the God of the **rock** of my salvation. ☐

2 Samuel 23:3, The God of Israel said, the **Rock** of Israel spake to me, He that ruleth over men must be just, ruling in the fear of God. ☐

Psalms 18:2, The LORD is my **rock**, and my fortress, and my deliverer; my God, my strength, in whom I will trust; my buckler, and the horn of my salvation, and my high tower. ☐

Psalms 18:31, For who is God save the LORD? or who is a **rock** save our God? ☐

Psalms 18:46, The LORD liveth; and blessed be my **rock**; and let the God of my salvation be exalted. ☐

Psalms 27:5, For in the time of trouble he shall hide me in his pavilion: in the secret of his tabernacle shall he hide me; he shall set me up upon a **rock**. ☐

Psalms 28:1, Unto thee will I cry, O LORD my **rock**; be not silent to me: lest, if thou be silent to me, I become like them that go down into the pit. ☐

Psalms 31:2, Bow down thine ear to me; deliver me speedily: be thou my strong **rock**, for a house of defence to save me. ☐

2 Corinthians 2:14, Now thanks be unto God, which always causeth us to triumph **in Christ**, and maketh manifest the savour of his knowledge by us in every place. ☐

2 Corinthians 3:14, But their minds were blinded: for until this day remaineth the same vail untaken away in the reading of the old testament; which vail is done away **in Christ**. ☐

2 Corinthians 5:17, Therefore if any man be **in Christ**, he is a new creature: old things are passed away; behold, all things are become new. ☐

2 Corinthians 5:19, To wit, that God was **in Christ**, reconciling the world unto himself, not imputing their trespasses unto them; and hath committed unto us the word of reconciliation. ☐

2 Corinthians 11:3, But I fear, lest by any means, as the serpent beguiled Eve through his subtilty, so your minds should be corrupted from the simplicity that is **in Christ**. ☐

Galatians 3:26, For ye are all the children of God by faith **in Christ Jesus**. ☐

Galatians 3:28, There is neither Jew nor Greek, there is neither bond nor free, there is neither male nor female: for ye are all one **in Christ Jesus**. ☐

Ephesians 1:1, Paul, an apostle of Jesus Christ by the will of God, to the saints which are at Ephesus, and to the faithful **in Christ Jesus**. ☐

Ephesians 1:3, Blessed be the God and Father of our Lord Jesus Christ, who hath blessed us with all spiritual blessings in heavenly places **in Christ**. ☐

Ephesians 1:10, That in the dispensation of the fulness of times he might gather together in one all things **in Christ**, both which are in heaven, and which are on earth; even in him. ☐

Ephesians 1:12, That we should be to the praise of his glory, who first trusted **in Christ**. ☐

Ephesians 1:20, Which he wrought **in Christ**, when he raised him from the dead, and set him at his own right hand in the heavenly places. ☐

In God We Trust

I BELIEVE
BIGGER
BETTER
BOLDER
BLESSINGS

MY SOUL *

24 DAY
MORNING
90 DAY CHALLENGE

Psalms 6:4, Return, O LORD, deliver **my soul**: oh save me for thy mercies' sake. ☐

Psalms 11:1, In the LORD put I my trust: how say ye to **my soul**, Flee as a bird to your mountain? ☐

Psalms 13:2, How long shall I take counsel in **my soul**, having sorrow in my heart daily? how long shall mine enemy be exalted over me? ☐

Psalms 23:3, He restoreth **my soul**: he leadeth me in the paths of righteousness for his name's sake. ☐

Psalms 25:1, Unto thee, O LORD, do I lift up **my soul**. ☐

Psalms 25:20, O keep **my soul**, and deliver me: let me not be ashamed; for I put my trust in thee. ☐

Psalms 26:9, Gather not **my soul** with sinners, nor my life with bloody men. ☐

Psalms 30:3, O LORD, thou hast brought up **my soul** from the grave: thou hast kept me alive, that I should not go down to the pit. ☐

Psalms 31:7, I will be glad and rejoice in thy mercy: for thou hast considered my trouble; thou hast known **my soul** in adversities. ☐

Psalms 31:9, Have mercy upon me, O LORD, for I am in trouble: mine eye is consumed with grief, yea **my soul** and my belly. ☐

Psalms 34:2, **My soul** shall make her boast in the LORD: the humble shall hear thereof, and be glad. ☐

Psalms 35:3, Draw out also the spear, and stop the way against them that persecute me: say unto **my soul**, I am thy salvation. ☐

DON'T BE OFFENDED
FOR THE WORD SAKE

In God We Trust

Matthew 8:10, When Jesus heard it, he marvelled, and said to them that followed, Verily I say unto you, I have not found so great **faith**, no, not in Israel. ☐

Mark 5:34, And he said unto her, Daughter, thy **faith** hath made thee whole; go in peace, and be whole of thy plague. ☐

Mark 11:22, And Jesus answering saith unto them, Have **faith** in God. ☐

Luke 7:9, When Jesus heard these things, he marvelled at him, and turned him about, and said unto the people that followed him, I say unto you, I have not found so great **faith**, no, not in Israel. ☐

Luke 7:50, And he said to the woman, Thy **faith** hath saved thee; go in peace. ☐

Luke 8:48, And he said unto her, Daughter, be of good comfort: thy **faith** hath made thee whole; go in peace. ☐

Luke 17:6, And the Lord said, If ye had **faith** as a grain of mustard seed, ye might say unto this sycamine tree, Be thou plucked up by the root, and be thou planted in the sea; and it should obey you. ☐

Luke 17:19, And he said unto him, Arise, go thy way: thy **faith** hath made thee whole. ☐

Luke 18:8, I tell you that he will avenge them speedily. Nevertheless when the Son of man cometh, shall he find **faith** on the earth? ☐

Luke 18:42, And Jesus said unto him, Receive thy sight: thy **faith** hath saved thee. ☐

Luke 22:32, But I have prayed for thee, that thy **faith** fail not: and when thou art converted, strengthen thy brethren. ☐

Acts 6:5, And the saying pleased the whole multitude: and they chose Stephen, a man full of **faith** and of the Holy Ghost, and Philip, and Prochorus, and Nicanor, and Timon, and Parmenas, and Nicolas a proselyte of Antioch: ☐

In God We Trust

Psalms 47:4, He shall choose our inheritance **for us**, the excellency of Jacob whom he loved. Selah. ☐

Psalms 62:8, Trust in him at all times; ye people, pour out your heart before him: God is a refuge **for us**. Selah. ☐

Psalms 68:28, Thy God hath commanded thy strength: strengthen, O God, that which thou hast wrought **for us**. ☐

Psalms 126:3, The LORD hath done great things **for us**; whereof we are glad. ☐

Isaiah 6:8, Also I heard the voice of the Lord, saying, Whom shall I send, and who will go **for us**? Then said I, Here am I; send me. ☐

Isaiah 26:12, LORD, thou wilt ordain peace **for us**: for thou also hast wrought all our works in us. ☐

Romans 4:24, But **for us** also, to whom it shall be imputed, if we believe on him that raised up Jesus our Lord from the dead. ☐

Romans 5:8, But God commendeth his love toward us, in that, while we were yet sinners, Christ died **for us**. ☐

Romans 8:26, Likewise the Spirit also helpeth our infirmities: for we know not what we should pray for as we ought: but the Spirit itself maketh intercession **for us** with groanings which cannot be uttered. ☐

Romans 8:31, What shall we then say to these things? If God be **for us**, who can be against us? ☐

Romans 8:32, He that spared not his own Son, but delivered him up **for us** all, how shall he not with him also freely give us all things? ☐

1 Corinthians 5:7, Purge out therefore the old leaven, that ye may be a new lump, as ye are unleavened. For even Christ our passover is sacrificed **for us**. ☐

In God We Trust

Deuteronomy 6:17, Ye shall diligently keep the commandments of the LORD your God, and his **testimonies**, and his statutes, which he hath commanded thee. □

1 Chronicles 29:19, And give unto Solomon my son a perfect heart, to keep thy commandments, thy **testimonies**, and thy statutes, and to do all these things, and to build the palace, for the which I have made provision. □

Psalms 25:10, All the paths of the LORD are mercy and truth unto such as keep his covenant and his **testimonies**. □

Psalms 93:5, Thy **testimonies** are very sure: holiness becometh thine house, O LORD, for ever. □

Psalms 99:7, He spake unto them in the cloudy pillar: they kept his **testimonies**, and the ordinance that he gave them. □

Psalms 119:2, Blessed are they that keep his **testimonies**, and that seek him with the whole heart. □

Psalms 119:14, I have rejoiced in the way of thy **testimonies**, as much as in all riches. □

Psalms 119:22, Remove from me reproach and contempt; for I have kept thy **testimonies**. □

Psalms 119:24, Thy **testimonies** also are my delight and my counsellors. □

Psalms 119:31, I have stuck unto thy **testimonies**: O LORD, put me not to shame. □

Psalms 119:36, Incline my heart unto thy **testimonies**, and not to covetousness. □

Psalms 119:46, I will speak of thy **testimonies** also before kings, and will not be ashamed. □

Psalms 102:1, Hear my prayer, O LORD, and let my **cry** come unto thee. ☐

Psalms 107:19, Then they **cry** unto the LORD in their trouble, and he saveth them out of their distresses. ☐

Psalms 107:28, Then they **cry** unto the LORD in their trouble, and he bringeth them out of their distresses. ☐

Psalms 119:169, Let my **cry** come near before thee, O LORD: give me understanding according to thy word. ☐

Psalms 141:1, LORD, I **cry** unto thee: make haste unto me; give ear unto my voice, when I **cry** unto thee. ☐

Psalms 142:6, Attend unto my **cry**; for I am brought very low: deliver me from my persecutors; for they are stronger than I. ☐

Psalms 145:19, He will fulfil the desire of them that fear him: he also will hear their **cry**, and will save them. ☐

Proverbs 8:1, Doth not wisdom **cry**? and understanding put forth her voice? ☐

Proverbs 21:13, Whoso stoppeth his ears at the **cry** of the poor, he also shall **cry** himself, but shall not be heard. ☐

Ecclesiastes 9:17, The words of wise men are heard in quiet more than the **cry** of him that ruleth among fools. ☐

Isaiah 12:6, **Cry** out and shout, thou inhabitant of Zion: for great is the Holy One of Israel in the midst of thee. ☐

Isaiah 58:1, **Cry** aloud, spare not, lift up thy voice like a trumpet, and shew my people their transgression, and the house of Jacob their sins. ☐

Philippians 1:29, For unto you it is given in the behalf of Christ, not only to **believe** on him, but also to suffer for his sake. ☐

1 Thessalonians 2:13, For this cause also thank we God without ceasing, because, when ye received the word of God which ye heard of us, ye received it not as the word of men, but as it is in truth, the word of God, which effectually worketh also in you that **believe**. ☐

1 Thessalonians 4:14, For if we **believe** that Jesus died and rose again, even so them also which sleep in Jesus will God bring with him. ☐

2 Thessalonians 1:10, When he shall come to be glorified in his saints, and to be admired in all them that **believe** (because our testimony among you was **believed**) in that day. ☐

Hebrews 11:6, But without faith it is impossible to please him: for he that cometh to God must **believe** that he is, and that he is a rewarder of them that diligently seek him. ☐

James 2:19, Thou believest that there is one God; thou doest well: the devils also **believe**, and tremble. ☐

1 Peter 1:21, Who by him do **believe** in God, that raised him up from the dead, and gave him glory; that your faith and hope might be in God. ☐

1 John 3:23, And this is his commandment, That we should **believe** on the name of his Son Jesus Christ, and love one another, as he gave us commandment. ☐

1 John 5:13, These things have I written unto you that **believe** on the name of the Son of God; that ye may know that ye have eternal life, and that ye may **believe** on the name of the Son of God. ☐

In God We Trust

Psalms 28:6, **Blessed** be the LORD, because he hath heard the voice of my supplications. ☐

Psalms 31:21, **Blessed** be the LORD: for he hath shewed me his marvellous kindness in a strong city. ☐

Psalms 41:13, **Blessed** be the LORD God of Israel from everlasting, and to everlasting. Amen, and Amen. ☐

Psalms 68:19, **Blessed** be the Lord, who daily loadeth us with benefits, even the God of our salvation. Selah. ☐

Psalms 68:35, O God, thou art terrible out of thy holy places: the God of Israel is he that giveth strength and power unto his people. **Blessed** be God. ☐

Psalms 72:18, **Blessed** be the LORD God, the God of Israel, who only doeth wondrous things. ☐

Psalms 72:19, And **blessed** be his glorious name for ever: and let the whole earth be filled with his glory; Amen, and Amen. ☐

Psalms 89:52, **Blessed** be the LORD for evermore. Amen, and Amen. ☐

Psalms 89:15, **Blessed** is the people that know the joyful sound: they shall walk, O LORD, in the light of thy countenance. ☐

Psalms 106:48, **Blessed** be the LORD God of Israel from everlasting to everlasting: and let all the people say, Amen. Praise ye the LORD. ☐

Psalms 144:1, **Blessed** be the LORD my strength, which teacheth my hands to war, and my fingers to fight. ☐

Psalms 18:46, The LORD liveth; and **blessed** be my rock; and let the God of my salvation be exalted. ☐

Luke 1:68, **Blessed** be the Lord God of Israel; for he hath visited and redeemed his people. ☐

Luke 6:20, And he lifted up his eyes on his disciples, and said, **Blessed** be ye poor: for yours is the kingdom of God. ☐

Psalms 72:8, He shall have **dominion** also from sea to sea, and from the river unto the ends of the earth. ☐

Psalms 103:22, Bless the LORD, all his works in all places of his **dominion**: bless the LORD, O my soul. ☐

Psalms 119:133, Order my steps in thy word: and let not any iniquity have **dominion** over me. ☐

Psalms 145:13, Thy kingdom is an everlasting kingdom, and thy **dominion** endureth throughout all generations. ☐

Romans 6:9, Knowing that Christ being raised from the dead dieth no more; death hath no more **dominion** over him. ☐

Romans 6:14, For sin shall not have **dominion** over you: for ye are not under the law, but under grace. ☐

2 Corinthians 1:24, Not for that we have **dominion** over your faith, but are helpers of your joy: for by faith ye stand. ☐

Ephesians 1:21, Far above all principality, and power, and might, and **dominion**, and every name that is named, not only in this world, but also in that which is to come. ☐

Colossians 1:16, For by him were all things created, that are in heaven, and that are in earth, visible and invisible, whether they be thrones, or **dominions**, or principalities, or powers: all things were created by him, and for him. ☐

1 Peter 5:11, To him be glory and **dominion** for ever and ever. Amen. ☐

Jude 1:25, To the only wise God our Saviour, be glory and majesty, **dominion** and power, both now and ever. Amen. ☐

TAKE HEED WHAT YOU HEAR

In God We Trust

Psalms 6:9, The LORD hath heard my supplication; the LORD will **receive** my prayer. ☐

Psalms 24:5, He shall **receive** the blessing from the LORD, and righteousness from the God of his salvation. ☐

Psalms 49:15, But God will redeem my soul from the power of the grave: for he shall **receive** me. Selah. ☐

Psalms 73:24, Thou shalt guide me with thy counsel, and afterward **receive** me to glory. ☐

Proverbs 1:3, To **receive** the instruction of wisdom, justice, and judgment, and equity. ☐

Proverbs 2:1, My son, if thou wilt **receive** my words, and hide my commandments with thee. ☐

Proverbs 4:10, Hear, O my son, and **receive** my sayings; and the years of thy life shall be many. ☐

Proverbs 8:10, **Receive** my instruction, and not silver; and knowledge rather than choice gold. ☐

Proverbs 10:8, The wise in heart will **receive** commandments: but a prating fool shall fall. ☐

Proverbs 19:20, Hear counsel, and **receive** instruction, that thou mayest be wise in thy latter end. ☐

Matthew 10:14, And whosoever shall not **receive** you, nor hear your words, when ye depart out of that house or city, shake off the dust of your feet. ☐

Matthew 21:22, And all things, whatsoever ye shall ask in prayer, believing, ye shall **receive**. ☐

Mark 11:24, Therefore I say unto you, What things soever ye desire, when ye pray, believe that ye **receive** them, and ye shall have them. ☐

Psalms 27:13, I had fainted, unless I had **believed** to see the goodness of the LORD in the land of the living. ☐

Psalms 78:32, For all this they sinned still, and **believed** not for his wondrous works. ☐

Psalms 106:12, Then **believed** they his words; they sang his praise. ☐

Psalms 116:10, I **believed**, therefore have I spoken: I was greatly afflicted. ☐

Psalms 119:66, Teach me good judgment and knowledge: for I have **believed** thy commandments. ☐

John 16:27, For the Father himself loveth you, because ye have loved me, and have **believed** that I came out from God. ☐

John 20:29, Jesus saith unto him, Thomas, because thou hast seen me, thou hast **believed**: blessed are they that have not seen, and yet have **believed**. ☐

Acts 4:32, And the multitude of them that **believed** were of one heart and of one soul: neither said any of them that ought of the things which he possessed was his own; but they had all things common. ☐

Acts 11:21, And the hand of the Lord was with them: and a great number **believed**, and turned unto the Lord. ☐

Acts 13:12, Then the deputy, when he saw what was done, **believed**, being astonished at the doctrine of the Lord. ☐

Romans 4:17, (As it is written, I have made thee a father of many nations,) before him whom he **believed**, even God, who quickeneth the dead, and calleth those things which be not as though they were. ☐

James 2:23, And the scripture was fulfilled which saith, Abraham **believed** God, and it was imputed unto him for righteousness: and he was called the Friend of God. ☐

Isaiah 32:17, And the work of **righteousness** shall be peace; and the effect of **righteousness** quietness and assurance forever. ☐

Isaiah 41:10, Fear thou not; for I am with thee: be not dismayed; for I am thy God: I will strengthen thee; yea, I will help thee; yea, I will uphold thee with the right hand of my **righteousness**. ☐

Isaiah 42:6, I the LORD have called thee in **righteousness**, and will hold thine hand, and will keep thee, and give thee for a covenant of the people, for a light of the Gentiles. ☐

Isaiah 42:21, The LORD is well pleased for his **righteousness** sake; he will magnify the law, and make it honourable. ☐

Isaiah 54:14, In **righteousness** shalt thou be established: thou shalt be far from oppression; for thou shalt not fear: and from terror; for it shall not come near thee. ☐

Isaiah 54:17, No weapon that is formed against thee shall prosper; and every tongue that shall rise against thee in judgment thou shalt condemn. This is the heritage of the servants of the LORD, and their **righteousness** is of me, saith the LORD. ☐

Isaiah 58:2, Yet they seek me daily, and delight to know my ways, as a nation that did **righteousness**, and forsook not the ordinance of their God: they ask of me the ordinances of justice; they take delight in approaching to God. ☐

Isaiah 58:8, Then shall thy light break forth as the morning, and thine health shall spring forth speedily: and thy **righteousness** shall go before thee; the glory of the LORD shall be thy reward. ☐

Isaiah 61:3, To appoint unto them that mourn in Zion, to give unto them beauty for ashes, the oil of joy for mourning, the garment of praise for the spirit of heaviness; that they might be called trees of **righteousness**, the planting of the LORD, that he might be glorified. ☐

Matthew 8:26, And he saith unto them, Why are ye fearful, O ye of little faith? Then he arose, and rebuked the winds and the sea; and there was a great calm. ☐

Matthew 9:2, And, behold, they brought to him a man sick of the palsy, lying on a bed: and Jesus seeing their faith said unto the sick of the palsy; Son, be of good cheer; thy sins be forgiven thee. ☐

Matthew 9:22, But Jesus turned him about, and when he saw her, he said, Daughter, be of good comfort; thy faith hath made thee whole. And the woman was made whole from that hour. ☐

Matthew 9:29, Then touched he their eyes, saying, According to your faith be it unto you. ☐

Matthew 14:31, And immediately Jesus stretched forth his hand, and caught him, and said unto him, O thou of little faith, wherefore didst thou doubt? ☐

Matthew 15:28, Then Jesus answered and said unto her, O woman, great is thy faith: be it unto thee even as thou wilt. And her daughter was made whole from that very hour. ☐

Matthew 16:8, Which when Jesus perceived, he said unto them, O ye of little faith, why reason ye among yourselves, because ye have brought no bread? ☐

Matthew 17:20, And Jesus said unto them, Because of your unbelief: for verily I say unto you, If ye have faith as a grain of mustard seed, ye shall say unto this mountain, Remove hence to yonder place; and it shall remove; and nothing shall be impossible unto you. ☐

Matthew 21:21, Jesus answered and said unto them, Verily I say unto you, If ye have faith, and doubt not, ye shall not only do this which is done to the fig tree, but also if ye shall say unto this mountain, Be thou removed, and be thou cast into the sea; it shall be done. ☐

Numbers 14:8, If the LORD delight **in us**, then he will bring us into this land, and give it us; a land which floweth with milk and honey. ☐

Isaiah 26:12, LORD, thou wilt ordain peace for us: for thou also hast wrought all our works **in us**. ☐

John 17:21, That they all may be one; as thou, Father, art in me, and I in thee, that they also may be one **in us**: that the world may believe that thou hast sent me. ☐

Romans 8:4, That the righteousness of the law might be fulfilled **in us**, who walk not after the flesh, but after the Spirit. ☐

Romans 8:18, For I reckon that the sufferings of this present time are not worthy to be compared with the glory which shall be revealed **in us**. ☐

2 Corinthians 1:5, For as the sufferings of Christ abound **in us**, so our consolation also aboundeth by Christ. ☐

2 Corinthians 6:12, Ye are not straitened **in us**, but ye are straitened in your own bowels. ☐

Ephesians 3:20, Now unto him that is able to do exceeding abundantly above all that we ask or think, according to the power that worketh **in us**. ☐

2 Timothy 1:14, That good thing which was committed unto thee keep by the Holy Ghost which dwelleth **in us**. ☐

James 4:5, Do ye think that the scripture saith in vain, The spirit that dwelleth **in us** lusteth to envy? ☐

1 John 1:8, If we say that we have no sin, we deceive ourselves, and the truth is not **in us**. ☐

1 John 1:10, If we say that we have not sinned, we make him a liar, and his word is not **in us**. ☐

In God We Trust
82

Psalms 78:35, And they remembered that God was their rock, and the high God their **redeemer**. □

Proverbs 23:11, For their **redeemer** is mighty; he shall plead their cause with thee. □

Psalms 31:5, Into thine hand I commit my spirit: thou hast **redeemed** me, O LORD God of truth. □

Isaiah 41:14, Fear not, thou worm Jacob, and ye men of Israel; I will help thee, saith the LORD, and thy **redeemer**, the Holy One of Israel. □

Psalms 71:23, My lips shall greatly rejoice when I sing unto thee; and my soul, which thou hast **redeemed**. □

Psalms 106:10, And he saved them from the hand of him that hated them, and **redeemed** them from the hand of the enemy. □

Psalms 107:2, Let the **redeemed** of the LORD say so, whom he hath **redeemed** from the hand of the enemy. □

Psalms 136:24, And hath **redeemed** us from our enemies: for his mercy endureth for ever. □

Isaiah 44:6, Thus saith the LORD the King of Israel, and his **redeemer** the LORD of hosts; I am the first, and I am the last; and beside me there is no God. □

Isaiah 44:24, Thus saith the LORD, thy **redeemer**, and he that formed thee from the womb, I am the LORD that maketh all things; that stretcheth forth the heavens alone; that spreadeth abroad the earth by myself. □

Isaiah 47:4, As for our **redeemer**, the LORD of hosts is his name, the Holy One of Israel. □

Isaiah 48:17, Thus saith the LORD, thy **Redeemer**, the Holy One of Israel; I am the LORD thy God which teacheth thee to profit, which leadeth thee by the way that thou shouldest go. □

In God We Trust

Deuteronomy 5:27, Go thou near, and hear all that the LORD our God shall say: and speak thou unto us all that the LORD our God shall speak unto thee; and we will hear it, and **do it**. ☐

1 Chronicles 28:10, Take heed now; for the LORD hath chosen thee to build an house for the sanctuary: be strong, and **do it**. ☐

1 Chronicles 28:20, And David said to Solomon his son, Be strong and of good courage, and **do it**: fear not, nor be dismayed: for the LORD God, even my God, will be with thee; he will not fail thee, nor forsake thee, until thou hast finished all the work for the service of the house of the LORD. ☐

Proverbs 21:15, It is joy to the just **to do** judgment: but destruction shall be to the workers of iniquity. ☐

Proverbs 21:3, **To do** justice and judgment is more acceptable to the LORD than sacrifice. ☐

Proverbs 24:8, He that deviseth **to do** evil shall be called a mischievous person. ☐

Ecclesiastes 3:12, I know that there is no good in them, but for a man to rejoice, and **to do** good in his life. ☐

Ecclesiastes 9:10, Whatsoever thy hand findeth **to do**, do it with thy might; for there is no work, nor device, nor knowledge, nor wisdom, in the grave, whither thou goest. ☐

Isaiah 1:17, Learn **to do** well; seek judgment, relieve the oppressed, judge the fatherless, plead for the widow. ☐

Mark 3:4, And he saith unto them, Is it lawful **to do** good on the sabbath days, or **to do** evil? to save life, or to kill? But they held their peace. ☐

1 Thessalonians 4:11, And that ye study to be quiet, and **to do** your own business, and to work with your own hands, as we commanded you. ☐

Hebrews 13:16, But **to do** good and to communicate forget not: for with such sacrifices God is well pleased. ☐

In God We Trust

Psalms 117:2, For his merciful kindness is **great** toward us: and the truth of the LORD endureth forever. Praise ye the LORD. □

Psalms 119:156, **Great** are thy tender mercies, O LORD: quicken me according to thy judgments. □

Psalms 119:162, I rejoice at thy word, as one that findeth **great** spoil. □

Psalms 119:165, **Great** peace have they which love thy law: and nothing shall offend them. □

Psalms 126:3, The LORD hath done **great** things for us; whereof we are glad. □

Psalms 135:5, For I know that the LORD is **great**, and that our Lord is above all gods. □

Psalms 136:4, To him who alone doeth **great** wonders: for his mercy endureth forever. □

Psalms 136:7, To him that made **great** lights: for his mercy endureth for ever. □

Psalms 139:17, How precious also are thy thoughts unto me, O God! how **great** is the sum of them! □

Psalms 145:3, **Great** is the LORD, and greatly to be praised; and his greatness is unsearchable. □

Psalms 145:7, They shall abundantly utter the memory of thy **great** goodness, and shall sing of thy righteousness. □

Psalms 145:8, The LORD is gracious, and full of compassion; slow to anger, and of **great** mercy. □

Psalms 147:5, **Great** is our Lord, and of **great** power: his understanding is infinite. □

Psalms 104:34, My meditation of him shall be sweet: **I will** be glad in the LORD. ☐

Psalms 108:1, O God, my heart is fixed; **I will** sing and give praise, even with my glory. ☐

Psalms 108:3, **I will** praise thee, O LORD, among the people: and **I will** sing praises unto thee among the nations. ☐

Psalms 109:30, **I will** greatly praise the LORD with my mouth; yea, **I will** praise him among the multitude. ☐

Psalms 111:1, Praise ye the LORD. **I will** praise the LORD with my whole heart, in the assembly of the upright, and in the congregation. ☐

Psalms 116:9, **I will** walk before the LORD in the land of the living. ☐

Psalms 116:13, **I will** take the cup of salvation, and call upon the name of the LORD. ☐

Psalms 116:14, **I will** pay my vows unto the LORD now in the presence of all his people. ☐

Psalms 116:17, **I will** offer to thee the sacrifice of thanksgiving, and will call upon the name of the LORD. ☐

Psalms 116:18, **I will** pay my vows unto the LORD now in the presence of all his people. ☐

Psalms 118:6, The LORD is on my side; **I will** not fear: what can man do unto me? ☐

Psalms 118:11, They compassed me about; yea, they compassed me about: but in the name of the LORD **I will** destroy them. ☐

Psalms 118:12, They compassed me about like bees; they are quenched as the fire of thorns: for in the name of the LORD **I will** destroy them. ☐

Psalms 119:159, Consider how I **love** thy precepts: quicken me, O LORD, according to thy lovingkindness. ☐

Psalms 119:165, Great peace have they which **love** thy law: and nothing shall offend them. ☐

Psalms 119:167, My soul hath kept thy testimonies; and I **love** them exceedingly. ☐

Psalms 122:6, Pray for the peace of Jerusalem: they shall prosper that **love** thee. ☐

Psalms 145:20, The LORD preserveth all them that **love** him: but all the wicked will he destroy. ☐

Proverbs 8:17, I **love** them that **love** me; and those that seek me early shall find me. ☐

Proverbs 8:21, That I may cause those that **love** me to inherit substance; and I will fill their treasures. ☐

Proverbs 8:36, But he that sinneth against me wrongeth his own soul: all they that hate me **love** death. ☐

Proverbs 10:12, Hatred stirreth up strifes: but **love** covereth all sins. ☐

Proverbs 15:17, Better is a dinner of herbs where **love** is, than a stalled ox and hatred therewith. ☐

Proverbs 16:13, Righteous lips are the delight of kings; and they **love** him that speaketh right. ☐

Proverbs 18:21, Death and life are in the power of the tongue: and they that **love** it shall eat the fruit thereof. ☐

Proverbs 20:13, **Love** not sleep, lest thou come to poverty; open thine eyes, and thou shalt be satisfied with bread. ☐

In God We Trust

Psalms 33:12, **Blessed** is the nation whose God is the LORD; and the people whom he hath chosen for his own inheritance. □

Psalms 34:8, O taste and see that the LORD is good: **blessed** is the man that trusteth in him. □

Psalms 37:22, For such as be **blessed** of him shall inherit the earth; and they that be cursed of him shall be cut off. □

Psalms 37:26, He is ever merciful, and lendeth; and his seed is **blessed**. □

Psalms 40:4, **Blessed** is that man that maketh the LORD his trust, and respecteth not the proud, nor such as turn aside to lies. □

Psalms 41:1, **Blessed** is he that considereth the poor: the LORD will deliver him in time of trouble. □

Psalms 41:2, The LORD will preserve him, and keep him alive; and he shall be **blessed** upon the earth: and thou wilt not deliver him unto the will of his enemies. □

Psalms 41:13, **Blessed** be the LORD God of Israel from everlasting, and to everlasting. Amen, and Amen. □

Psalms 45:2, Thou art fairer than the children of men: grace is poured into thy lips: therefore God hath **blessed** thee forever. □

Psalms 49:18, Though while he lived he **blessed** his soul: and men will praise thee, when thou doest well to thyself. □

Psalms 66:20, **Blessed** be God, which hath not turned away my prayer, nor his mercy from me. □

Psalms 68:19, **Blessed** be the Lord, who daily loadeth us with benefits, even the God of our salvation. Selah. □

Psalms 72:17, His name shall endure for ever: his name shall be continued as long as the sun: and men shall be **blessed** in him: all nations shall call him **blessed**. □

Psalms 29:1, Give unto the LORD, O ye mighty, give unto the LORD glory and **strength**. ☐

Psalms 29:11, The LORD will give **strength** unto his people; the LORD will bless his people with peace. ☐

Psalms 31:24, Be of good courage, and he shall **strengthen** your heart, all ye that hope in the LORD. ☐

Psalms 38:10, My heart panteth, my **strength** faileth me: as for the light of mine eyes, it also is gone from me. ☐

Psalms 46:1, God is our refuge and **strength**, a very present help in trouble. ☐

Psalms 52:7, Lo, this is the man that made not God his **strength**; but trusted in the abundance of his riches, and strengthened himself in his wickedness. ☐

Psalms 59:9, Because of his **strength** will I wait upon thee: for God is my defence. ☐

Psalms 59:17, Unto thee, O my **strength**, will I sing: for God is my defence, and the God of my mercy. ☐

Psalms 62:7, In God is my salvation and my glory: the rock of my **strength**, and my refuge, is in God. ☐

Psalms 68:28, Thy God hath commanded thy **strength**: **strengthen**, O God, that which thou hast wrought for us. ☐

Psalms 71:9, Cast me not off in the time of old age; forsake me not when my **strength** faileth. ☐

Psalms 71:16, I will go in the **strength** of the Lord GOD: I will make mention of thy righteousness, even of thine only. ☐

Psalms 73:26, My flesh and my heart faileth: but God is the **strength** of my heart, and my portion forever. ☐

In God We Trust
89

Psalms 89:26, He shall cry unto me, Thou art my father, my God, and the **rock** of my salvation. ☐

Psalms 92:15, To shew that the LORD is upright: he is my **rock**, and there is no unrighteousness in him. ☐

Psalms 94:22, But the LORD is my defence; and my God is the **rock** of my refuge. ☐

Psalms 95:1, O come, let us sing unto the LORD: let us make a joyful noise to the **rock** of our salvation. ☐

Psalms 105:41, He opened the **rock**, and the waters gushed out; they ran in the dry places like a river. ☐

Psalms 114:8, Which turned the **rock** into a standing water, the flint into a fountain of waters. ☐

Isaiah 51:1, Hearken to me, ye that follow after righteousness, ye that seek the LORD: look unto the **rock** whence ye are hewn, and to the hole of the pit whence ye are digged. ☐

Matthew 7:24, Therefore whosoever heareth these sayings of mine, and doeth them, I will liken him unto a wise man, which built his house upon a **rock**. ☐

Matthew 7:25, And the rain descended, and the floods came, and the winds blew, and beat upon that house; and it fell not: for it was founded upon a **rock**. ☐

Matthew 16:18, And I say also unto thee, That thou art Peter, and upon this **rock** I will build my church; and the gates of hell shall not prevail against it. ☐

Luke 8:13, They on the **rock** are they, which, when they hear, receive the word with joy; and these have no root, which for a while believe, and in time of temptation fall away. ☐

In God We Trust

FORGIVENESS
FORGIVEN

31 DAY

MORNING
90 DAY CHALLENGE

Psalms 130:4, But there is **forgiveness** with thee, that thou mayest be feared. ☐

Matthew 9:2, And, behold, they brought to him a man sick of the palsy, lying on a bed: and Jesus seeing their faith said unto the sick of the palsy; Son, be of good cheer; thy sins be **forgiven** thee. ☐

Matthew 9:5, For whether is easier, to say, Thy sins be **forgiven** thee; or to say, Arise, and walk? ☐

Matthew 12:31, Wherefore I say unto you, All manner of sin and blasphemy shall be **forgiven** unto men: but the blasphemy against the Holy Ghost shall not be **forgiven** unto men. ☐

Matthew 12:32, And whosoever speaketh a word against the Son of man, it shall be **forgiven** him: but whosoever speaketh against the Holy Ghost, it shall not be **forgiven** him, neither in this world, neither in the world to come. ☐

Mark 2:5, When Jesus saw their faith, he said unto the sick of the palsy, Son, thy sins be **forgiven** thee. ☐

Acts 5:31, Him hath God exalted with his right hand to be a Prince and a Saviour, for to give repentance to Israel, and **forgiveness** of sins. ☐

Acts 13:38, Be it known unto you therefore, men and brethren, that through this man is preached unto you the **forgiveness** of sins. ☐

Acts 26:18, To open their eyes, and to turn them from darkness to light, and from the power of Satan unto God, that they may receive **forgiveness** of sins, and inheritance among them which are sanctified by faith that is in me. ☐

Ephesians 1:7, In whom we have redemption through his blood, the **forgiveness** of sins, according to the riches of his grace. ☐

Colossians 1:14, In whom we have redemption through his blood, even the **forgiveness** of sins. ☐

Proverbs 4:8, Exalt her, and she shall promote thee: she shall bring thee to **honour**, when thou dost embrace her. ☐

Proverbs 5:9, Lest thou give thine **honour** unto others, and thy years unto the cruel. ☐

Proverbs 8:18, Riches and **honour** are with me; yea, durable riches and righteousness. ☐

Proverbs 11:16, A gracious woman retaineth **honour**: and strong men retain riches. ☐

Proverbs 15:33, The fear of the LORD is the instruction of wisdom; and before **honour** is humility. ☐

Proverbs 18:12, Before destruction the heart of man is haughty, and before **honour** is humility. ☐

Proverbs 20:3, It is an **honour** for a man to cease from strife: but every fool will be meddling. ☐

Proverbs 21:21, He that followeth after righteousness and mercy findeth life, righteousness, and **honour**. ☐

Proverbs 22:4, By humility and the fear of the LORD are riches, and **honour**, and life. ☐

Proverbs 26:1, As snow in summer, and as rain in harvest, so **honour** is not seemly for a fool. ☐

Proverbs 26:8, As he that bindeth a stone in a sling, so is he that giveth **honour** to a fool. ☐

Proverbs 29:23, A man's pride shall bring him low: but **honour** shall uphold the humble in spirit. ☐

Proverbs 31:25, Strength and **honour** are her clothing; and she shall rejoice in time to come. ☐

Psalms 89:3, I have made a **covenant** with my chosen, I have sworn unto David my servant. ☐

Psalms 89:28, My mercy will I keep for him for evermore, and my **covenant** shall stand fast with him. ☐

Psalms 89:34, My **covenant** will I not break, nor alter the thing that is gone out of my lips. ☐

Psalms 89:39, Thou hast made void the **covenant** of thy servant: thou hast profaned his crown by casting it to the ground. ☐

Psalms 103:18, To such as keep his **covenant**, and to those that remember his commandments to do them. ☐

Psalms 105:8, He hath remembered his **covenant** for ever, the word which he commanded to a thousand generations. ☐

Psalms 106:45, And he remembered for them his **covenant**, and repented according to the multitude of his mercies. ☐

Psalms 111:5, He hath given meat unto them that fear him: he will ever be mindful of his **covenant**. ☐

Psalms 111:9, He sent redemption unto his people: he hath commanded his **covenant** for ever: holy and reverend is his name. ☐

Psalms 132:12, If thy children will keep my **covenant** and my testimony that I shall teach them, their children shall also sit upon thy throne for evermore. ☐

Isaiah 59:21, As for me, this is my **covenant** with them, saith the LORD; My spirit that is upon thee, and my words which I have put in thy mouth, shall not depart out of thy mouth, nor out of the mouth of thy seed, nor out of the mouth of thy seed's seed, saith the LORD, from henceforth and forever. ☐

Jeremiah 11:2, Hear ye the words of this **covenant**, and speak unto the men of Judah, and to the inhabitants of Jerusalem. ☐

In God We Trust

Acts 6:7, And the word of God increased; and the number of the disciples multiplied in Jerusalem greatly; and a great company of the priests were obedient to the **faith**. ☐

Acts 6:8, And Stephen, full of **faith** and power, did great wonders and miracles among the people. ☐

Acts 11:24, For he was a good man, and full of the Holy Ghost and of **faith**: and much people was added unto the Lord. ☐

Acts 14:9, The same heard Paul speak: who stedfastly beholding him, and perceiving that he had **faith** to be healed. ☐

Acts 14:22, Confirming the souls of the disciples, and exhorting them to continue in the **faith**, and that we must through much tribulation enter into the kingdom of God. ☐

Acts 16:5, And so were the churches established in the **faith**, and increased in number daily. ☐

Acts 20:21, Testifying both to the Jews, and also to the Greeks, repentance toward God, and **faith** toward our Lord Jesus Christ. ☐

Acts 26:18, To open their eyes, and to turn them from darkness to light, and from the power of Satan unto God, that they may receive forgiveness of sins, and inheritance among them which are sanctified by **faith** that is in me. ☐

Romans 1:8, First, I thank my God through Jesus Christ for you all, that your **faith** is spoken of throughout the whole world. ☐

Romans 1:12, That is, that I may be comforted together with you by the mutual **faith** both of you and me. ☐

Romans 1:17, For therein is the righteousness of God revealed from **faith** to **faith**: as it is written, The just shall live by **faith**. ☐

Romans 3:3, For what if some did not believe? shall their unbelief make the **faith** of God without effect? ☐

In God We Trust
94

Ephesians 4:4, There is one body, and one Spirit, even as ye are called in one **hope** of your calling. ☐

Colossians 1:27, To whom God would make known what is the riches of the glory of this mystery among the Gentiles; which is Christ in you, the **hope** of glory. ☐

1 Thessalonians 1:3, Remembering without ceasing your work of faith, and labour of love, and patience of **hope** in our Lord Jesus Christ, in the sight of God and our Father. ☐

1 Thessalonians 2:19, For what is our **hope**, or joy, or crown of rejoicing? Are not even ye in the presence of our Lord Jesus Christ at his coming? ☐

1 Thessalonians 4:13, But I would not have you to be ignorant, brethren, concerning them which are asleep, that ye sorrow not, even as others which have no **hope**. ☐

1 Thessalonians 5:8, But let us, who are of the day, be sober, putting on the breastplate of faith and love; and for an helmet, the **hope** of salvation. ☐

2 Thessalonians 2:16, Now our Lord Jesus Christ himself, and God, even our Father, which hath loved us, and hath given us everlasting consolation and good **hope** through grace. ☐

Titus 1:2, In **hope** of eternal life, which God, that cannot lie, promised before the world began. ☐

Titus 2:13, Looking for that blessed **hope**, and the glorious appearing of the great God and our Saviour Jesus Christ. ☐

Titus 3:7, That being justified by his grace, we should be made heirs according to the **hope** of eternal life. ☐

Hebrews 6:11, And we desire that every one of you do shew the same diligence to the full assurance of **hope** unto the end. ☐

Hebrews 7:19, For the law made nothing perfect, but the bringing in of a better **hope** did; by the which we draw nigh unto God. ☐

In God We Trust

Matthew 18:5, And whoso shall **receive** one such little child in my name receiveth me. □

Matthew 19:29, And every one that hath forsaken houses, or brethren, or sisters, or father, or mother, or wife, or children, or lands, for my name's sake, shall **receive** a hundredfold, and shall inherit everlasting life. □

Mark 4:20, And these are they which are sown on good ground; such as hear the word, and **receive** it, and bring forth fruit, some thirtyfold, some sixty, and some an hundred. □

Mark 10:30, But he shall **receive** an hundredfold now in this time, houses, and brethren, and sisters, and mothers, and children, and lands, with persecutions; and in the world to come eternal life. □

Luke 6:34, And if ye lend to them of whom ye hope to **receive**, what thank have ye? for sinners also lend to sinners, to **receive** as much again. □

Luke 16:9, And I say unto you, Make to yourselves friends of the mammon of unrighteousness; that, when ye fail, they may **receive** you into everlasting habitations. □

Luke 18:41, Saying, What wilt thou that I shall do unto thee? And he said, Lord, that I may **receive** my sight. □

Luke 18:42, And Jesus said unto him, **Receive** thy sight: thy faith hath saved thee. □

John 5:43, I am come in my Father's name, and ye **receive** me not: if another shall come in his own name, him ye will **receive**. □

John 5:44, How can ye believe, which **receive** honour one of another, and seek not the honour that cometh from God only? □

John 14:3, And if I go and prepare a place for you, I will come again, and **receive** you unto myself; that where I am, there ye may be also. □

1 Kings 9:4, And if thou wilt walk before me, as David thy father walked, in **integrity** of heart, and in uprightness, to do according to all that I have commanded thee, and wilt keep my statutes and my judgments. ☐

Job 2:3, And the LORD said unto Satan, Hast thou considered my servant Job, that there is none like him in the earth, a perfect and an upright man, one that feareth God, and escheweth evil? and still he holdeth fast his **integrity**, although thou movedst me against him, to destroy him without cause. ☐

Job 31:6, Let me be weighed in an even balance, that God may know mine **integrity**. ☐

Psalms 7:8, The LORD shall judge the people: judge me, O LORD, according to my righteousness, and according to mine **integrity** that is in me. ☐

Psalms 25:21, Let **integrity** and uprightness preserve me; for I wait on thee. ☐

Psalms 26:1, Judge me, O LORD; for I have walked in mine **integrity**: I have trusted also in the LORD; therefore I shall not slide. ☐

Psalms 26:11, But as for me, I will walk in mine **integrity**: redeem me, and be merciful unto me. ☐

Psalms 41:12, And as for me, thou upholdest me in mine **integrity**, and settest me before thy face for ever. ☐

Psalms 78:72, So he fed them according to the **integrity** of his heart; and guided them by the skilfulness of his hands. ☐

Proverbs 11:3, The **integrity** of the upright shall guide them: but the perverseness of transgressors shall destroy them. ☐

Proverbs 19:1, Better is the poor that walketh in his **integrity**, than he that is perverse in his lips, and is a fool. ☐

Proverbs 20:7, The just man walketh in his **integrity**: his children are blessed after him. ☐

REDEEM - REDEEMED *
REDEEMER
REDEEMING

33 DAY
AFTERNOON
90 DAY CHALLENGE

2 Samuel 4:9, And David answered Rechab and Baanah his brother, the sons of Rimmon the Beerothite, and said unto them, As the LORD liveth, who hath **redeemed** my soul out of all adversity. ☐

1 Kings 1:29, And the king sware, and said, As the LORD liveth, that hath **redeemed** my soul out of all distress. ☐

Job 19:25, For I know that my **redeemer** liveth, and that he shall stand at the latter day upon the earth. ☐

Psalms 25:22, **Redeem** Israel, O God, out of all his troubles. ☐

Psalms 26:11, But as for me, I will walk in mine integrity: **redeem** me, and be merciful unto me. ☐

Psalms 49:15, But God will **redeem** my soul from the power of the grave: for he shall receive me. Selah. ☐

Isaiah 52:3, For thus saith the LORD, Ye have sold yourselves for nought; and ye shall be **redeemed** without money. ☐

Isaiah 63:4, For the day of vengeance is in mine heart, and the year of my **redeemed** is come. ☐

Lamentations 3:58, O Lord, thou hast pleaded the causes of my soul; thou hast **redeemed** my life. ☐

Hosea 13:14, I will ransom them from the power of the grave; I will **redeem** them from death: O death, I will be thy plagues; O grave, I will be thy destruction: repentance shall be hid from mine eyes. ☐

Galatians 3:13, Christ hath **redeemed** us from the curse of the law, being made a curse for us: for it is written, Cursed is every one that hangeth on a tree. ☐

Colossians 4:5, Walk in wisdom toward them that are without, **redeeming** the time. ☐

In God We Trust

Psalms 42:11, Why art thou cast down, O my soul? and why art thou disquieted within me? hope thou in God: for I shall yet praise him, who is the **health** of my countenance, and my God. ☐

Proverbs 3:8, It shall be **health** to thy navel, and marrow to thy bones. ☐

Proverbs 4:22, For they are life unto those that find them, and **health** to all their flesh. ☐

Proverbs 12:18, There is that speaketh like the piercings of a sword: but the tongue of the wise is **health**. ☐

Proverbs 13:17, A wicked messenger falleth into mischief: but a faithful ambassador is **health**. ☐

Isaiah 58:8, Then shall thy light break forth as the morning, and thine **health** shall spring forth speedily: and thy righteousness shall go before thee; the glory of the LORD shall be thy reward. ☐

Jeremiah 8:15, We looked for peace, but no good came; and for a time of **health**, and behold trouble! ☐

Jeremiah 30:17, For I will restore **health** unto thee, and I will heal thee of thy wounds, saith the LORD; because they called thee an Outcast, saying, This is Zion, whom no man seeketh after. ☐

Jeremiah 33:6, Behold, I will bring it **health** and cure, and I will cure them, and will reveal unto them the abundance of peace and truth. ☐

III John 2, Beloved, I wish above all things
that thou mayest prosper and be in **health**,
even as thy soul prospereth. ☐

In God We Trust

Genesis 1:11, And God said, Let the earth bring forth grass, the herb yielding seed, and the **fruit** tree yielding **fruit** after his kind, whose seed is in itself, upon the earth: and it was so. ☐

Psalms 1:3, And he shall be like a tree planted by the rivers of water, that bringeth forth his **fruit** in his season; his leaf also shall not wither; and whatsoever he doeth shall prosper. ☐

Psalms 92:14, They shall still bring forth **fruit** in old age; they shall be fat and flourishing. ☐

Psalms 104:13, He watereth the hills from his chambers: the earth is satisfied with the **fruit** of thy works. ☐

Psalms 105:35, And did eat up all the herbs in their land, and devoured the **fruit** of their ground. ☐

Psalms 127:3, Lo, children are an heritage of the LORD: and the **fruit** of the womb is his reward. ☐

Psalms 132:11, The LORD hath sworn in truth unto David; he will not turn from it; Of the **fruit** of thy body will I set upon thy throne. ☐

Proverbs 1:31, Therefore shall they eat of the **fruit** of their own way, and be filled with their own devices. ☐

Proverbs 8:19, My **fruit** is better than gold, yea, than fine gold; and my revenue than choice silver. ☐

Proverbs 10:16, The labour of the righteous tendeth to life: the **fruit** of the wicked to sin. ☐

Proverbs 11:30, The **fruit** of the righteous is a tree of life; and he that winneth souls is wise. ☐

Proverbs 12:12, The wicked desireth the net of evil men: but the root of the righteous yieldeth **fruit**. ☐

In God We Trust

Deuteronomy 32:1, Give ear, O ye heavens, and I will speak; and hear, O earth, the words of **my mouth.** ☐

Psalms 19:14, Let the words of **my mouth**, and the meditation of my heart, be acceptable in thy sight, O LORD, my strength, and my redeemer. ☐

Proverbs 8:6, Hear; for I will speak of excellent things; and the opening of **my lips** shall be right things. ☐

Psalms 141:3, Set a watch, O LORD, before **my mouth**; keep the door of **my lips.** ☐

Psalms 34:1, I will bless the LORD at all times: his praise shall continually be in **my mouth.** ☐

Psalms 39:1, I said, I will take heed to my ways, that I sin not with my tongue: I will keep **my mouth** with a bridle, while the wicked is before me. ☐

Psalms 63:3, Because thy lovingkindness is better than life, **my lips** shall praise thee. ☐

Psalms 71:8, Let **my mouth** be filled with thy praise and with thy honour all the day. ☐

Psalms 71:15, **My mouth** shall shew forth thy righteousness and thy salvation all the day; for I know not the numbers thereof. ☐

Psalms 51:15, O Lord, open thou **my lips**; and **my mouth** shall shew forth thy praise. ☐

Psalms 63:3, Because thy lovingkindness is better than life, **my lips** shall praise thee. ☐

Proverbs 8:8, All the words of **my mouth** are in righteousness; there is nothing forward or perverse in them. ☐

Isaiah 45:23, I have sworn by myself, the word is gone out of **my mouth** in righteousness, and shall not return, That unto me every knee shall bow, every tongue shall swear. ☐

In God We Trust

TESTIMONIES
TESTIFY
TESTIMONY *

34 DAY
EVENING
90 DAY CHALLENGE

Psalms 119:167, My soul hath kept thy **testimonies**; and I love them exceedingly. ☐

Psalms 119:168, I have kept thy precepts and thy **testimonies**: for all my ways are before thee. ☐

Psalms 81:8, Hear, O my people, and I will **testify** unto thee: O Israel, if thou wilt hearken unto me. ☐

Psalms 19:7, The law of the LORD is perfect, converting the soul: the **testimony** of the LORD is sure, making wise the simple. ☐

Psalms 81:5, This he ordained in Joseph for a **testimony**, when he went out through the land of Egypt: where I heard a language that I understood not. ☐

Psalms 119:88, Quicken me after thy lovingkindness; so shall I keep the **testimony** of thy mouth. ☐

Psalms 132:12, If thy children will keep my covenant and my **testimony** that I shall teach them, their children shall also sit upon thy throne for evermore. ☐

Isaiah 8:16, Bind up the **testimony**, seal the law among my disciples. ☐

Isaiah 8:20, To the law and to the **testimony**: if they speak not according to this word, it is because there is no light in them. ☐

Matthew 8:4, And Jesus saith unto him, See thou tell no man; but go thy way, shew thyself to the priest, and offer the gift that Moses commanded, for a **testimony** unto them. ☐

1 Corinthians 1:6, Even as the **testimony** of Christ was confirmed in you. ☐

Acts 20:24, But none of these things move me, neither count I my life dear unto myself, so that I might finish my course with joy, and the ministry, which I have received of the Lord Jesus, to **testify** the gospel of the grace of God. ☐

In God We Trust

Proverbs 3:9, Honour the LORD with thy substance, and with the firstfruits of all thine **increase**. ☐

Proverbs 9:9, Give instruction to a wise man, and he will be yet wiser: teach a just man, and he will **increase** in learning. ☐

Proverbs 13:11, Wealth gotten by vanity shall be diminished: but he that gathereth by labour shall **increase**.☐

Proverbs 14:4, Where no oxen are, the crib is clean: but much **increase** is by the strength of the ox. ☐

Proverbs 28:28, When the wicked rise, men hide themselves: but when they perish, the righteous **increase**. ☐

Luke 17:5, And the apostles said unto the Lord, **increase** our faith. ☐

John 3:30, He must **increase**, but I must decrease. ☐

1 Corinthians 3:6, I have planted, Apollos watered; but God gave the **increase**. ☐

1 Corinthians 3:7, So then neither is he that planteth any thing, neither he that watereth; but God that giveth the **increase**. ☐

2 Corinthians 9:10, Now he that ministereth seed to the sower both minister bread for your food, and multiply your seed sown, and **increase** the fruits of your righteousness. ☐

Colossians 2:19, And not holding the Head, from which all the body by joints and bands having nourishment ministered, and knit together, **increaseth** with the **increase** of God. ☐

1 Thessalonians 3:12, And the Lord make you to **increase** and abound in love one toward another, and toward all men, even as we do toward you. ☐

1 Thessalonians 4:10, And indeed ye do it toward all the brethren which are in all Macedonia: but we beseech you, brethren, that ye **increase** more and more. ☐

Leviticus 26:4, Then I will give you rain in **due season**, and the land shall yield her increase, and the trees of the field shall yield their fruit. □

Numbers 28:2, Command the children of Israel, and say unto them, My offering, and my bread for my sacrifices made by fire, for a sweet savour unto me, shall ye observe to offer unto me in their **due season**. □

Deuteronomy 11:14, That I will give you the rain of your land in his **due season**, the first rain and the latter rain, that thou mayest gather in thy corn, and thy wine, and thine oil. □

Psalms 104:27, These wait all upon thee; that thou mayest give them their meat in **due season**. □

Psalms 145:15, The eyes of all wait upon thee; and thou givest them their meat in **due season**. □

Proverbs 15:23, A man hath joy by the answer of his mouth: and a word spoken in **due season**, how good is it! □

Ecclesiastes 10:17, Blessed art thou, O land, when thy king is the son of nobles, and thy princes eat in **due season**, for strength, and not for drunkenness! □

Matthew 24:45, Who then is a faithful and wise servant, whom his lord hath made ruler over his household, to give them meat in **due season**? □

Luke 12:42, And the Lord said, Who then is that faithful and wise steward, whom his lord shall make ruler over his household, to give them their portion of meat in **due season**?□

Galatians 6:9, And let us not be weary in well doing: for in **due season** we shall reap, if we faint not. □

Isaiah 35:4, Say to them that are of a fearful heart, Be **strong**, fear not: behold, your God will come with vengeance, even God with a recompence; he will come and save you. ☐

Daniel 11:32, And such as do wickedly against the covenant shall he corrupt by flatteries: but the people that do know their God shall be **strong**, and do exploits. ☐

Joel 3:10, Beat your plowshares into swords, and your pruninghooks into spears: let the weak say, I am **strong**. ☐

Nahum 1:7, The LORD is good, a **strong** hold in the day of trouble; and he knoweth them that trust in him. ☐

Romans 4:20, He staggered not at the promise of God through unbelief; but was **strong** in faith, giving glory to God; ☐

Romans 15:1, We then that are **strong** ought to bear the infirmities of the weak, and not to please ourselves. ☐

1 Corinthians 4:10, We are fools for Christ's sake, but ye are wise in Christ; we are weak, but ye are **strong**; ye are honourable, but we are despised. ☐

2 Corinthians 12:10, Therefore I take pleasure in infirmities, in reproaches, in necessities, in persecutions, in distresses for Christ's sake: for when I am weak, then am I **strong**. ☐

Ephesians 6:10, Finally, my brethren, be **strong** in the Lord, and in the power of his might. ☐

2 Timothy 2:1, Thou therefore, my son, be **strong** in the grace that is in Christ Jesus. ☐

In God We Trust
105

Psalms 66:7, He ruleth by his **power** for ever; his eyes behold the nations: let not the rebellious exalt themselves. Selah. ☐

Psalms 68:35, O God, thou art terrible out of thy holy places: the God of Israel is he that giveth strength and **power** unto his people. Blessed be God. ☐

Psalms 79:11, Let the sighing of the prisoner come before thee; according to the greatness of thy **power** preserve thou those that are appointed to die. ☐

Psalms 90:11, Who knoweth the **power** of thine anger? even according to thy fear, so is thy wrath. ☐

Psalms 111:6, He hath shewed his people the **power** of his works, that he may give them the heritage of the heathen. ☐

Psalms 145:11, They shall speak of the glory of thy kingdom, and talk of thy **power**. ☐

Psalms 147:5, Great is our Lord, and of great **power**: his understanding is infinite. ☐

Psalms 150:1, Praise ye the LORD. Praise God in his sanctuary: praise him in the firmament of his **power**. ☐

Proverbs 3:27, Withhold not good from them to whom it is due, when it is in the **power** of thine hand to do it. ☐

Proverbs 18:21, Death and life are in the **power** of the tongue: and they that love it shall eat the fruit thereof. ☐

Isaiah 40:29, He giveth **power** to the faint; and to them that have no might he increaseth strength. ☐

Jeremiah 51:15, He hath made the earth by his **power**, he hath established the world by his wisdom, and hath stretched out the heaven by his understanding. ☐

In God We Trust

Proverbs 12:16, A fool's wrath is presently known: but a **prudent** man covereth shame. ☐

Proverbs 12:23, A **prudent** man concealeth knowledge: but the heart of fools proclaimeth foolishness. ☐

Proverbs 13:16, Every **prudent** man dealeth with knowledge: but a fool layeth open his folly. ☐

Proverbs 14:8, The wisdom of the **prudent** is to understand his way: but the folly of fools is deceit. ☐

Proverbs 14:15, The simple believeth every word: but the **prudent** man looketh well to his going. ☐

Proverbs 14:18, The simple inherit folly: but the **prudent** are crowned with knowledge. ☐

Proverbs 15:5, A fool despiseth his father's instruction: but he that regardeth reproof is **prudent**. ☐

Proverbs 16:21, The wise in heart shall be called **prudent**: and the sweetness of the lips increaseth learning. ☐

Proverbs 18:15, The heart of the **prudent** getteth knowledge; and the ear of the wise seeketh knowledge. ☐

Proverbs 19:14, House and riches are the inheritance of fathers: and a **prudent** wife is from the LORD. ☐

Proverbs 22:3, A **prudent** man foreseeth the evil, and hideth himself: but the simple pass on, and are punished. ☐

Isaiah 5:21, Woe unto them that are wise in their own eyes, and **prudent** in their own sight! ☐

Hosea 14:9, Who is wise, and he shall understand these things? **prudent**, and he shall know them? for the ways of the LORD are right, and the just shall walk in them: but the transgressors shall fall therein. ☐

In God We Trust

Genesis 17:7, And I will establish my covenant between me and thee and thy seed after thee in their generations for an everlasting covenant, **to be** a God unto thee, and to thy seed after thee. ☐

Deuteronomy 26:17, Thou hast avouched the LORD this day **to be** thy God, and to walk in his ways, and to keep his statutes, and his commandments, and his judgments, and to hearken unto his voice. ☐

Deuteronomy 26:18, And the LORD hath avouched thee this day **to be** his peculiar people, as he hath promised thee, and that thou shouldest keep all his commandments. ☐

Psalms 18:3, I will call upon the LORD, who is worthy **to be** praised: so shall I be saved from mine enemies. ☐

Psalms 19:10, More **to be** desired are they than gold, yea, than much fine gold: sweeter also than honey and the honeycomb. ☐

Psalms 45:17, I will make thy name **to be** remembered in all generations: therefore shall the people praise thee for ever and ever. ☐

Psalms 48:1, Great is the LORD, and greatly **to be** praised in the city of our God, in the mountain of his holiness. ☐

Psalms 55:22, Cast thy burden upon the LORD, and he shall sustain thee: he shall never suffer the righteous **to be** moved. ☐

Psalms 66:8, O bless our God, ye people, and make the voice of his praise **to be** heard. ☐

Psalms 76:7, Thou, even thou, art **to be** feared: and who may stand in thy sight when once thou art angry? ☐

Psalms 89:7, God is greatly **to be** feared in the assembly of the saints, and **to be** had in reverence of all them that are about him. ☐

SEEK THE LORD CONTINUALLY

I BELIEVE **BIGGER** BETTER **BOLDER BLESSINGS**

IMPOSSIBLE *
POSSIBLE *

37 DAY
MORNING
90 DAY CHALLENGE

Matthew 17:20, And Jesus said unto them, Because of your unbelief: for verily I say unto you, If ye have faith as a grain of mustard seed, ye shall say unto this mountain, Remove hence to yonder place; and it shall remove; and nothing shall be **impossible** unto you. ☐

Matthew 19:26, But Jesus beheld them, and said unto them, With men this is **impossible**; but with God all things are **possible**. ☐

Matthew 24:24, For there shall arise false Christs, and false prophets, and shall shew great signs and wonders; insomuch that, if it were **possible**, they shall deceive the very elect. ☐

Matthew 26:39, And he went a little further, and fell on his face, and prayed, saying, O my Father, if it be **possible**, let this cup pass from me: nevertheless not as I will, but as thou wilt. ☐

Luke 1:37, For with God nothing shall be **impossible**. ☐

Luke 17:1, Then said he unto the disciples, It is **impossible** but that offences will come: but woe unto him, through whom they come! ☐

Mark 9:23, Jesus said unto him, If thou canst believe, all things are **possible** to him that believeth. ☐

Mark 10:27, And Jesus looking upon them saith, With men it is **impossible**, but not with God: for with God all things are **possible**. ☐

Mark 13:22, For false Christs and false prophets shall rise, and shall shew signs and wonders, to seduce, if it were **possible**, even the elect. ☐

Mark 14:36, And he said, Abba, Father, all things are **possible** unto thee; take away this cup from me: nevertheless not what I will, but what thou wilt. ☐

Romans 12:18, If it be **possible**, as much as lieth in you, live peaceably with all men. ☐

Genesis 2:9, And out of the ground made the LORD God to grow every tree that is **pleasant** to the sight, and good for food; the tree of life also in the midst of the garden, and the tree of knowledge of good and evil.☐

Psalms 133:1, Behold, how good and how **pleasant** it is for brethren to dwell together in unity! ☐

Psalms 135:3, Praise the LORD; for the LORD is good: sing praises unto his name; for it is **pleasant**.☐

Psalms 147:1, Praise ye the LORD: for it is good to sing praises unto our God; for it is **pleasant**; and praise is comely.☐

Proverbs 2:10, When wisdom entereth into thine heart, and knowledge is **pleasant** unto thy soul.☐

Proverbs 15:26, The thoughts of the wicked are an abomination to the LORD: but the words of the pure are **pleasant** words.☐

Proverbs 16:24, **Pleasant** words are as a honeycomb, sweet to the soul, and health to the bones. ☐

Proverbs 24:4, And by knowledge shall the chambers be filled with all precious and **pleasant** riches. ☐

Proverbs 3:17, Her ways are ways of **pleasantness**, and all her paths are peace.☐

Proverbs 22:18, For it is a **pleasant** thing if thou keep them within thee; they shall withal be fitted in thy lips. ☐

1 Chronicles 28:10, Take heed now; for the LORD hath chosen thee to build a house for the sanctuary: be **strong**, and do it.☐

1 Chronicles 28:20, And David said to Solomon his son, Be **strong** and of good courage, and do it: fear not, nor be dismayed: for the LORD God, even my God, will be with thee; he will not fail thee, nor forsake thee, until thou hast finished all the work for the service of the house of the LORD.☐

2 Chronicles 15:7, Be ye **strong** therefore, and let not your hands be weak: for your work shall be rewarded. ☐

2 Chronicles 32:7, Be **strong** and courageous, be not afraid nor dismayed for the king of Assyria, nor for all the multitude that is with him: for there be more with us than with him. ☐

Psalms 24:8, Who is this King of glory? The LORD **strong** and mighty, the LORD mighty in battle.☐

Psalms 31:21, Blessed be the LORD: for he hath shewed me his marvellous kindness in a **strong** city. ☐

Psalms 71:7, I am as a wonder unto many; but thou art my **strong** refuge.☐

Psalms 136:12, With a **strong** hand, and with a stretched out arm: for his mercy endureth for ever. ☐

Proverbs 14:26, In the fear of the LORD is **strong** confidence: and his children shall have a place of refuge.☐

Proverbs 18:10, The name of the LORD is a **strong** tower: the righteous runneth into it, and is safe. ☐

Proverbs 18:11, The rich man's wealth is his **strong** city, and as an high wall in his own conceit.☐

Proverbs 30:25, The ants are a people not **strong**, yet they prepare their meat in the summer. ☐

John 9:38, And he said, Lord, I **believe**. And he worshipped him. ☐

John 10:38, But if I do, though ye **believe** not me, **believe** the works: that ye may know, and **believe**, that the Father is in me, and I in him. ☐

John 11:27, She saith unto him, Yea, Lord: I **believe** that thou art the Christ, the Son of God, which should come into the world. ☐

John 11:40, Jesus saith unto her, Said I not unto thee, that, if thou wouldest **believe**, thou shouldest see the glory of God? ☐

John 12:47, And if any man hear my words, and **believe** not, I judge him not: for I came not to judge the world, but to save the world. ☐

John 13:19, Now I tell you before it come, that, when it is come to pass, ye may **believe** that I am he. ☐

John 14:1, Let not your heart be troubled: ye **believe** in God, **believe** also in me. ☐

John 14:29, And now I have told you before it come to pass, that, when it is come to pass, ye might **believe**. ☐

John 16:30, Now are we sure that thou knowest all things, and needest not that any man should ask thee: by this we **believe** that thou camest forth from God. ☐

John 16:31, Jesus answered them, Do ye now **believe**? ☐

Acts 8:37, And Philip said, If thou believest with all thine heart, thou mayest. And he answered and said, I **believe** that Jesus Christ is the Son of God. ☐

Acts 13:39, And by him all that **believe** are justified from all things, from which ye could not be justified by the law of Moses. ☐

Acts 15:7, And when there had been much disputing, Peter rose up, and said unto them, Men and brethren, ye know how that a good while ago God made choice among us, that the Gentiles by my mouth should hear the word of the gospel, and **believe**. ☐

QUIET *
QUIETNESS
QUIETLY

38 DAY
AFTERNOON
90 DAY CHALLENGE

1 Chronicles 22:9, Behold, a son shall be born to thee, who shall be a man of rest; and I will give him rest from all his enemies round about: for his name shall be Solomon, and I will give peace and **quietness** unto Israel in his days. ☐

Psalms 35:20, For they speak not peace: but they devise deceitful matters against them that are **quiet** in the land. ☐

Psalms 107:30, Then are they glad because they be **quiet**; so he bringeth them unto their desired haven. ☐

Proverbs 1:33, But whoso hearkeneth unto me shall dwell safely, and shall be **quiet** from fear of evil. ☐

Proverbs 17:1, Better is a dry morsel, and **quietness** therewith, than an house full of sacrifices with strife. ☐

Ecclesiastes 4:6, Better is an handful with **quietness**, than both the hands full with travail and vexation of spirit. ☐

Ecclesiastes 9:17, The words of wise men are heard in **quiet** more than the cry of him that ruleth among fools. ☐

Isaiah 30:15, For thus saith the Lord GOD, the Holy One of Israel; In returning and rest shall ye be saved; in **quietness** and in confidence shall be your strength: and ye would not. ☐

Isaiah 32:17, And the work of righteousness shall be peace; and the effect of righteousness **quietness** and assurance forever. ☐

Isaiah 32:18, And my people shall dwell in a peaceable habitation, and in sure dwellings, and in **quiet** resting places. ☐

Lamentations 3:26, It is good that a man should both hope and **quietly** wait for the salvation of the LORD. ☐

Acts 24:2, And when he was called forth, Tertullus began to accuse him, saying, Seeing that by thee we enjoy great **quietness**, and that very worthy deeds are done unto this nation by thy providence. ☐

In God We Trust

Isaiah 45:19, I have not spoken in secret, in a dark place of the earth: I said not unto the seed of Jacob, Seek ye me in vain: I the LORD speak righteousness, I **declare** things that are right.☐

Isaiah 57:12, I will **declare** thy righteousness, and thy works; for they shall not profit thee.☐

John 17:26, And I have **declared** unto them thy name, and will **declare** it: that the love wherewith thou hast loved me may be in them, and I in them.☐

Acts 13:32, And we **declare** unto you glad tidings, how that the promise which was made unto the fathers.☐

Romans 3:25, Whom God hath set forth to be a propitiation through faith in his blood, to **declare** his righteousness for the remission of sins that are past, through the forbearance of God.☐

Romans 3:26, To **declare**, I say, at this time his righteousness: that he might be just, and the justifier of him which believeth in Jesus.☐

1 Corinthians 3:13, Every man's work shall be made manifest: for the day shall **declare** it, because it shall be revealed by fire; and the fire shall try every man's work of what sort it is.☐

1 John 1:5, This then is the message which we have heard of him, and **declare** unto you, that God is light, and in him is no darkness at all.☐

In God We Trust

Psalms 76:9, When God arose to judgment, to save all the **meek** of the earth. Selah. ☐

Psalms 147:6, The LORD lifteth up the **meek**: he casteth the wicked down to the ground. ☐

Psalms 149:4, For the LORD taketh pleasure in his people: he will beautify the **meek** with salvation. ☐

Isaiah 29:19, The **meek** also shall increase their joy in the LORD, and the poor among men shall rejoice in the Holy One of Israel. ☐

Isaiah 61:1, The Spirit of the Lord GOD is upon me; because the LORD hath anointed me to preach good tidings unto the **meek**; he hath sent me to bind up the brokenhearted, to proclaim liberty to the captives, and the opening of the prison to them that are bound. ☐

Matthew 5:5, Blessed are the **meek**: for they shall inherit the earth. ☐

Matthew 11:29, Take my yoke upon you, and learn of me; for I am **meek** and lowly in heart: and ye shall find rest unto your souls. ☐

James 1:21, Wherefore lay apart all filthiness and superfluity of naughtiness, and receive with **meekness** the engrafted word, which is able to save your souls. ☐

James 3:13, Who is a wise man and endued with knowledge among you? let him shew out of a good conversation his works with **meekness** of wisdom. ☐

1 Peter 3:4, But let it be the hidden man of the heart, in that which is not corruptible, even the ornament of a **meek** and quiet spirit, which is in the sight of God of great price. ☐

1 Peter 3:15, But sanctify the Lord God in your hearts: and be ready always to give an answer to every man that asketh you a reason of the hope that is in you with **meekness** and fear. ☐

In God We Trust

MINDFUL *
MINDS
MINDED *

 DAY

AFTERNOON
90 DAY CHALLENGE

2 Corinthians 11:3, But I fear, lest by any means, as the serpent be-guiled Eve through his subtilty, so your **minds** should be corrupted from the simplicity that is in Christ. ☐

Galatians 5:10, I have confidence in you through the Lord, that ye will be none otherwise **minded**: but he that troubleth you shall bear his judgment, whosoever he be. ☐

2 Timothy 3:8, Now as Jannes and Jambres withstood Moses, so do these also resist the truth: men of corrupt **minds**, reprobate concerning the faith. ☐

Titus 2:6, Young men likewise exhort to be sober **minded**. ☐

Hebrews 10:16, This is the covenant that I will make with them after those days, saith the Lord, I will put my laws into their hearts, and in their **minds** will I write them. ☐

Hebrews 12:3, For consider him that endured such contradiction of sinners against himself, lest ye be wearied and faint in your **minds**. ☐

2 Peter 3:1, This second epistle, beloved, I now write unto you; in both which I stir up your pure **minds** by way of remembrance. ☐

2 Peter 3:2, That ye may be **mindful** of the words which were spoken before by the holy prophets, and of the commandment of us the apostles of the Lord and Saviour. ☐

Philippians 3:15, Let us therefore, as many as be perfect, be thus **minded**: and if in any thing ye be otherwise **minded**, God shall reveal even this unto you. ☐

Philippians 4:7, And the peace of God, which passeth all understanding, shall keep your hearts and **minds** through Christ Jesus. ☐

James 1:8, A double **minded** man is unstable in all his ways. ☐

James 4:8, Draw nigh to God, and he will draw nigh to you. Cleanse your hands, ye sinners; and purify your hearts, ye double **minded**. ☐

Romans 8:25, But if we **hope** for that we see not, then do we with patience wait for it. ☐

Romans 12:12, Rejoicing in **hope**; patient in tribulation; continuing instant in prayer. ☐

Romans 15:4, For whatsoever things were written aforetime were written for our learning, that we through patience and comfort of the scriptures might have **hope**. ☐

Romans 15:13, Now the God of **hope** fill you with all joy and peace in believing, that ye may abound in **hope**, through the power of the Holy Ghost. ☐

1 Corinthians 9:10, Or saith he it altogether for our sakes? For our sakes, no doubt, this is written: that he that ploweth should plow in **hope**; and that he that thresheth in **hope** should be partaker of his **hope**. ☐

1 Corinthians 13:7, Beareth all things, believeth all things, **hopeth** all things, endureth all things. ☐

1 Corinthians 13:13, And now abideth faith, **hope**, charity, these three; but the greatest of these is charity. ☐

1 Corinthians 15:19, If in this life only we have **hope** in Christ, we are of all men most miserable. ☐

2 Corinthians 1:7, And our **hope** of you is stedfast, knowing, that as ye are partakers of the sufferings, so shall ye be also of the consolation. ☐

2 Corinthians 3:12, Seeing then that we have such **hope**, we use great plainness of speech. ☐

Galatians 5:5, For we through the Spirit wait for the **hope** of righteousness by faith. ☐

Ephesians 2:12, That at that time ye were without Christ, being aliens from the commonwealth of Israel, and strangers from the covenants of promise, having no **hope**, and without God in the world. ☐

In God We Trust

2 Corinthians 13:5, Examine yourselves, whether ye be in the **faith**; prove your own selves. Know ye not your own selves, how that Jesus Christ is in you, except ye be reprobates? ☐

Galatians 2:16, Knowing that a man is not justified by the works of the law, but by the **faith** of Jesus Christ, even we have believed in Jesus Christ, that we might be justified by the **faith** of Christ, and not by the works of the law: for by the works of the law shall no flesh be justified. ☐

Galatians 2:20, I am crucified with Christ: nevertheless I live; yet not I, but Christ liveth in me: and the life which I now live in the flesh I live by the **faith** of the Son of God, who loved me, and gave himself for me. ☐

Galatians 3:2, This only would I learn of you, Received ye the Spirit by the works of the law, or by the hearing of **faith**? ☐

Galatians 3:5, He therefore that ministereth to you the Spirit, and worketh miracles among you, doeth he it by the works of the law, or by the hearing of **faith**? ☐

Galatians 3:7, Know ye therefore that they which are of **faith**, the same are the children of Abraham. ☐

Galatians 3:9, So then they which be of **faith** are blessed with faithful Abraham. ☐

Galatians 3:11, But that no man is justified by the law in the sight of God, it is evident: for, The just shall live by **faith**. ☐

Galatians 3:22, But the scripture hath concluded all under sin, that the promise by **faith** of Jesus Christ might be given to them that believe. ☐

Galatians 3:24, Wherefore the law was our schoolmaster to bring us unto Christ, that we might be justified by **faith**. ☐

Galatians 3:26, For ye are all the children of God by **faith** in Christ Jesus. ☐

Galatians 5:5, For we through the Spirit wait for the hope of righteousness by **faith**. ☐

Genesis 14:19, And he blessed him, and said, Blessed be Abram of the most high God, possessor of heaven and earth. ☐

Psalms 7:17, I will praise the LORD according to his righteousness: and will sing praise to the name of the LORD most high. ☐

Psalms 9:2, I will be glad and rejoice in thee: I will sing praise to thy name, O thou most high. ☐

Psalms 47:2, For the LORD most high is terrible; he is a great King over all the earth. ☐

Psalms 57:2, I will cry unto God most high; unto God that performeth all things for me. ☐

Psalms 73:11, And they say, How doth God know? and is there knowledge in the most high? ☐

Psalms 91:1, He that dwelleth in the secret place of the most high shall abide under the shadow of the Almighty. ☐

Psalms 91:9, Because thou hast made the LORD, which is my refuge, even the most high, thy habitation. ☐

Psalms 92:8, But thou, LORD, art most high for evermore. ☐

Psalms 107:11, Because they rebelled against the words of God, and contemned the counsel of the most high. ☐

Daniel 7:18, But the saints of the most high shall take the kingdom, and possess the kingdom for ever, even for ever and ever. ☐

Acts 16:17, The same followed Paul and us, and cried, saying, These men are the servants of the most high God, which shew unto us the way of salvation. ☐

Jude 1:20, But ye, beloved, building up yourselves on your most holy faith, praying in the Holy Ghost. ☐

In God We Trust

Matthew 17:9, And as they came down from the mountain, Jesus charged them, saying, Tell the vision to no man, until the **Son of man** be risen again from the dead. ☐

Matthew 18:11, For the **Son of man** is come to save that which was lost. ☐

Matthew 20:28, Even as the **Son of man** came not to be ministered unto, but to minister, and to give his life a ransom for many. ☐

Matthew 24:27, For as the lightning cometh out of the east, and shineth even unto the west; so shall also the coming of the **Son of man** be. ☐

Matthew 24:30, And then shall appear the sign of the **Son of man** in heaven: and then shall all the tribes of the earth mourn, and they shall see the **Son of man** coming in the clouds of heaven with power and great glory. ☐

Matthew 26:2, Ye know that after two days is the feast of the passover, and the **Son of man** is betrayed to be crucified. ☐

Matthew 26:24, The **Son of man** goeth as it is written of him: but woe unto that man by whom the **Son of man** is betrayed! it had been good for that man if he had not been born. ☐

Mark 10:45, For even the **Son of man** came not to be ministered unto, but to minister, and to give his life a ransom for many. ☐

John 1:51, And he saith unto him, Verily, verily, I say unto you, Hereafter ye shall see heaven open, and the angels of God ascending and descending upon the **Son of man.** ☐

John 3:13, And no man hath ascended up to heaven, but he that came down from heaven, even the **Son of man** which is in heaven. ☐

John 5:27, And hath given him authority to execute judgment also, because he is the **Son of man.** ☐

John 12:23, And Jesus answered them, saying, The hour is come, that the **Son of man** should be glorified. ☐

Isaiah 61:10, I will greatly rejoice in the LORD, my soul shall be joyful in my God; for he hath clothed me with the garments of salvation, he hath covered me with the robe of righteousness, as a bridegroom decketh himself with ornaments, and as a bride adorneth herself with her jewels. □

Matthew 5:6, Blessed are they which do hunger and thirst after righteousness: for they shall be filled. □

Matthew 6:33, But seek ye first the kingdom of God, and his righteousness; and all these things shall be added unto you. □

Romans 1:17, For therein is the righteousness of God revealed from faith to faith: as it is written, The just shall live by faith. □

Romans 3:22, Even the righteousness of God which is by faith of Jesus Christ unto all and upon all them that believe: for there is no difference. □

Romans 3:25, Whom God hath set forth to be a propitiation through faith in his blood, to declare his righteousness for the remission of sins that are past, through the forbearance of God. □

Romans 3:26, To declare, I say, at this time his righteousness: that he might be just, and the justifier of him which believeth in Jesus. □

Romans 4:3, For what saith the scripture? Abraham believed God, and it was counted unto him for righteousness. □

Romans 4:6, Even as David also describeth the blessedness of the man, unto whom God imputeth righteousness without works. □

Romans 4:13, For the promise, that he should be the heir of the world, was not to Abraham, or to his seed, through the law, but through the righteousness of faith. □

Romans 5:17, For if by one man's offence death reigned by one; much more they which receive abundance of grace and of the gift of righteousness shall reign in life by one, Jesus Christ. □

Exodus 24:7, And he took the book of the covenant, and read in the audience of the people: and they said, All that the LORD hath said will we do, and be **obedient**. □

Proverbs 25:12, As an earring of gold, and an ornament of fine gold, so is a wise reprover upon an **obedient** ear. □

Isaiah 1:19, If ye be willing and **obedient**, ye shall eat the good of the land. □

Isaiah 42:24, Who gave Jacob for a spoil, and Israel to the robbers? did not the LORD, he against whom we have sinned? for they would not walk in his ways, neither were they **obedient** unto his law. □

Acts 6:7, And the word of God increased; and the number of the disciples multiplied in Jerusalem greatly; and a great company of the priests were **obedient** to the faith. □

Romans 15:18, For I will not dare to speak of any of those things which Christ hath not wrought by me, to make the Gentiles **obedient**, by word and deed. □

2 Corinthians 2:9, For to this end also did I write, that I might know the proof of you, whether ye be **obedient** in all things. □

Ephesians 6:5, Servants, be **obedient** to them that are your masters according to the flesh, with fear and trembling, in singleness of your heart, as unto Christ. □

Philippians 2:8, And being found in fashion as a man, he humbled himself, and became **obedient** unto death, even the death of the cross. □

Titus 2:9, Exhort servants to be **obedient** unto their own masters, and to please them well in all things; not answering again. □

1 Peter 1:14, As **obedient** children, not fashioning yourselves according to the former lusts in your ignorance. □

TRUST IN
TRUST IN THE LORD
TRUST *

41 DAY
EVENING
90 DAY CHALLENGE

Proverbs 29:25, The fear of man bringeth a snare: but whoso putteth his **trust in the LORD** shall be safe. ☐

Proverbs 30:5, Every word of God is pure: he is a shield unto them that put their **trust in** him. ☐

Proverbs 31:11, The heart of her husband doth safely **trust in** her, so that he shall have no need of spoil. ☐

Isaiah 36:6, Lo, thou trustest in the staff of this broken reed, on Egypt; whereon if a man lean, it will go into his hand, and pierce it: so is Pharaoh king of Egypt to all that **trust in** him. ☐

Isaiah 36:7, But if thou say to me, We **trust in the LORD** our God: is it not he, whose high places and whose altars Hezekiah hath taken away, and said to Judah and to Jerusalem, Ye shall worship before this altar? ☐

Isaiah 36:15, Neither let Hezekiah make you **trust in the LORD**, saying, The LORD will surely deliver us: this city shall not be delivered into the hand of the king of Assyria. ☐

Nahum 1:7, The LORD is good, a strong hold in the day of trouble; and he knoweth them that **trust in** him. ☐

Zephaniah 3:12, I will also leave in the midst of thee an afflicted and poor people, and they shall **trust in** the name of the LORD. ☐

Philippians 2:19, But I **trust in the Lord** Jesus to send Timotheus shortly unto you, that I also may be of good comfort, when I know your state. ☐

Philippians 2:24, But I **trust in the Lord** that I also myself shall come shortly. ☐

1 Timothy 6:17, Charge them that are rich in this world, that they be not highminded, nor **trust in** uncertain riches, but in the living God, who giveth us richly all things to enjoy. ☐

Hebrews 2:13, And again, I will put my **trust in** him. And again, Behold I and the children which God hath given me. ☐

In God We Trust

Proverbs 28:5, Evil men understand not judgment: but they that **seek** the LORD understand all things. ☐

Proverbs 29:10, The bloodthirsty hate the upright: but the just **seek** his soul. ☐

Proverbs 29:26, Many **seek** the ruler's favour; but every man's judgment cometh from the LORD. ☐

Ecclesiastes 1:13, And I gave my heart to **seek** and search out by wisdom concerning all things that are done under heaven: this sore travail hath God given to the sons of man to be exercised therewith. ☐

Ecclesiastes 7:25, I applied mine heart to know, and to search, and to **seek** out wisdom, and the reason of things, and to know the wickedness of folly, even of foolishness and madness. ☐

Isaiah 34:16, **Seek** ye out of the book of the LORD, and read: no one of these shall fail, none shall want her mate: for my mouth it hath commanded, and his spirit it hath gathered them. ☐

Isaiah 51:1, Hearken to me, ye that follow after righteousness, ye that **seek** the LORD: look unto the rock whence ye are hewn, and to the hole of the pit whence ye are digged. ☐

Isaiah 55:6, **Seek** ye the LORD while he may be found, call ye upon him while he is near. ☐

Isaiah 58:2, Yet they **seek** me daily, and delight to know my ways, as a nation that did righteousness, and forsook not the ordinance of their God: they ask of me the ordinances of justice; they take delight in approaching to God. ☐

Colossians 3:1, If ye then be risen with Christ, **seek** those things which are above, where Christ sitteth on the right hand of God. ☐

Hebrews 11:6, But without faith it is impossible to please him: for he that cometh to God must believe that he is, and that he is a rewarder of them that diligently **seek** him. ☐

In God We Trust
124

Isaiah 49:4, Then I said, I have laboured in vain, I have spent my strength for nought, and in vain: yet surely my judgment is with the LORD, and my work with **my God**. ☐

Isaiah 49:5, And now, saith the LORD that formed me from the womb to be his servant, to bring Jacob again to him, Though Israel be not gathered, yet shall I be glorious in the eyes of the LORD, and **my God** shall be my strength. ☐

Isaiah 57:21, There is no peace, saith **my God**, to the wicked. ☐

Isaiah 61:10, I will greatly rejoice in the LORD, my soul shall be joyful in **my God**; for he hath clothed me with the garments of salvation, he hath covered me with the robe of righteousness, as a bridegroom decketh himself with ornaments, and as a bride adorneth herself with her jewels. ☐

Daniel 6:22, **My God** hath sent his angel, and hath shut the lions' mouths, that they have not hurt me: forasmuch as before him innocency was found in me; and also before thee, O king, have I done no hurt. ☐

Daniel 9:4, And I prayed unto the LORD **my God**, and made my confession, and said, O Lord, the great and dreadful God, keeping the covenant and mercy to them that love him, and to them that keep his commandments. ☐

Romans 1:8, First, I thank **my God** through Jesus Christ for you all, that your faith is spoken of throughout the whole world. ☐

1 Corinthians 1:4, I thank **my God** always on your behalf, for the grace of God which is given you by Jesus Christ. ☐

Philippians 4:19, But **my God** shall supply all your need according to his riches in glory by Christ Jesus. ☐

In God We Trust

Psalms 18:6, In my distress I called upon the LORD, and cried unto my God: he heard my voice out of his temple, and my cry came before him, even into **his ears.** ☐

Psalms 34:15, The eyes of the LORD are upon the righteous, and **his ears** are open unto their cry. ☐

Psalms 78:1, Give **ear**, O my people, to my law: incline your **ears** to the words of my mouth. ☐

Psalms 92:11, Mine eye also shall see my desire on mine enemies, and mine **ears** shall hear my desire of the wicked that rise up against me. ☐

Psalms 130:2, Lord, hear my voice: let thine **ears** be attentive to the voice of my supplications. ☐

Psalms 135:17, They have **ears**, but they hear not; neither is there any breath in their mouths. ☐

Proverbs 21:13, Whoso stoppeth **his ears** at the cry of the poor, he also shall cry himself, but shall not be heard. ☐

Proverbs 23:9, Speak not in the **ears** of a fool: for he will despise the wisdom of thy words. ☐

Proverbs 23:12, Apply thine heart unto instruction, and thine **ears** to the words of knowledge. ☐

Mark 7:33, And he took him aside from the multitude, and put his fingers into **his ears**, and he spit, and touched his tongue. ☐

Mark 7:35, And straightway **his ears** were opened, and the string of his tongue was loosed, and he spake plain. ☐

1 Peter 3:12, For the eyes of the Lord are over the righteous, and **his ears** are open unto their prayers: but the face of the Lord is against them that do evil. ☐

Hosea 3:5, Afterward shall the children of Israel return, and seek the LORD their God, and David their king; and shall fear the LORD and his **goodness** in the latter days. ☐

Ephesians 6:7, With **good** will doing service, as to the Lord, and not to men. ☐

Philippians 1:6, Being confident of this very thing, that he which hath begun a **good** work in you will perform it until the day of Jesus Christ. ☐

Philippians 2:13, For it is God which worketh in you both to will and to do of his **good** pleasure. ☐

Colossians 1:10, That ye might walk worthy of the Lord unto all pleasing, being fruitful in every **good** work, and increasing in the knowledge of God. ☐

1 Thessalonians 5:15, See that none render evil for evil unto any man; but ever follow that which is **good**, both among yourselves, and to all men. ☐

1 Thessalonians 5:21, Prove all things; hold fast that which is **good**. ☐

2 Thessalonians 1:11, Wherefore also we pray always for you, that our God would count you worthy of this calling, and fulfil all the **good** pleasure of his **goodness**, and the work of faith with power. ☐

2 Thessalonians 2:17, Comfort your hearts, and stablish you in every **good** word and work. ☐

1 Timothy 6:12, Fight the **good** fight of faith, lay hold on eternal life, whereunto thou art also called, and hast professed a **good** profession before many witnesses. ☐

1 Timothy 6:13, I give thee charge in the sight of God, who quickeneth all things, and before Christ Jesus, who before Pontius Pilate witnessed a **good** confession. ☐

2 Timothy 1:14, That **good** thing which was committed unto thee keep by the Holy Ghost which dwelleth in us. ☐

Psalms 72:18, **Blessed** be the LORD God, the God of Israel, who only doeth wondrous things. ☐

Psalms 72:19, And **blessed** be his glorious name for ever: and let the whole earth be filled with his glory; Amen, and Amen. ☐

Psalms 84:4, **Blessed** are they that dwell in thy house: they will be still praising thee. Selah. ☐

Psalms 84:5, **Blessed** is the man whose strength is in thee; in whose heart are the ways of them. ☐

Psalms 84:12, O LORD of hosts, **blessed** is the man that trusteth in thee. ☐

Psalms 89:15, **Blessed** is the people that know the joyful sound: they shall walk, O LORD, in the light of thy countenance. ☐

Psalms 106:3, **Blessed** are they that keep judgment, and he that doeth righteousness at all times. ☐

Psalms 112:1, Praise ye the LORD. **Blessed** is the man that feareth the LORD, that delighteth greatly in his commandments. ☐

Psalms 112:2, His seed shall be mighty upon earth: the generation of the upright shall be **blessed**. ☐

Psalms 113:2, **Blessed** be the name of the LORD from this time forth and for evermore. ☐

Psalms 115:15, Ye are **blessed** of the LORD which made heaven and earth. ☐

Psalms 118:26, **Blessed** be he that cometh in the name of the LORD: we have **blessed** you out of the house of the LORD. ☐

Psalms 119:1, **Blessed** are the undefiled in the way, who walk in the law of the LORD. ☐

Psalms 72:17, His name shall endure for ever: his name shall be continued as long as the sun: and men shall be blessed **in him**: all nations shall call him blessed. ☐

Psalms 91:2, I will say of the LORD, He is my refuge and my fortress: my God; **in him** will I trust. ☐

Psalms 92:15, To shew that the LORD is upright: he is my rock, and there is no unrighteousness **in him**. ☐

Proverbs 30:5, Every word of God is pure: he is a shield unto them that put their trust **in him**. ☐

Jeremiah 4:2, And thou shalt swear, The LORD liveth, in truth, in judgment, and in righteousness; and the nations shall bless themselves **in him**, and **in him** shall they glory. ☐

Lamentations 3:24, The LORD is my portion, saith my soul; therefore will I hope **in him**. ☐

Nahum 1:7, The LORD is good, a strong hold in the day of trouble; and he knoweth them that trust **in him**. ☐

John 1:4, **In him** was life; and the life was the light of men. ☐

John 3:16, For God so loved the world, that he gave his only begotten Son, that whosoever believeth **in him** should not perish, but have everlasting life. ☐

John 4:14, But whosoever drinketh of the water that I shall give him shall never thirst; but the water that I shall give him shall be **in him** a well of water springing up into everlasting life. ☐

John 6:56, He that eateth my flesh, and drinketh my blood, dwelleth in me, and I **in him**. ☐

John 7:18, He that speaketh of himself seeketh his own glory: but he that seeketh his glory that sent him, the same is true, and no unrighteousness is **in him**. ☐

In God We Trust

POOR *
RICH *
RICHES

44 DAY
MORNING
90 DAY CHALLENGE

Psalms 49:16, Be not thou afraid when one is made **rich**, when the glory of his house is increased. ☐

Proverbs 10:22, The blessing of the LORD, it maketh **rich**, and he addeth no sorrow with it. ☐

Proverbs 22:7, The **rich** ruleth over the **poor**, and the borrower is servant to the lender. ☐

Proverbs 22:16, He that oppresseth the **poor** to increase his **riches**, and he that giveth to the **rich**, shall surely come to want. ☐

Proverbs 23:4, Labour not to be **rich**: cease from thine own wisdom. ☐

Proverbs 28:6, Better is the **poor** that walketh in his uprightness, than he that is perverse in his ways, though he be **rich**. ☐

Proverbs 28:11, The **rich** man is wise in his own conceit; but the **poor** that hath understanding searcheth him out. ☐

Proverbs 28:20, A faithful man shall abound with blessings: but he that maketh haste to be **rich** shall not be innocent. ☐

Proverbs 28:22, He that hasteth to be **rich** hath an evil eye, and considereth not that poverty shall come upon him. ☐

Ecclesiastes 5:12, The sleep of a labouring man is sweet, whether he eat little or much: but the abundance of the **rich** will not suffer him to sleep. ☐

Ecclesiastes 10:6, Folly is set in great dignity, and the **rich** sit in low place. ☐

Jeremiah 9:23, Thus saith the LORD, Let not the wise man glory in his wisdom, neither let the mighty man glory in his might, let not the **rich** man glory in his **riches**. ☐

Romans 10:12, For there is no difference between the Jew and the Greek: for the same Lord over all is **rich** unto all that call upon him. ☐

In God We Trust

Psalms 86:11, Teach me thy way, O LORD; I will walk in thy truth: unite my heart to fear thy name. □

Psalms 86:12, I will praise thee, O Lord my God, with all my heart: and I will glorify thy name for evermore. □

Psalms 89:25, I will set his hand also in the sea, and his right hand in the rivers. □

Psalms 89:27, Also I will make him my firstborn, higher than the kings of the earth. □

Psalms 91:2, I will say of the LORD, He is my refuge and my fortress: my God; in him will I trust. □

Psalms 91:14, Because he hath set his love upon me, therefore will I deliver him: I will set him on high, because he hath known my name. □

Psalms 91:15, He shall call upon me, and I will answer him: I will be with him in trouble; I will deliver him, and honour him. □

Psalms 92:4, For thou, LORD, hast made me glad through thy work: I will triumph in the works of thy hands. □

Psalms 101:1, I will sing of mercy and judgment: unto thee, O LORD, will I sing. □

Psalms 101:2, I will behave myself wisely in a perfect way. O when wilt thou come unto me? I will walk within my house with a perfect heart. □

Psalms 101:3, I will set no wicked thing before mine eyes: I hate the work of them that turn aside; it shall not cleave to me. □

Psalms 101:4, A froward heart shall depart from me: I will not know a wicked person. □

Psalms 104:33, I will sing unto the LORD as long as I live: I will sing praise to my God while I have my being. □

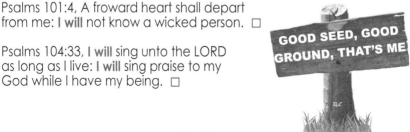

GOOD SEED, GOOD GROUND, THAT'S ME

In God We Trust
131

Genesis 6:8, But Noah found **grace** in the eyes of the LORD. ☐

Genesis 39:4, And Joseph found **grace** in his sight, and he served him: and he made him overseer over his house, and all that he had he put into his hand. ☐

Exodus 33:13, Now therefore, I pray thee, if I have found **grace** in thy sight, shew me now thy way, that I may know thee, that I may find **grace** in thy sight: and consider that this nation is thy people. ☐

Psalms 45:2, Thou art fairer than the children of men: **grace** is poured into thy lips: therefore God hath blessed thee forever. ☐

Psalms 84:11, For the LORD God is a sun and shield: the LORD will give **grace** and glory: no good thing will he withhold from them that walk uprightly. ☐

Proverbs 1:9, For they shall be an ornament of **grace** unto thy head, and chains about thy neck. ☐

Proverbs 3:22, So shall they be life unto thy soul, and **grace** to thy neck. ☐

Proverbs 3:34, Surely he scorneth the scorners: but he giveth **grace** unto the lowly. ☐

Proverbs 4:9, She shall give to thine head an ornament of **grace**: a crown of glory shall she deliver to thee. ☐

Proverbs 22:11, He that loveth pureness of heart, for the **grace** of his lips the king shall be his friend. ☐

Zechariah 4:7, Who art thou, O great mountain? before Zerubbabel thou shalt become a plain: and he shall bring forth the headstone thereof with shoutings, crying, **Grace**, **grace** unto it. ☐

Luke 2:40, And the child grew, and waxed strong in spirit, filled with wisdom: and the **grace** of God was upon him. ☐

John 1:16, And of his fulness have all we received, and **grace** for **grace**. ☐

GREAT *

Psalms 57:10, For thy mercy is **great** unto the heavens, and thy truth unto the clouds.☐

Psalms 68:11, The Lord gave the word: **great** was the company of those that published it.☐

Psalms 71:19, Thy righteousness also, O God, is very high, who hast done **great** things: O God, who is like unto thee! ☐

Psalms 77:13, Thy way, O God, is in the sanctuary: who is so **great** a God as our God? ☐

Psalms 86:13, For **great** is thy mercy toward me: and thou hast delivered my soul from the lowest hell.☐

Psalms 92:5, O LORD, how **great** are thy works! and thy thoughts are very deep.☐

Psalms 95:3, For the LORD is a **great** God, and a **great** King above all gods.☐

Psalms 96:4, For the LORD is **great**, and greatly to be praised: he is to be feared above all gods.☐

Psalms 99:2, The LORD is **great** in Zion; and he is high above all the people.☐

Psalms 99:3, Let them praise thy **great** and terrible name; for it is holy. ☐

Psalms 103:11, For as the heaven is high above the earth, so **great** is his mercy toward them that fear him. ☐

Psalms 104:1, Bless the LORD, O my soul. O LORD my God, thou art very **great**; thou art clothed with honour and majesty. ☐

Psalms 108:4, For thy mercy is **great** above the heavens: and thy truth reacheth unto the clouds. ☐

Psalms 111:2, The works of the LORD are **great**, sought out of all them that have pleasure therein. ☐

Psalms 115:13, He will bless them that fear the LORD, both small and **great**. ☐

In God We Trust
133

Psalms 33:18, Behold, the eye of the LORD is upon them that fear him, upon them that hope in his **mercy**. ☐

Psalms 57:3, He shall send from heaven, and save me from the reproach of him that would swallow me up. Selah. God shall send forth his **mercy** and his truth. ☐

Psalms 66:20, Blessed be God, which hath not turned away my prayer, nor his **mercy** from me. ☐

Psalms 77:8, Is his **mercy** clean gone for ever? doth his promise fail forever more? ☐

Psalms 98:3, He hath remembered his **mercy** and his truth toward the house of Israel: all the ends of the earth have seen the salvation of our God. ☐

Psalms 100:5, For the LORD is good; his **mercy** is everlasting; and his truth endureth to all generations. ☐

Psalms 103:11, For as the heaven is high above the earth, so great is his **mercy** toward them that fear him. ☐

Psalms 106:1, Praise ye the LORD. O give thanks unto the LORD; for he is good: for his **mercy** endureth forever. ☐

Psalms 107:1, O give thanks unto the LORD, for he is good: for his **mercy** endureth forever. ☐

Psalms 118:1, O give thanks unto the LORD; for he is good: because his **mercy** endureth forever. ☐

Psalms 118:2, Let Israel now say, that his **mercy** endureth forever. ☐

Psalms 118:4, Let them now that fear the LORD say, that his **mercy** endureth forever. ☐

Psalms 118:29, O give thanks unto the LORD; for he is good: for his **mercy** endureth forever. ☐

I BELIEVE
BIGGER
BETTER
BOLDER
BLESSINGS

SEEK *

_45_ DAY
EVENING
90 DAY CHALLENGE

Deuteronomy 4:29, But if from thence thou shalt **seek** the LORD thy God, thou shalt find him, if thou **seek** him with all thy heart and with all thy soul. ☐

1 Chronicles 16:10, Glory ye in his holy name: let the heart of them rejoice that **seek** the LORD. ☐

1 Chronicles 16:11, **Seek** the LORD and his strength, **seek** his face continually. ☐

1 Chronicles 22:19, Now set your heart and your soul to **seek** the LORD your God; arise therefore, and build ye the sanctuary of the LORD God, to bring the ark of the covenant of the LORD, and the holy vessels of God, into the house that is to be built to the name of the LORD. ☐

2 Chronicles 7:14, If my people, which are called by my name, shall humble themselves, and pray, and **seek** my face, and turn from their wicked ways; then will I hear from heaven, and will forgive their sin, and will heal their land. ☐

2 Chronicles 12:14, And he did evil, because he prepared not his heart to **seek** the LORD. ☐

2 Chronicles 15:2, And he went out to meet Asa, and said unto him, Hear ye me, Asa, and all Judah and Benjamin; The LORD is with you, while ye be with him; and if ye **seek** him, he will be found of you; but if ye forsake him, he will forsake you. ☐

2 Chronicles 15:12, And they entered into a covenant to **seek** the LORD God of their fathers with all their heart and with all their soul. ☐

2 Chronicles 31:21, And in every work that he began in the service of the house of God, and in the law, and in the commandments, to **seek** his God, he did it with all his heart, and prospered. ☐

Job 5:8, I would **seek** unto God, and unto God would I commit my cause. ☐

Job 8:5, If thou wouldest **seek** unto God quickly, and make thy supplication to the Almighty. ☐

Isaiah 52:9, Break forth into **joy**, sing together, ye waste places of Jerusalem: for the LORD hath comforted his people, he hath redeemed Jerusalem. ☐

Isaiah 55:12, For ye shall go out with **joy**, and be led forth with peace: the mountains and the hills shall break forth before you into singing, and all the trees of the field shall clap their hands. ☐

Habakkuk 3:18, Yet I will rejoice in the LORD, I will **joy** in the God of my salvation.☐

Matthew 13:20, But he that received the seed into stony places, the same is he that heareth the word, and anon with **joy** receiveth it. ☐

Matthew 25:21, His lord said unto him, Well done, thou good and faithful servant: thou hast been faithful over a few things, I will make thee ruler over many things: enter thou into the **joy** of thy lord.☐

Matthew 25:23, His lord said unto him, Well done, good and faithful servant; thou hast been faithful over a few things, I will make thee ruler over many things: enter thou into the **joy** of thy lord.☐

Luke 1:14, And thou shalt have **joy** and gladness; and many shall rejoice at his birth.☐

Luke 2:10, And the angel said unto them, Fear not: for, behold, I bring you good tidings of great **joy**, which shall be to all people.☐

Luke 8:13, They on the rock are they, which, when they hear, receive the word with **joy**; and these have no root, which for a while believe, and in time of temptation fall away. ☐

Luke 15:10, Likewise, I say unto you, there is **joy** in the presence of the angels of God over one sinner that repenteth. ☐

John 15:11, These things have I spoken unto you, that my **joy** might remain in you, and that your **joy** might be full.☐

In God We Trust

FOOL *
FOOLISH *
FOOLISHNESS *

46 DAY
AFTERNOON
90 DAY CHALLENGE

Psalms 14:1, The **fool** hath said in his heart, There is no God. They are corrupt, they have done abominable works, there is none that doeth good. ☐

Psalms 38:5, My wounds stink and are corrupt because of my **foolishness**. ☐

Psalms 53:1, The **fool** hath said in his heart, There is no God. Corrupt are they, and have done abominable iniquity: there is none that doeth good. ☐

Psalms 69:5, O God, thou knowest my **foolishness**; and my sins are not hid from thee. ☐

Psalms 73:3, For I was envious at the **foolish**, when I saw the prosperity of the wicked. ☐

Psalms 92:6, A brutish man knoweth not; neither doth a **fool** understand this. ☐

Proverbs 7:22, He goeth after her straightway, as an ox goeth to the slaughter, or as a **fool** to the correction of the stocks. ☐

Proverbs 10:8, The wise in heart will receive commandments: but a prating **fool** shall fall. ☐

Proverbs 10:10, He that winketh with the eye causeth sorrow: but a prating **fool** shall fall. ☐

Proverbs 10:14, Wise men lay up knowledge: but the mouth of the **foolish** is near destruction. ☐

Proverbs 10:18, He that hideth hatred with lying lips, and he that uttereth a slander, is a **fool**. ☐

Proverbs 10:23, It is as sport to a **fool** to do mischief: but a man of understanding hath wisdom. ☐

Proverbs 11:29, He that troubleth his own house shall inherit the wind: and the **fool** shall be servant to the wise of heart. ☐

Psalms 24:10, Who is this King of glory? The LORD of hosts, **he is** the King of glory. Selah. ☐

Psalms 28:8, The LORD is their strength, and **he is** the saving strength of his anointed. ☐

Psalms 33:20, Our soul waiteth for the LORD: **he is** our help and our shield. ☐

Psalms 45:11, So shall the king greatly desire thy beauty: for **he is** thy Lord; and worship thou him. ☐

Psalms 95:7, For **he is** our God; and we are the people of his pasture, and the sheep of his hand. Today if ye will hear his voice. ☐

Psalms 96:4, For the LORD is great, and greatly to be praised: **he is** to be feared above all gods. ☐

Psalms 99:5, Exalt ye the LORD our God, and worship at his footstool; for **he is** holy. ☐

Psalms 100:3, Know ye that the LORD **he is** God: it is he that hath made us, and not we ourselves; we are his people, and the sheep of his pasture. ☐

Proverbs 30:5, Every word of God is pure: **he is** a shield unto them that put their trust in him. ☐

Hebrews 10:23, Let us hold fast the profession of our faith without wavering; for **he is** faithful that promised. ☐

In God We Trust

I BELIEVE
BIGGER
BETTER
BOLDER
BLESSINGS

TEACH *

47 DAY
MORNING
90 DAY CHALLENGE

Job 6:24, **Teach** me, and I will hold my tongue: and cause me to understand wherein I have erred.☐

Job 33:33, If not, hearken unto me: hold thy peace, and I shall **teach** thee wisdom.☐

Psalms 25:4, Shew me thy ways, O LORD; **teach** me thy paths.☐

Psalms 25:5, Lead me in thy truth, and **teach** me: for thou art the God of my salvation; on thee do I wait all the day.☐

Psalms 25:8, Good and upright is the LORD: therefore will he **teach** sinners in the way.☐

Psalms 25:9, The meek will he guide in judgment: and the meek will he **teach** his way.☐

Psalms 27:11, **Teach** me thy way, O LORD, and lead me in a plain path, because of mine enemies. ☐

Psalms 32:8, I will instruct thee and **teach** thee in the way which thou shalt go: I will guide thee with mine eye.☐

Psalms 34:11, Come, ye children, hearken unto me: I will **teach** you the fear of the LORD.☐

Psalms 45:4, And in thy majesty ride prosperously because of truth and meekness and righteousness; and thy right hand shall **teach** thee terrible things.☐

Psalms 51:13, Then will I **teach** transgressors thy ways; and sinners shall be converted unto thee.☐

Psalms 86:11, **Teach** me thy way, O LORD; I will walk in thy truth: unite my heart to fear thy name.☐

Psalms 90:12, So **teach** us to number our days, that we may apply our hearts unto wisdom.☐

MINDFUL *
MINDS
MINDED *

47 DAY
AFTERNOON
90 DAY CHALLENGE

1 Chronicles 16:15, Be ye **mindful** always of his covenant; the word which he commanded to a thousand generations. ☐

Nehemiah 9:17, And refused to obey, neither were **mindful** of thy wonders that thou didst among them; but hardened their necks, and in their rebellion appointed a captain to return to their bondage: but thou art a God ready to pardon, gracious and merciful, slow to anger, and of great kindness, and forsookest them not. ☐

Psalms 8:4, What is man, that thou art **mindful** of him? and the son of man, that thou visitest him? ☐

Psalms 111:5, He hath given meat unto them that fear him: he will ever be **mindful** of his covenant. ☐

Psalms 115:12, The LORD hath been **mindful** of us: he will bless us; he will bless the house of Israel; he will bless the house of Aaron. ☐

Isaiah 17:10, Because thou hast forgotten the God of thy salvation, and hast not been **mindful** of the rock of thy strength, therefore shalt thou plant pleasant plants, and shalt set it with strange slips. ☐

Romans 8:6, For to be carnally **minded** is death; but to be spiritually **minded** is life and peace. ☐

2 Corinthians 4:4, In whom the god of this world hath blinded the **minds** of them which believe not, lest the light of the glorious gospel of Christ, who is the image of God, should shine unto them. ☐

2 Timothy 1:4, Greatly desiring to see thee, being **mindful** of thy tears, that I may be filled with joy. ☐

Hebrews 2:6, But one in a certain place testified, saying, What is man, that thou art **mindful** of him? or the son of man, that thou visitest him? ☐

2 Peter 3:2, That ye may be **mindful** of the words which were spoken before by the holy prophets, and of the commandment of us the apostles of the Lord and Saviour. ☐

Psalms 54:3, For strangers are risen up against me, and oppressors seek after **my soul**: they have not set God before them. Selah.☐

Psalms 54:4, Behold, God is mine helper: the Lord is with them that uphold **my soul**.☐

Psalms 66:16, Come and hear, all ye that fear God, and I will declare what he hath done for **my soul**.☐

Psalms 69:10, When I wept, and chastened **my soul** with fasting, that was to my reproach.☐

Psalms 71:23, My lips shall greatly rejoice when I sing unto thee; and **my soul**, which thou hast redeemed.☐

Psalms 86:2, Preserve **my soul**; for I am holy: O thou my God, save thy servant that trusteth in thee.☐

Psalms 86:4, Rejoice the soul of thy servant: for unto thee, O Lord, do I lift up **my soul**.☐

Psalms 86:13, For great is thy mercy toward me: and thou hast delivered **my soul** from the lowest hell.☐

Psalms 88:3, For **my soul** is full of troubles: and my life draweth nigh unto the grave.☐

Psalms 94:17, Unless the LORD had been my help, **my soul** had almost dwelt in silence.☐

Psalms 94:19, In the multitude of my thoughts within me thy comforts delight **my soul**.☐

Psalms 103:22, Bless the LORD, all his works in all places of his dominion: bless the LORD, O **my soul**.☐

Psalms 104:1, Bless the LORD, O **my soul**. O LORD my God, thou art very great; thou art clothed with honour and majesty.☐

Psalms 96:4, For the LORD is great, and greatly **to be** praised: he is **to be** feared above all gods. □

Psalms 106:8, Nevertheless he saved them for his name's sake, that he might make his mighty power **to be** known. □

Psalms 111:4, He hath made his wonderful works **to be** remembered: the LORD is gracious and full of compassion. □

Psalms 113:3, From the rising of the sun unto the going down of the same the LORD'S name is **to be** praised. □

Psalms 119:128, Therefore I esteem all thy precepts concerning all things **to be** right; and I hate every false way. □

Psalms 121:3, He will not suffer thy foot **to be** moved: he that keepeth thee will not slumber. □

Psalms 145:3, Great is the LORD, and greatly **to be** praised; and his greatness is unsearchable. □

Proverbs 8:11, For wisdom is better than rubies; and all the things that may be desired are not **to be** compared to it. □

Proverbs 16:7, When a man's ways please the LORD, he maketh even his enemies **to be** at peace with him. □

Matthew 6:1, Take heed that ye do not your alms before men, **to be** seen of them: otherwise ye have no reward of your Father which is in heaven. □

Matthew 15:31, Insomuch that the multitude wondered, when they saw the dumb to speak, the maimed **to be** whole, the lame to walk, and the blind to see: and they glorified the God of Israel. □

Acts 27:22, And now I exhort you **to be** of good cheer: for there shall be no loss of any man's life among you, but of the ship. □

Romans 6:11, Likewise reckon ye also yourselves **to be** dead indeed unto sin, but alive unto God through Jesus Christ our Lord. □

Job 29:12, Because I delivered the poor that **cried**, and the fatherless, and him that had none to help him.☐

Psalms 18:6, In my distress I called upon the LORD, and **cried** unto my God: he heard my voice out of his temple, and my **cry** came before him, even into his ears. ☐

Psalms 30:2, O LORD my God, I **cried** unto thee, and thou hast healed me.☐

Psalms 30:8, I **cried** to thee, O LORD; and unto the LORD I made supplication.☐

Psalms 34:6, This poor man **cried**, and the LORD heard him, and saved him out of all his troubles. ☐

Psalms 77:1, I **cried** unto God with my voice, even unto God with my voice; and he gave ear unto me. ☐

Psalms 107:6, Then they **cried** unto the LORD in their trouble, and he delivered them out of their distresses. ☐

Psalms 119:145, I **cried** with my whole heart; hear me, O LORD: I will keep thy statutes.☐

Psalms 119:146, I **cried** unto thee; save me, and I shall keep thy testimonies.☐

Psalms 119:147, I prevented the dawning of the morning, and **cried**: I hoped in thy word.☐

Psalms 120:1, In my distress I **cried** unto the LORD, and he heard me. ☐

BE GRATEFUL ALWAYS

In God We Trust

Proverbs 12:14, A man shall be satisfied with good by the **fruit** of his mouth: and the recompence of a man's hands shall be rendered unto him. ☐

Proverbs 13:2, A man shall eat good by the **fruit** of his mouth: but the soul of the transgressors shall eat violence. ☐

Proverbs 18:21, Death and life are in the power of the tongue: and they that love it shall eat the **fruit** thereof. ☐

Proverbs 27:18, Whoso keepeth the fig tree shall eat the **fruit** thereof: so he that waiteth on his master shall be honoured. ☐

Proverbs 31:16, She considereth a field, and buyeth it: with the **fruit** of her hands she planteth a vineyard. ☐

Proverbs 31:31, Give her of the **fruit** of her hands; and let her own works praise her in the gates. ☐

Isaiah 3:10, Say ye to the righteous, that it shall be well with him: for they shall eat the **fruit** of their doings. ☐

Isaiah 57:19, I create the **fruit** of the lips; Peace, peace to him that is far off, and to him that is near, saith the LORD; and I will heal him. ☐

Matthew 7:17, Even so every good tree bringeth forth good **fruit**; but a corrupt tree bringeth forth evil **fruit**. ☐

Matthew 7:18, A good tree cannot bring forth evil **fruit**, neither can a corrupt tree bring forth good **fruit**. ☐

Matthew 12:33, Either make the tree good, and his **fruit** good; or else make the tree corrupt, and his **fruit** corrupt: for the tree is known by his **fruit**. ☐

Matthew 13:8, But other fell into good ground, and brought forth **fruit**, some an hundredfold, some sixtyfold, some thirtyfold. ☐

Mark 4:7, And some fell among thorns, and the thorns grew up, and choked it, and it yielded no **fruit**. ☐

Proverbs 4:5, Get wisdom, get **understanding**: forget it not; neither decline from the words of my mouth.☐

Proverbs 4:7, Wisdom is the principal thing; therefore get wisdom: and with all thy getting get **understanding**. ☐

Proverbs 5:1, My son, attend unto my wisdom, and bow thine ear to my **understanding**.☐

Proverbs 6:32, But whoso committeth adultery with a woman lacketh **understanding**: he that doeth it destroyeth his own soul. ☐

Proverbs 7:4, Say unto wisdom, Thou art my sister; and call **understanding** thy kinswoman.☐

Proverbs 7:7, And beheld among the simple ones, I discerned among the youths, a young man void of **understanding**.☐

Proverbs 8:1, Doth not wisdom cry? and **understanding** put forth her voice?☐

Proverbs 8:5, O ye simple, **understand** wisdom: and, ye fools, be ye of an **understanding** heart. ☐

Proverbs 8:14, Counsel is mine, and sound wisdom: I am **understanding**; I have strength.☐

Proverbs 9:6, Forsake the foolish, and live; and go in the way of **understanding**. ☐

Proverbs 9:10, The fear of the LORD is the beginning of wisdom: and the knowledge of the holy is **understanding**.☐

Proverbs 9:16, Whoso is simple, let him turn in hither: and as for him that wanteth **understanding**, she saith to him. ☐

Proverbs 10:13, In the lips of him that hath **understanding** wisdom is found: but a rod is for the back of him that is void of **understanding**.☐

In God We Trust

Matthew 10:41, He that **receiveth** a prophet in the name of a prophet shall **receive** a prophet's reward; and he that **receiveth** a righteous man in the name of a righteous man shall **receive** a righteous man's reward. ☐

1 Corinthians 3:14, If any man's work abide which he hath built thereupon, he shall **receive** a reward. ☐

2 Corinthians 6:17, Wherefore come out from among them, and be ye separate, saith the Lord, and touch not the unclean thing; and I will **receive** you. ☐

2 Corinthians 7:2, **Receive** us; we have wronged no man, we have corrupted no man, we have defrauded no man. ☐

2 Corinthians 8:4, Praying us with much intreaty that we would **receive** the gift, and take upon us the fellowship of the ministering to the saints. ☐

Galatians 4:5, To redeem them that were under the law, that we might **receive** the adoption of sons. ☐

Ephesians 6:8, Knowing that whatsoever good thing any man doeth, the same shall he **receive** of the Lord, whether he be bond or free. ☐

Philippians 2:29, **Receive** him therefore in the Lord with all gladness; and hold such in reputation. ☐

Colossians 3:24, Knowing that of the Lord ye shall **receive** the reward of the inheritance: for ye serve the Lord Christ. ☐

Colossians 3:25, But he that doeth wrong shall **receive** for the wrong which he hath done: and there is no respect of persons. ☐

James 1:7, For let not that man think that he shall **receive** any thing of the Lord. ☐

James 1:21, Wherefore lay apart all filthiness and superfluity of naughtiness, and **receive** with meekness the engrafted word, which is able to save your souls. ☐

In God We Trust

Esther 8:16, The Jews had light, and gladness, and joy, and **honour**.☐

Psalms 7:5, Let the enemy persecute my soul, and take it; yea, let him tread down my life upon the earth, and lay mine **honour** in the dust. Selah.☐

Psalms 8:5, For thou hast made him a little lower than the angels, and hast crowned him with glory and **honour**. ☐

Psalms 21:5, His glory is great in thy salvation: **honour** and majesty hast thou laid upon him.☐

Psalms 26:8, LORD, I have loved the habitation of thy house, and the place where thine **honour** dwelleth.☐

Psalms 49:20, Man that is in **honour**, and understandeth not, is like the beasts that perish.☐

Psalms 66:2, Sing forth the **honour** of his name: make his praise glorious.☐

Psalms 71:8, Let my mouth be filled with thy praise and with thy **honour** all the day.☐

Psalms 91:15, He shall call upon me, and I will answer him: I will be with him in trouble; I will deliver him, and **honour** him.☐

Psalms 104:1, Bless the LORD, O my soul. O LORD my God, thou art very great; thou art clothed with **honour** and majesty.☐

Psalms 112:9, He hath dispersed, he hath given to the poor; his righteousness endureth for ever; his horn shall be exalted with **honour**.☐

Psalms 145:5, I will speak of the glorious **honour** of thy majesty, and of thy wondrous works.☐

Psalms 149:9, To execute upon them the judgment written: this **honour** have all his saints. Praise ye the LORD.☐

Proverbs 3:16, Length of days is in her right hand; and in her left hand riches and **honour**. ☐

Romans 3:22, Even the righteousness of God which is by **faith** of Jesus Christ unto all and upon all them that believe: for there is no difference. ☐

Romans 3:25, Whom God hath set forth to be a propitiation through **faith** in his blood, to declare his righteousness for the remission of sins that are past, through the forbearance of God. ☐

Romans 4:5, But to him that worketh not, but believeth on him that justifieth the ungodly, his **faith** is counted for righteousness. ☐

Romans 4:13, For the promise, that he should be the heir of the world, was not to Abraham, or to his seed, through the law, but through the righteousness of **faith**. ☐

Romans 4:19, And being not weak in **faith**, he considered not his own body now dead, when he was about an hundred years old, neither yet the deadness of Sara's womb. ☐

Romans 4:20, He staggered not at the promise of God through unbelief; but was strong in **faith**, giving glory to God. ☐

Romans 5:1, Therefore being justified by **faith**, we have peace with God through our Lord Jesus Christ. ☐

Romans 5:2, By whom also we have access by **faith** into this grace wherein we stand, and rejoice in hope of the glory of God. ☐

Romans 10:8, But what saith it? The word is nigh thee, even in thy mouth, and in thy heart: that is, the word of **faith**, which we preach. ☐

Romans 10:17, So then **faith** cometh by hearing, and hearing by the word of God. ☐

Romans 12:3, For I say, through the grace given unto me, to every man that is among you, not to think of himself more highly than he ought to think; but to think soberly, according as God hath dealt to every man the measure of **faith**. ☐

In God We Trust

Proverbs 11:5, The **righteousness** of the perfect shall direct his way: but the wicked shall fall by his own wickedness.☐

Proverbs 11:6, The **righteousness** of the upright shall deliver them: but transgressors shall be taken in their own naughtiness. ☐

Proverbs 11:18, The wicked worketh a deceitful work: but to him that soweth **righteousness** shall be a sure reward. ☐

Proverbs 11:19, As **righteousness** tendeth to life: so he that pursueth evil pursueth it to his own death.☐

Proverbs 12:17, He that speaketh truth sheweth forth **righteousness**: but a false witness deceit.☐

Proverbs 12:28, In the way of **righteousness** is life; and in the pathway thereof there is no death. ☐

Proverbs 13:6, **Righteousness** keepeth him that is upright in the way: but wickedness overthroweth the sinner. ☐

Proverbs 14:34, **Righteousness** exalteth a nation: but sin is a reproach to any people.☐

Proverbs 15:9, The way of the wicked is an abomination unto the LORD: but he loveth him that followeth after **righteousness**.☐

Proverbs 16:8, Better is a little with **righteousness** than great revenues without right.☐

Proverbs 21:21, He that followeth after **righteousness** and mercy findeth life, **righteousness**, and honour. ☐

Proverbs 25:5, Take away the wicked from before the king, and his throne shall be established in **righteousness**.☐

Isaiah 11:4, But with **righteousness** shall he judge the poor, and reprove with equity for the meek of the earth: and he shall smite the earth with the rod of his mouth, and with the breath of his lips shall he slay the wicked.☐

In God We Trust

Psalms 69:18, Draw nigh unto my soul, and redeem it: deliver me because of mine **enemies**. ☐

Psalms 74:23, Forget not the voice of thine **enemies**: the tumult of those that rise up against thee increaseth continually. ☐

Psalms 71:10, For mine **enemies** speak against me; and they that lay wait for my soul take counsel together. ☐

Psalms 78:53, And he led them on safely, so that they feared not: but the sea overwhelmed their **enemies**. ☐

Psalms 83:2, For, lo, thine **enemies** make a tumult: and they that hate thee have lifted up the head. ☐

Psalms 89:10, Thou hast broken Rahab in pieces, as one that is slain; thou hast scattered thine **enemies** with thy strong arm. ☐

Psalms 92:9, For, lo, thine **enemies**, O LORD, for, lo, thine **enemies** shall perish; all the workers of iniquity shall be scattered. ☐

Psalms 92:11, Mine eye also shall see my desire on mine **enemies**, and mine ears shall hear my desire of the wicked that rise up against me. ☐

Psalms 97:3, A fire goeth before him, and burneth up his **enemies** round about. ☐

Psalms 106:11, And the waters covered their **enemies**: there was not one of them left. ☐

Psalms 110:1, The LORD said unto my Lord, Sit thou at my right hand, until I make thine **enemies** thy footstool. ☐

Psalms 110:2, The LORD shall send the rod of thy strength out of Zion: rule thou in the midst of thine **enemies**. ☐

Psalms 112:8, His heart is established, he shall not be afraid, until he see his desire upon his **enemies**. ☐

Psalms 5:11, But let all those that put their trust in thee rejoice: let them ever shout for **joy**, because thou defendest them: let them also that love thy name be **joyful** in thee. ☐

Psalms 16:11, Thou wilt shew me the path of life: in thy presence is fulness of **joy**; at thy right hand there are pleasures for evermore. ☐

Psalms 30:5, For his anger endureth but a moment; in his favour is life: weeping may endure for a night, but **joy** cometh in the morning. ☐

Psalms 32:11, Be glad in the LORD, and rejoice, ye righteous: and shout for **joy**, all ye that are upright in heart. ☐

Psalms 35:27, Let them shout for **joy**, and be glad, that favour my righteous cause: yea, let them say continually, Let the LORD be magnified, which hath pleasure in the prosperity of his servant. ☐

Psalms 48:2, Beautiful for situation, the **joy** of the whole earth, is mount Zion, on the sides of the north, the city of the great King. ☐

Psalms 51:8, Make me to hear **joy** and gladness; that the bones which thou hast broken may rejoice. ☐

Psalms 51:12, Restore unto me the **joy** of thy salvation; and uphold me with thy free spirit. ☐

Psalms 67:4, O let the nations be glad and sing for **joy**: for thou shalt judge the people righteously, and govern the nations upon earth. Selah. ☐

Psalms 126:5, They that sow in tears shall reap in **joy**. ☐

Psalms 132:9, Let thy priests be clothed with righteousness; and let thy saints shout for **joy**. ☐

Psalms 137:6, If I do not remember thee, let my tongue cleave to the roof of my mouth; if I prefer not Jerusalem above my chief **joy**. ☐

Proverbs 12:20, Deceit is in the heart of them that imagine evil: but to the counsellors of peace is **joy**. ☐

Romans 1:5, By whom we have received grace and apostleship, for **obedience** to the faith among all nations, for his name. ☐

Romans 5:19, For as by one man's disobedience many were made sinners, so by the **obedience** of one shall many be made righteous. ☐

Romans 6:16, Know ye not, that to whom ye yield yourselves servants to obey, his servants ye are to whom ye obey; whether of sin unto death, or of **obedience** unto righteousness? ☐

Romans 16:19, For your **obedience** is come abroad unto all men. I am glad therefore on your behalf: but yet I would have you wise unto that which is good, and simple concerning evil. ☐

Romans 16:26, But now is made manifest, and by the scriptures of the prophets, according to the commandment of the everlasting God, made known to all nations for the **obedience** of faith. ☐

2 Corinthians 7:15, And his inward affection is more abundant toward you, whilst he remembereth the **obedience** of you all, how with fear and trembling ye received him. ☐

2 Corinthians 10:5, Casting down imaginations, and every high thing that exalteth itself against the knowledge of God, and bringing into captivity every thought to the **obedience** of Christ. ☐

2 Corinthians 10:6, And having in a readiness to revenge all disobedience, when your **obedience** is fulfilled. ☐

Philemon 1:21, Having confidence in thy **obedience** I wrote unto thee, knowing that thou wilt also do more than I say. ☐

Hebrews 5:8, Though he were a Son, yet learned he **obedience** by the things which he suffered. ☐

1 Peter 1:2, Elect according to the foreknowledge of God the Father, through sanctification of the Spirit, unto **obedience** and sprinkling of the blood of Jesus Christ: Grace unto you, and peace, be multiplied. ☐

In God We Trust

Colossians 1:4, Since we heard of your faith **in Christ Jesus**, and of the love which ye have to all the saints. □

Colossians 1:28, Whom we preach, warning every man, and teaching every man in all wisdom; that we may present every man perfect **in Christ Jesus.** □

Colossians 2:5, For though I be absent in the flesh, yet am I with you in the spirit, joying and beholding your order, and the stedfastness of your faith **in Christ.** □

1 Thessalonians 4:16, For the Lord himself shall descend from heaven with a shout, with the voice of the archangel, and with the trump of God: and the dead **in Christ** shall rise first. □

1 Thessalonians 5:18, In every thing give thanks: for this is the will of God **in Christ Jesus** concerning you. □

1 Timothy 1:14, And the grace of our Lord was exceeding abundant with faith and love which is **in Christ Jesus.** □

1 Timothy 3:13, For they that have used the office of a deacon well purchase to themselves a good degree, and great boldness in the faith which is **in Christ Jesus.** □

2 Timothy 1:1, Paul, an apostle of Jesus Christ by the will of God, according to the promise of life which is **in Christ Jesus.** □

2 Timothy 1:9, Who hath saved us, and called us with an holy calling, not according to our works, but according to his own purpose and grace, which was given us **in Christ Jesus** before the world began. □

2 Timothy 1:13, Hold fast the form of sound words, which thou hast heard of me, in faith and love which is **in Christ Jesus.** □

2 Timothy 2:10, Therefore I endure all things for the elect's sakes, that they may also obtain the salvation which is **in Christ Jesus** with eternal glory. □

Psalms 102:18, This shall be **written** for the generation to come: and the people which shall be created shall praise the LORD. □

John 20:31, But these are **written**, that ye might believe that Jesus is the Christ, the Son of God; and that believing ye might have life through his name. □

Romans 15:9, And that the Gentiles might glorify God for his mercy; as **it is written**, For this cause I will confess to thee among the Gentiles, and sing unto thy name. □

1 Corinthians 1:19, For **it is written**, I will destroy the wisdom of the wise, and will bring to nothing the understanding of the prudent. □

1 Corinthians 1:31, That, according as **it is written**, He that glorieth, let him glory in the Lord. □

1 Corinthians 2:9, But as **it is written**, Eye hath not seen, nor ear heard, neither have entered into the heart of man, the things which God hath prepared for them that love him. □

1 Corinthians 3:19, For the wisdom of this world is foolishness with God. For **it is written**, He taketh the wise in their own craftiness. □

1 Corinthians 15:45, And so **it is written**, The first man Adam was made a living soul; the last Adam was made a quickening spirit. □

2 Corinthians 4:13, We having the same spirit of faith, according as **it is written**, I believed, and therefore have I spoken; we also believe, and therefore speak. □

2 Corinthians 9:9, As **it is written**, He hath dispersed abroad; he hath given to the poor: his righteousness remaineth forever. □

Galatians 3:13, Christ hath redeemed us from the curse of the law, being made a curse for us: for **it is written**, Cursed is every one that hangeth on a tree. □

In God We Trust

POOR *
RICH *
RICHES

DAY
AFTERNOON
90 DAY CHALLENGE

Deuteronomy 15:11, For the **poor** shall never cease out of the land: therefore I command thee, saying, Thou shalt open thine hand wide unto thy brother, to thy **poor**, and to thy needy, in thy land. ☐

1 Samuel 2:7, The LORD maketh **poor**, and maketh **rich**: he bringeth low, and lifteth up. ☐

Psalms 37:14, The wicked have drawn out the sword, and have bent their bow, to cast down the **poor** and needy, and to slay such as be of upright conversation. ☐

Psalms 40:17, But I am **poor** and needy; yet the Lord thinketh upon me: thou art my help and my deliverer; make no tarrying, O my God. ☐

Psalms 41:1, Blessed is he that considereth the **poor**: the LORD will deliver him in time of trouble. ☐

Psalms 49:2, Both low and high, **rich** and **poor**, together. ☐

Psalms 68:10, Thy congregation hath dwelt therein: thou, O God, hast prepared of thy goodness for the **poor**. ☐

Psalms 69:29, But I am **poor** and sorrowful: let thy salvation, O God, set me up on high. ☐

Psalms 69:33, For the LORD heareth the **poor**, and despiseth not his prisoners. ☐

Psalms 70:5, But I am **poor** and needy: make haste unto me, O God: thou art my help and my deliverer; O LORD, make no tarrying. ☐

Psalms 72:13, He shall spare the **poor** and needy, and shall save the souls of the needy. ☐

Psalms 82:3, Defend the **poor** and fatherless: do justice to the afflicted and needy. ☐

Psalms 82:4, Deliver the **poor** and needy: rid them out of the hand of the wicked. ☐

In God We Trust

FRIEND - FRIENDS
FRIENDSHIP *
FRIENDLY

52 DAY
EVENING
90 DAY CHALLENGE

Proverbs 6:3, Do this now, my son, and deliver thyself, when thou art come into the hand of thy **friend**; go, humble thyself, and make sure thy **friend**. ☐

Proverbs 17:17, A **friend** loveth at all times, and a brother is born for adversity. ☐

Proverbs 17:18, A man void of understanding striketh hands, and becometh surety in the presence of his **friend**. ☐

Proverbs 18:24, A man that hath **friends** must shew himself **friendly**: and there is a **friend** that sticketh closer than a brother. ☐

Proverbs 19:6, Many will intreat the favour of the prince: and every man is a **friend** to him that giveth gifts. ☐

Proverbs 22:11, He that loveth pureness of heart, for the grace of his lips the king shall be his **friend**. ☐

Proverbs 22:24, Make no **friendship** with an angry man; and with a furious man thou shalt not go. ☐

Proverbs 27:6, Faithful are the wounds of a **friend**; but the kisses of an enemy are deceitful. ☐

Proverbs 27:9, Ointment and perfume rejoice the heart: so doth the sweetness of a man's **friend** by hearty counsel. ☐

Proverbs 27:10, Thine own **friend**, and thy father's **friend**, forsake not; neither go into thy brother's house in the day of thy calamity: for better is a neighbour that is near than a brother far off. ☐

Proverbs 27:14, He that blesseth his **friend** with a loud voice, rising early in the morning, it shall be counted a curse to him. ☐

Proverbs 27:17, Iron sharpeneth iron; so a man sharpeneth the countenance of his **friend**. ☐

Song of Solomon 5:16, His mouth is most sweet: yea, he is altogether lovely. This is my beloved, and this is my **friend**, O daughters of Jerusalem. ☐

Matthew 5:12, Rejoice, and be exceeding glad: for **great** is your reward in heaven: for so persecuted they the prophets which were before you. □

Matthew 19:2, And **great** multitudes followed him; and he healed them there. □

Matthew 20:26, But it shall not be so among you: but whosoever will be **great** among you, let him be your minister. □

Mark 5:19, Howbeit Jesus suffered him not, but saith unto him, Go home to thy friends, and tell them how **great** things the Lord hath done for thee, and hath had compassion on thee. □

Mark 13:26, And then shall they see the Son of man coming in the clouds with **great** power and glory. □

Acts 6:7, And the word of God increased; and the number of the disciples multiplied in Jerusalem **greatly**; and a **great** company of the priests were obedient to the faith. □

Acts 6:8, And Stephen, full of faith and power, did **great** wonders and miracles among the people. □

2 Corinthians 1:10, Who delivered us from so **great** a death, and doth deliver: in whom we trust that he will yet deliver us. □

2 Corinthians 7:4, **Great** is my boldness of speech toward you, **great** is my glorying of you: I am filled with comfort, I am exceeding joyful in all our tribulation. □

Ephesians 2:4, But God, who is rich in mercy, for his **great** love wherewith he loved us. □

Titus 2:13, Looking for that blessed hope, and the glorious appearing of the **great** God and our Saviour Jesus Christ. □

Hebrews 2:3, How shall we escape, if we neglect so **great** salvation; which at the first began to be spoken by the Lord, and was confirmed unto us by them that heard him. □

In God We Trust

Matthew 5:22, **But I say unto you,** That whosoever is angry with his brother without a cause shall be in danger of the judgment: and whosoever shall say to his brother, Raca, shall be in danger of the council: but whosoever shall say, Thou fool, shall be in danger of hell fire. ☐

Matthew 5:28, **But I say unto you,** That whosoever looketh on a woman to lust after her hath committed adultery with her already in his heart. ☐

Matthew 5:32, **But I say unto you,** That whosoever shall put away his wife, saving for the cause of fornication, causeth her to commit adultery: and whosoever shall marry her that is divorced committeth adultery. ☐

Matthew 5:34, **But I say unto you,** Swear not at all; neither by heaven; for it is God's throne. ☐

Matthew 5:39, **But I say unto you,** That ye resist not evil: but whosoever shall smite thee on thy right cheek, turn to him the other also. ☐

Matthew 5:44, **But I say unto you,** Love your enemies, bless them that curse you, do good to them that hate you, and pray for them which despitefully use you, and persecute you. ☐

Matthew 11:22, **But I say unto you,** It shall be more tolerable for Tyre and Sidon at the day of judgment, than for you. ☐

Matthew 11:24, **But I say unto you,** That it shall be more tolerable for the land of Sodom in the day of judgment, than for thee. ☐

Matthew 12:6, **But I say unto you,** That in this place is one greater than the temple. ☐

Matthew 12:36, **But I say unto you,** That every idle word that men shall speak, they shall give account thereof in the day of judgment. ☐

Matthew 17:12 **But I say unto you,** That Elias is come already, and they knew him not, but have done unto him whatsoever they listed. Likewise shall also the Son of man suffer of them. ☐

In God We Trust

STRENGTH *
STRENGTHEN *

Psalms 18:1, I will love thee, O LORD, my **strength**. ☐

Psalms 18:2, The LORD is my rock, and my fortress, and my deliverer; my God, my **strength**, in whom I will trust; my buckler, and the horn of my salvation, and my high tower. ☐

Psalms 18:32, It is God that girdeth me with **strength**, and maketh my way perfect.☐

Psalms 19:14, Let the words of my mouth, and the meditation of my heart, be acceptable in thy sight, O LORD, my **strength**, and my redeemer. ☐

Psalms 21:13, Be thou exalted, LORD, in thine own **strength**: so will we sing and praise thy power. ☐

Psalms 22:19, But be not thou far from me, O LORD: O my **strength**, haste thee to help me. ☐

Psalms 27:1, The LORD is my light and my salvation; whom shall I fear? the LORD is the **strength** of my life; of whom shall I be afraid? ☐

Psalms 27:14, Wait on the LORD: be of good courage, and he shall **strengthen** thine heart: wait, I say, on the LORD. ☐

Psalms 28:7, The LORD is my **strength** and my shield; my heart trusted in him, and I am helped: therefore my heart greatly rejoiceth; and with my song will I praise him. ☐

Psalms 28:8, The LORD is their **strength**, and he is the saving **strength** of his anointed. ☐

Psalms 37:39, But the salvation of the righteous is of the LORD: he is their **strength** in the time of trouble. ☐

Matthew 5:44, But I say unto you, **Love** your enemies, bless them that curse you, do good to them that hate you, and pray for them which despitefully use you, and persecute you. ☐

Matthew 19:19, Honour thy father and thy mother: and, Thou shalt **love** thy neighbour as thyself. ☐

Matthew 22:37, Jesus said unto him, Thou shalt **love** the Lord thy God with all thy heart, and with all thy soul, and with all thy mind. ☐

Matthew 22:39, And the second is like unto it, Thou shalt **love** thy neighbour as thyself. ☐

Mark 12:30, And thou shalt **love** the Lord thy God with all thy heart, and with all thy soul, and with all thy mind, and with all thy strength: this is the first commandment. ☐

Mark 12:31, And the second is like, namely this, Thou shalt **love** thy neighbour as thyself. There is none other commandment greater than these. ☐

Luke 6:27, But I say unto you which hear, **love** your enemies, do good to them which hate you. ☐

Luke 6:32, For if ye **love** them which **love** you, what thank have ye? for sinners also **love** those that **love** them. ☐

Luke 10:27, And he answering said, Thou shalt **love** the Lord thy God with all thy heart, and with all thy soul, and with all thy strength, and with all thy mind; and thy neighbour as thyself. ☐

John 13:34, A new commandment I give unto you, That ye **love** one another; as I have **loved** you, that ye also **love** one another. ☐

John 13:35, By this shall all men know that ye are my disciples, if ye have **love** one to another. ☐

John 14:15, If ye **love** me, keep my commandments. ☐

In God We Trust

2 Samuel 23:2, The Spirit of the LORD spake by me, and his word was in **my tongue**. ☐

Job 6:24, Teach me, and I will hold **my tongue**: and cause me to understand wherein I have erred. ☐

Job 6:30, Is there iniquity in **my tongue**? cannot my taste discern perverse things? ☐

Job 27:4, My lips shall not speak wickedness, nor **my tongue** utter deceit. ☐

Job 33:2, Behold, now I have opened my mouth, **my tongue** hath spoken in my mouth. ☐

Psalms 39:1, I said, I will take heed to my ways, that I sin not with **my tongue**: I will keep my mouth with a bridle, while the wicked is before me. ☐

Psalms 39:3, My heart was hot within me, while I was musing the fire burned: then spake I with **my tongue**. ☐

Psalms 45:1, My heart is inditing a good matter: I speak of the things which I have made touching the king: **my tongue** is the pen of a ready writer. ☐

Psalms 51:14, Deliver me from bloodguiltiness, O God, thou God of my salvation: and **my tongue** shall sing aloud of thy righteousness. ☐

Psalms 35:28, And **my tongue** shall speak of thy righteousness and of thy praise all the day long. ☐

Psalms 66:17, I cried unto him with my mouth, and he was extolled with **my tongue**. ☐

Psalms 71:24, **My tongue** also shall talk of thy righteousness all the day long: for they are confounded, for they are brought unto shame, that seek my hurt. ☐

Psalms 49:6, They that **trust in** their wealth, and boast themselves in the multitude of their riches. ☐

Psalms 52:8, But I am like a green olive tree in the house of God: I **trust in** the mercy of God for ever and ever. ☐

Psalms 55:23, But thou, O God, shalt bring them down into the pit of destruction: bloody and deceitful men shall not live out half their days; but I will **trust in** thee. ☐

Psalms 62:8, **Trust in** him at all times; ye people, pour out your heart before him: God is a refuge for us. Selah. ☐

Psalms 64:10, The righteous shall be glad in the LORD, and shall **trust in** him; and all the upright in heart shall glory. ☐

Psalms 73:28, But it is good for me to draw near to God: I have put my **trust in the Lord** GOD, that I may declare all thy works. ☐

Psalms 115:10, O house of Aaron, **trust in the LORD**: he is their help and their shield. ☐

Psalms 115:11, Ye that fear the LORD, **trust in the LORD**: he is their help and their shield. ☐

Psalms 118:8, It is better to **trust in the LORD** than to put confidence in man. ☐

Psalms 118:9, It is better to **trust in the LORD** than to put confidence in princes. ☐

Psalms 119:42, So shall I have wherewith to answer him that reproacheth me: for I **trust in** thy word. ☐

Psalms 125:1, They that **trust in the LORD** shall be as mount Zion, which cannot be removed, but abideth forever. ☐

Proverbs 28:25, He that is of a proud heart stirreth up strife: but he that putteth his **trust in the LORD** shall be made fat. ☐

In God We Trust

HEALETH *
HEALED
HEAL *

55 DAY
MORNING
90 DAY CHALLENGE

Exodus 15:26, And said, If thou wilt diligently hearken to the voice of the LORD thy God, and wilt do that which is right in his sight, and wilt give ear to his commandments, and keep all his statutes, I will put none of these diseases upon thee, which I have brought upon the Egyptians: for I am the LORD that **healeth** thee. □

2 Chronicles 30:20, And the LORD hearkened to Hezekiah, and **healed** the people. □

Psalms 103:3, Who forgiveth all thine iniquities; who **healeth** all thy diseases; □

Psalms 147:3, He **healeth** the broken in heart, and bindeth up their wounds. □

Psalms 107:20, He sent his word, and **healed** them, and delivered them from their destructions. □

Isaiah 6:10, Make the heart of this people fat, and make their ears heavy, and shut their eyes; lest they see with their eyes, and hear with their ears, and understand with their heart, and convert, and be **healed**. □

Isaiah 30:26, Moreover the light of the moon shall be as the light of the sun, and the light of the sun shall be sevenfold, as the light of seven days, in the day that the LORD bindeth up the breach of his people, and **healeth** the stroke of their wound. □

Isaiah 53:5, But he was wounded for our transgressions, he was bruised for our iniquities: the chastisement of our peace was upon him; and with his stripes we are **healed**. □

Jeremiah 6:14, They have **healed** also the hurt of the daughter of my people slightly, saying, Peace, peace; when there is no peace. □

Jeremiah 17:14, **Heal** me, O LORD, and I shall be **healed**; save me, and I shall be saved: for thou art my praise. □

2 Corinthians 13:3, Since ye seek a proof of Christ speaking in me, which to you-ward is not weak, but is mighty **in you**. ☐

2 Corinthians 13:5, Examine yourselves, whether ye be in the faith; prove your own selves. Know ye not your own selves, how that Jesus Christ is **in you**, except ye be reprobates? ☐

Galatians 4:19, My little children, of whom I travail in birth again until Christ be formed **in you**. ☐

Galatians 5:10, I have confidence **in you** through the Lord, that ye will be none otherwise minded: but he that troubleth you shall bear his judgment, whosoever he be. ☐

Ephesians 4:6, One God and Father of all, who is above all, and through all, and **in you** all. ☐

Philippians 1:6, Being confident of this very thing, that he which hath begun a good work **in you** will perform it until the day of Jesus Christ. ☐

Philippians 2:5, Let this mind be **in you**, which was also in Christ Jesus. ☐

Philippians 2:13, For it is God which worketh **in you** both to will and to do of his good pleasure. ☐

Colossians 1:27, To whom God would make known what is the riches of the glory of this mystery among the Gentiles; which is Christ **in you**, the hope of glory. ☐

Colossians 3:16, Let the word of Christ dwell **in you** richly in all wisdom; teaching and admonishing one another in psalms and hymns and spiritual songs, singing with grace in your hearts to the Lord. ☐

2 Thessalonians 1:12, That the name of our Lord Jesus Christ may be glorified **in you**, and ye in him, according to the grace of our God and the Lord Jesus Christ. ☐

Philemon 1:6, That the communication of thy faith may become effectual by the acknowledging of every good thing which is **in you** in Christ Jesus. ☐

1 Kings 8:50, And **forgive** thy people that have sinned against thee, and all their transgressions wherein they have transgressed against thee, and give them compassion before them who carried them captive, that they may have compassion on them. ☐

2 Chronicles 6:30, Then hear thou from heaven thy dwelling place, and **forgive**, and render unto every man according unto all his ways, whose heart thou knowest; for thou only knowest the hearts of the children of men. ☐

2 Chronicles 7:14, If my people, which are called by my name, shall humble themselves, and pray, and seek my face, and turn from their wicked ways; then will I hear from heaven, and will **forgive** their sin, and will heal their land. ☐

Psalms 25:18, Look upon mine affliction and my pain; and **forgive** all my sins. ☐

Psalms 86:5, For thou, Lord, art good, and ready to **forgive**; and plenteous in mercy unto all them that call upon thee. ☐

Jeremiah 31:34, And they shall teach no more every man his neighbour, and every man his brother, saying, Know the LORD: for they shall all know me, from the least of them unto the greatest of them, saith the LORD: for I will **forgive** their iniquity, and I will remember their sin no more. ☐

Matthew 6:12, And **forgive** us our debts, as we **forgive** our debtors. ☐

Matthew 6:14, For if ye **forgive** men their trespasses, your heavenly Father will also **forgive** you. ☐

Matthew 6:15, But if ye **forgive** not men their trespasses, neither will your Father **forgive** your trespasses. ☐

Matthew 18:21-22, Then came Peter to him, and said, Lord, how oft shall my brother sin against me, and I **forgive** him? till seven times? Jesus said unto him, I say not unto thee, Until seven times: but, Until seventy times seven. ☐

DECLARE *

MORNING
90 DAY CHALLENGE

Psalms 2:7, I will **declare** the decree: the LORD hath said unto me, Thou art my Son; this day have I begotten thee. ☐

Psalms 9:11, Sing praises to the LORD, which dwelleth in Zion: **declare** among the people his doings. ☐

Psalms 19:1, The heavens **declare** the glory of God; and the firmament sheweth his handywork. ☐

Psalms 22:22, I will **declare** thy name unto my brethren: in the midst of the congregation will I praise thee. ☐

Psalms 22:31, They shall come, and shall **declare** his righteousness unto a people that shall be born, that he hath done this. ☐

Psalms 38:18, For I will **declare** mine iniquity; I will be sorry for my sin. ☐

Psalms 40:5, Many, O LORD my God, are thy wonderful works which thou hast done, and thy thoughts which are to us-ward: they cannot be reckoned up in order unto thee: if I would **declare** and speak of them, they are more than can be numbered. ☐

Psalms 50:6, And the heavens shall **declare** his righteousness: for God is judge himself. Selah. ☐

Psalms 50:16, But unto the wicked God saith, What hast thou to do to **declare** my statutes, or that thou shouldest take my covenant in thy mouth? ☐

Psalms 64:9, And all men shall fear, and shall **declare** the work of God; for they shall wisely consider of his doing. ☐

Psalms 66:16, Come and hear, all ye that fear God, and I will **declare** what he hath done for my soul. ☐

Psalms 73:28, But it is good for me to draw near to God: I have put my trust in the Lord GOD, that I may **declare** all thy works. ☐

In God We Trust
166

Deuteronomy 8:17, And thou say in thine heart, My **power** and the might of mine hand hath gotten me this wealth. ☐

Deuteronomy 8:18, But thou shalt remember the LORD thy God: for it is he that giveth thee **power** to get wealth, that he may establish his covenant which he sware unto thy fathers, as it is this day. ☐

Leviticus 26:19, And I will break the pride of your **power**; and I will make your heaven as iron, and your earth as brass. ☐

Nehemiah 1:10, Now these are thy servants and thy people, whom thou hast redeemed by thy great **power**, and by thy strong hand. ☐

Job 5:20, In famine he shall redeem thee from death: and in war from the **power** of the sword. ☐

Psalms 21:13, Be thou exalted, LORD, in thine own strength: so will we sing and praise thy **power**. ☐

Psalms 49:15, But God will redeem my soul from the **power** of the grave: for he shall receive me. Selah. ☐

Psalms 59:11, Slay them not, lest my people forget: scatter them by thy **power**; and bring them down, O Lord our shield. ☐

Psalms 59:16, But I will sing of thy **power**; yea, I will sing aloud of thy mercy in the morning: for thou hast been my defence and refuge in the day of my trouble. ☐

Psalms 62:11, God hath spoken once; twice have I heard this; that **power** belongeth unto God. ☐

Psalms 63:2, To see thy **power** and thy glory, so as I have seen thee in the sanctuary. ☐

Psalms 66:3, Say unto God, How terrible art thou in thy works! through the greatness of thy **power** shall thine enemies submit themselves unto thee. ☐

1 Samuel 2:1, And Hannah prayed, and said, My heart rejoiceth in the LORD, mine horn is exalted in the LORD: **my mouth** is enlarged over mine enemies; because I rejoice in thy salvation. ☐

Psalms 78:1, Give ear, O my people, to my law: incline your ears to the words of **my mouth**. ☐

Psalms 78:2, I will open **my mouth** in a parable: I will utter dark sayings of old. ☐

Psalms 89:1, I will sing of the mercies of the LORD for ever: with **my mouth** will I make known thy faithfulness to all generations. ☐

Psalms 71:23, **My lips** shall greatly rejoice when I sing unto thee; and my soul, which thou hast redeemed. ☐

Psalms 40:3, And he hath put a new song in **my mouth**, even praise unto our God: many shall see it, and fear, and shall trust in the LORD. ☐

Psalms 49:3, **My mouth** shall speak of wisdom; and the meditation of my heart shall be of understanding. ☐

Psalms 54:2, Hear my prayer, O God; give ear to the words of **my mouth**. ☐

Psalms 66:14, Which **my lips** have uttered, and **my mouth** hath spoken, When I was in trouble. ☐

Psalms 66:17, I cried unto him with **my mouth**, and he was extolled with my tongue. ☐

Psalms 89:34, My covenant will I not break, nor alter the thing that is gone out of **my lips**. ☐

Psalms 109:30, I will greatly praise the LORD with **my mouth**; yea, I will praise him among the multitude. ☐

Psalms 119:103, How sweet are thy words unto my taste! yea, sweeter than honey to **my mouth**! ☐

I BELIEVE
BIGGER
BETTER
BOLDER
BLESSINGS

I SAY

57 DAY

MORNING
90 DAY CHALLENGE

Matthew 8:10, When Jesus heard it, he marvelled, and said to them that followed, Verily **I say** unto you, I have not found so great faith, no, not in Israel. ☐

Matthew 8:11, And **I say** unto you, That many shall come from the east and west, and shall sit down with Abraham, and Isaac, and Jacob, in the kingdom of heaven. ☐

Matthew 10:42, And whosoever shall give to drink unto one of these little ones a cup of cold water only in the name of a disciple, verily **I say** unto you, he shall in no wise lose his reward. ☐

Matthew 12:31, Wherefore **I say** unto you, All manner of sin and blasphemy shall be forgiven unto men: but the blasphemy against the Holy Ghost shall not be forgiven unto men. ☐

Matthew 12:36, But **I say** unto you, That every idle word that men shall speak, they shall give account thereof in the day of judgment. ☐

Matthew 13:17, For verily **I say** unto you, That many prophets and righteous men have desired to see those things which ye see, and have not seen them; and to hear those things which ye hear, and have not heard them. ☐

Matthew 16:18, And **I say** also unto thee, That thou art Peter, and upon this rock I will build my church; and the gates of hell shall not prevail against it. ☐

Matthew 16:28, Verily **I say** unto you, There be some standing here, which shall not taste of death, till they see the Son of man coming in his kingdom. ☐

Matthew 17:20, And Jesus said unto them, Because of your unbelief: for verily **I say** unto you, If ye have faith as a grain of mustard seed, ye shall say unto this mountain, Remove hence to yonder place; and it shall remove; and nothing shall be impossible unto you. ☐

SOW IN YOUR HEART, GOD'S WORD

In God We Trust
169

Mark 16:17, And these signs shall follow them that **believe**; In my name shall they cast out devils; they shall speak with new tongues. ☐

Luke 8:12, Those by the way side are they that hear; then cometh the devil, and taketh away the word out of their hearts, lest they should **believe** and be saved. ☐

Luke 8:50, But when Jesus heard it, he answered him, saying, Fear not: **believe** only, and she shall be made whole. ☐

Luke 24:25, Then he said unto them, O fools, and slow of heart to **believe** all that the prophets have spoken. ☐

John 1:12, But as many as received him, to them gave he power to become the sons of God, even to them that **believe** on his name. ☐

John 3:12, If I have told you earthly things, and ye **believe** not, how shall ye **believe**, if I tell you of heavenly things? ☐

John 4:42, And said unto the woman, Now we **believe**, not because of thy saying: for we have heard him ourselves, and know that this is indeed the Christ, the Saviour of the world. ☐

John 5:47, But if ye **believe** not his writings, how shall ye **believe** my words? ☐

John 6:29, Jesus answered and said unto them, This is the work of God, that ye **believe** on him whom he hath sent. ☐

John 6:69, And we **believe** and are sure that thou art that Christ, the Son of the living God. ☐

John 8:24, I said therefore unto you, that ye shall die in your sins: for if ye **believe** not that I am he, ye shall die in your sins. ☐

John 9:35, Jesus heard that they had cast him out; and when he had found him, he said unto him, Dost thou **believe** on the Son of God? ☐

John 9:36, He answered and said, Who is he, Lord, that I might **believe** on him? ☐

Ephesians 2:6, And hath raised us up together, and made us sit together in heavenly places **in Christ Jesus**.☐

Ephesians 2:10, For we are his workmanship, created **in Christ Jesus** unto good works, which God hath before ordained that we should walk in them. ☐

Ephesians 2:13, But now **in Christ Jesus** ye who sometimes were far off are made nigh by the blood of Christ. ☐

Ephesians 3:6, That the Gentiles should be fellowheirs, and of the same body, and partakers of his promise **in Christ** by the gospel.☐

Ephesians 3:11, According to the eternal purpose which he purposed **in Christ Jesus** our Lord.☐

Philippians 1:1, Paul and Timotheus, the servants of Jesus Christ, to all the saints **in Christ Jesus** which are at Philippi, with the bishops and deacons.☐

Philippians 1:13, So that my bonds **in Christ** are manifest in all the palace, and in all other places. ☐

Philippians 2:1, If there be therefore any consolation **in Christ**, if any comfort of love, if any fellowship of the Spirit, if any bowels and mercies.☐

Philippians 2:5, Let this mind be in you, which was also **in Christ Jesus**: ☐

Philippians 3:3, For we are the circumcision, which worship God in the spirit, and rejoice **in Christ Jesus**, and have no confidence in the flesh. ☐

Philippians 3:14, I press toward the mark for the prize of the high calling of God **in Christ Jesus**.☐

Philippians 4:21, Salute every saint **in Christ Jesus**. The brethren which are with me greet you. ☐

Colossians 1:2, To the saints and faithful brethren **in Christ** which are at Colosse: Grace be unto you, and peace, from God our Father and the Lord Jesus Christ.☐

In God We Trust

Matthew 16:18, And I say also unto thee, That thou art Peter, and upon this rock I will build my church; and the gates of hell shall not prevail against it. ☐

Matthew 16:19, And I will give unto thee the keys of the kingdom of heaven: and whatsoever thou shalt bind on earth shall be bound in heaven: and whatsoever thou shalt loose on earth shall be loosed in heaven. ☐

Matthew 18:26, The servant therefore fell down, and worshipped him, saying, Lord, have patience with me, and I will pay thee all. ☐

Matthew 18:29, And his fellowservant fell down at his feet, and besought him, saying, Have patience with me, and I will pay thee all. ☐

Matthew 20:4, And said unto them; Go ye also into the vineyard, and whatsoever is right I will give you. And they went their way. ☐

Matthew 20:14, Take that thine is, and go thy way: I will give unto this last, even as unto thee. ☐

Matthew 20:15, Is it not lawful for me to do what I will with mine own? Is thine eye evil, because I am good? ☐

Matthew 25:21, His lord said unto him, Well done, thou good and faithful servant: thou hast been faithful over a few things, I will make thee ruler over many things: enter thou into the joy of thy lord. ☐

Matthew 26:31, Then saith Jesus unto them, All ye shall be offended because of me this night: for it is written, I will smite the shepherd, and the sheep of the flock shall be scattered abroad. ☐

In God We Trust
172

Psalms 6:2, Have mercy upon me, O LORD; for I am weak: O LORD, **heal** me; for my bones are vexed. ☐

Psalms 41:4, I said, LORD, be merciful unto me: **heal** my soul; for I have sinned against thee. ☐

Ecclesiastes 3:3, A time to kill, and a time to **heal**; a time to break down, and a time to build up. ☐

Isaiah 19:22, And the LORD shall smite Egypt: he shall smite and **heal** it: and they shall return even to the LORD, and he shall be intreated of them, and shall **heal** them. ☐

Isaiah 57:18, I have seen his ways, and will **heal** him: I will lead him also, and restore comforts unto him and to his mourners. ☐

Isaiah 57:19, I create the fruit of the lips; Peace, peace to him that is far off, and to him that is near, saith the LORD; and I will **heal** him. ☐

Luke 4:18, The Spirit of the Lord is upon me, because he hath anointed me to preach the gospel to the poor; he hath sent me to **heal** the brokenhearted, to preach deliverance to the captives, and recovering of sight to the blind, to set at liberty them that are bruised. ☐

1 Corinthians 12:9, To another faith by the same Spirit; to another the gifts of **healing** by the same Spirit. ☐

1 Corinthians 12:30, Have all the gifts of **healing**? do all speak with tongues? do all interpret? ☐

Acts 4:22, For the man was above forty years old, on whom this miracle of **healing** was shewed. ☐

Revelation 22:2, In the midst of the street of it, and on either side of the river, was there the tree of life, which bare twelve manner of fruits, and yielded her fruit every month: and the leaves of the tree were for the **healing** of the nations. ☐

Ecclesiastes 3:13, And also that every man should eat and drink, and enjoy the **good** of all his labour, it is the gift of God. ☐

Ecclesiastes 4:9, Two are better than one; because they have a **good** reward for their labour. ☐

Ecclesiastes 7:1, A **good** name is better than precious ointment; and the day of death than the day of one's birth. ☐

Ecclesiastes 9:18, Wisdom is better than weapons of war: but one sinner destroyeth much **good**. ☐

Ecclesiastes 12:14, For God shall bring every work into judgment, with every secret thing, whether it be **good**, or whether it be evil. ☐

Isaiah 39:8, Then said Hezekiah to Isaiah, **Good** is the word of the LORD which thou hast spoken. He said moreover, For there shall be peace and truth in my days. ☐

Isaiah 61:1, The Spirit of the Lord GOD is upon me; because the LORD hath anointed me to preach **good** tidings unto the meek; he hath sent me to bind up the brokenhearted, to proclaim liberty to the captives, and the opening of the prison to them that are bound. ☐

Jeremiah 33:9, And it shall be to me a name of joy, a praise and an honour before all the nations of the earth, which shall hear all the **good** that I do unto them: and they shall fear and tremble for all the **goodness** and for all the prosperity that I procure unto it. ☐

Matthew 5:16, Let your light so shine before men, that they may see your **good** works, and glorify your Father which is in heaven. ☐

Matthew 5:44, But I say unto you, Love your enemies, bless them that curse you, do **good** to them that hate you, and pray for them which despitefully use you, and persecute you. ☐

1 Timothy 6:19, Laying up in store for themselves a **good** foundation against the time to come, that they may lay hold on eternal life. ☐

In God We Trust

Exodus 15:2, The LORD is my strength and song, and he is become my salvation: he is **my God**, and I will prepare him an habitation; my father's God, and I will exalt him. ☐

Joshua 14:8, Nevertheless my brethren that went up with me made the heart of the people melt: but I wholly followed the LORD **my God**. ☐

2 Samuel 22:7, In my distress I called upon the LORD, and cried to **my God**: and he did hear my voice out of his temple, and my cry did enter into his ears. ☐

1 Kings 5:4, But now the LORD **my God** hath given me rest on every side, so that there is neither adversary nor evil occurrent. ☐

Psalms 5:2, Hearken unto the voice of my cry, my King, and **my God**: for unto thee will I pray. ☐

Psalms 7:1, O LORD **my God**, in thee do I put my trust: save me from all them that persecute me, and deliver me. ☐

Psalms 18:2, The LORD is my rock, and my fortress, and my deliverer; **my God**, my strength, in whom I will trust; my buckler, and the horn of my salvation, and my high tower. ☐

Psalms 18:6, In my distress I called upon the LORD, and cried unto **my God**: he heard my voice out of his temple, and my cry came before him, even into his ears. ☐

Psalms 18:28, For thou wilt light my candle: the LORD **my God** will enlighten my darkness. ☐

Psalms 22:1, **My God**, **my God**, why hast thou forsaken me? why art thou so far from helping me, and from the words of my roaring? ☐

JOY *
JOYFUL *
JOYED

59 DAY

AFTERNOON
90 DAY CHALLENGE

Psalms 98:4, Make a **joyful** noise unto the LORD, all the earth: make a loud noise, and rejoice, and sing praise. ☐

Psalms 98:6, With trumpets and sound of cornet make a **joyful** noise before the LORD, the King. ☐

Psalms 98:8, Let the floods clap their hands: let the hills be **joyful** together. ☐

Psalms 100:1, Make a **joyful** noise unto the LORD, all ye lands. ☐

Psalms 113:9, He maketh the barren woman to keep house, and to be a **joyful** mother of children. Praise ye the LORD. ☐

Psalms 137:6, If I do not remember thee, let my tongue cleave to the roof of my mouth; if I prefer not Jerusalem above my chief **joy**. ☐

Isaiah 49:13, Sing, O heavens; and be **joyful**, O earth; and break forth into singing, O mountains: for the LORD hath comforted his people, and will have mercy upon his afflicted. ☐

Isaiah 56:7, Even them will I bring to my holy mountain, and make them **joyful** in my house of prayer: their burnt offerings and their sacrifices shall be accepted upon mine altar; for mine house shall be called an house of prayer for all people. ☐

Isaiah 61:10, I will greatly rejoice in the LORD, my soul shall be **joyful** in my God; for he hath clothed me with the garments of salvation, he hath covered me with the robe of righteousness, as a bridegroom decketh himself with ornaments, and as a bride adorneth herself with her jewels. ☐

2 Corinthians 7:4, Great is my boldness of speech toward you, great is my glorying of you: I am filled with comfort, I am exceeding **joyful** in all our tribulation. ☐

2 Corinthians 7:13, Therefore we were comforted in your comfort: yea, and exceedingly the more **joyed** we for the **joy** of Titus, because his spirit was refreshed by you all. ☐

In God We Trust

I BELIEVE
BIGGER
BETTER
BOLDER
BLESSINGS

HUMBLE *

*59*DAY
EVENING
90 DAY CHALLENGE

Deuteronomy 8:2, And thou shalt remember all the way which the LORD thy God led thee these forty years in the wilderness, to **humble** thee, and to prove thee, to know what was in thine heart, whether thou wouldest keep his commandments, or no. ☐

Deuteronomy 8:16, Who fed thee in the wilderness with manna, which thy fathers knew not, that he might **humble** thee, and that he might prove thee, to do thee good at thy latter end. ☐

2 Chronicles 7:14, If my people, which are called by my name, shall **humble** themselves, and pray, and seek my face, and turn from their wicked ways; then will I hear from heaven, and will forgive their sin, and will heal their land. ☐

Psalms 9:12, When he maketh inquisition for blood, he remembereth them: he forgetteth not the cry of the **humble**. ☐

Psalms 10:12, Arise, O LORD; O God, lift up thine hand: forget not the **humble**. ☐

Psalms 10:17, LORD, thou hast heard the desire of the **humble**: thou wilt prepare their heart, thou wilt cause thine ear to hear. ☐

Psalms 34:2, My soul shall make her boast in the LORD: the **humble** shall hear thereof, and be glad. ☐

Psalms 69:32, The **humble** shall see this, and be glad: and your heart shall live that seek God. ☐

Proverbs 6:3, Do this now, my son, and deliver thyself, when thou art come into the hand of thy friend; go, **humble** thyself, and make sure thy friend. ☐

Proverbs 16:19, Better it is to be of an **humble** spirit with the lowly, than to divide the spoil with the proud. ☐

Proverbs 29:23, A man's pride shall bring him low: but honour shall uphold the **humble** in spirit. ☐

DON'T FALL BY THE WAY SIDE

ILC

In God We Trust

Psalms 52:9, I will praise thee for ever, because thou hast done it: and I will wait on thy name; for it is good before thy saints. ☐

Psalms 54:6, I will freely sacrifice unto thee: I will praise thy name, O LORD; for it is good. ☐

Psalms 55:16, As for me, I will call upon God; and the LORD shall save me. ☐

Psalms 55:23, But thou, O God, shalt bring them down into the pit of destruction: bloody and deceitful men shall not live out half their days; but I will trust in thee. ☐

Psalms 56:11, In God have I put my trust: I will not be afraid what man can do unto me. ☐

Psalms 57:2, I will cry unto God most high; unto God that performeth all things for me. ☐

Psalms 57:7, My heart is fixed, O God, my heart is fixed: I will sing and give praise. ☐

Psalms 57:9, I will praise thee, O Lord, among the people: I will sing unto thee among the nations. ☐

Psalms 59:16, But I will sing of thy power; yea, I will sing aloud of thy mercy in the morning: for thou hast been my defence and refuge in the day of my trouble. ☐

Psalms 61:4, I will abide in thy tabernacle for ever: I will trust in the covert of thy wings. Selah. ☐

Psalms 63:4, Thus will I bless thee while I live: I will lift up my hands in thy name. ☐

Psalms 66:13, I will go into thy house with burnt offerings I will pay thee my vows. ☐

Psalms 66:16, Come and hear, all ye that fear God, and I will declare what he hath done for my soul. ☐

Psalms 18:50, **Great** deliverance giveth he to his king; and showeth mercy to his anointed, to David, and to his seed for evermore. ☐

Psalms 19:11, Moreover by them is thy servant warned: and in keeping of them there is **great** reward. ☐

Psalms 19:13, Keep back thy servant also from presumptuous sins; let them not have dominion over me: then shall I be upright, and I shall be innocent from the **great** transgression. ☐

Psalms 21:1, The king shall joy in thy strength, O LORD; and in thy salvation how **greatly** shall he rejoice! ☐

Psalms 21:5, His glory is **great** in thy salvation: honour and majesty hast thou laid upon him. ☐

Psalms 22:25, My praise shall be of thee in the **great** congregation: I will pay my vows before them that fear him. ☐

Psalms 25:11, For thy name's sake, O LORD, pardon mine iniquity; for it is **great**. ☐

Psalms 31:19, Oh how **great** is thy goodness, which thou hast laid up for them that fear thee; which thou hast wrought for them that trust in thee before the sons of men! ☐

Psalms 35:18, I will give thee thanks in the **great** congregation: I will praise thee among much people. ☐

Psalms 36:6, Thy righteousness is like the **great** mountains; thy judgments are a **great** deep: O LORD, thou preservest man and beast. ☐

Psalms 47:2, For the LORD most high is terrible; he is a **great** King over all the earth. ☐

Psalms 48:1, **Great** is the LORD, and **greatly** to be praised in the city of our God, in the mountain of his holiness. ☐

In God We Trust

Deuteronomy 6:3, Hear therefore, O Israel, and observe **to do it**; that it may be well with thee, and that ye may increase mightily, as the LORD God of thy fathers hath promised thee, in the land that floweth with milk and honey. ☐

Deuteronomy 12:32, What thing soever I command you, observe **to do it**: thou shalt not add thereto, nor diminish from it. ☐

Deuteronomy 30:14, But the word is very nigh unto thee, in thy mouth, and in thy heart, that thou mayest **do it**. ☐

Deuteronomy 15:5, Only if thou carefully hearken unto the voice of the LORD thy God, to observe **to do** all these commandments which I command thee this day. ☐

Ezra 7:10, For Ezra had prepared his heart to seek the law of the LORD, and **to do it**, and to teach in Israel statutes and judgments. ☐

Psalms 37:8, Cease from anger, and forsake wrath: fret not thyself in any wise **to do** evil. ☐

Psalms 40:8, I delight **to do** thy will, O my God: yea, thy law is within my heart. ☐

Psalms 103:18, To such as keep his covenant, and to those that remember his commandments **to do** them. ☐

Psalms 119:132, Look thou upon me, and be merciful unto me, as thou usest **to do** unto those that love thy name. ☐

Psalms 143:10, Teach me **to do** thy will; for thou art my God: thy spirit is good; lead me into the land of uprightness. ☐

Proverbs 2:14, Who rejoice **to do** evil, and delight in the frowardness of the wicked. ☐

Proverbs 3:27, Withhold not good from them to whom it is due, when it is in the power of thine hand **to do it**. ☐

John 1:17, For the law was given by Moses, but **grace** and truth came by Jesus Christ. ☐

Acts 4:33, And with great power gave the apostles witness of the resurrection of the Lord Jesus: and great **grace** was upon them all. ☐

Acts 11:23, Who, when he came, and had seen the **grace** of God, was glad, and exhorted them all, that with purpose of heart they would cleave unto the Lord. ☐

Acts 14:3, Long time therefore abode they speaking boldly in the Lord, which gave testimony unto the word of his **grace**, and granted signs and wonders to be done by their hands. ☐

Acts 15:11, But we believe that through the **grace** of the Lord Jesus Christ we shall be saved, even as they. ☐

Acts 15:40, And Paul chose Silas, and departed, being recommended by the brethren unto the **grace** of God. ☐

Acts 20:24, But none of these things move me, neither count I my life dear unto myself, so that I might finish my course with joy, and the ministry, which I have received of the Lord Jesus, to testify the gospel of the **grace** of God. ☐

Romans 1:5, By whom we have received **grace** and apostleship, for obedience to the faith among all nations, for his name. ☐

Romans 1:7, To all that be in Rome, beloved of God, called to be saints: **Grace** to you and peace from God our Father, and the Lord Jesus Christ. ☐

Romans 3:24, Being justified freely by his **grace** through the redemption that is in Christ Jesus: ☐

Romans 4:16, Therefore it is of faith, that it might be by **grace**; to the end the promise might be sure to all the seed; not to that only which is of the law, but to that also which is of the faith of Abraham; who is the father of us all, ☐

Psalms 59:17, Unto thee, O my strength, will I sing: for God is my defence, and the God of my **mercy**. ☐

Psalms 61:7, He shall abide before God for ever: O prepare **mercy** and truth, which may preserve him. ☐

Psalms 62:12, Also unto thee, O Lord, belongeth **mercy**: for thou renderest to every man according to his work. ☐

Psalms 69:13, But as for me, my prayer is unto thee, O LORD, in an acceptable time: O God, in the multitude of thy **mercy** hear me, in the truth of thy salvation. ☐

Psalms 85:7, Shew us thy **mercy**, O LORD, and grant us thy salvation. ☐

Psalms 85:10, **Mercy** and truth are met together; righteousness and peace ave kissed each other. ☐

Psalms 86:5, For thou, Lord, art good, and ready to forgive; and plenteous in **mercy** unto all them that call upon thee. ☐

Psalms 86:13, For great is thy **mercy** toward me: and thou hast delivered my soul from the lowest hell. ☐

Psalms 86:15, But thou, O Lord, art a God full of compassion, and gracious, longsuffering, and plenteous in **mercy** and truth. ☐

Psalms 89:2, For I have said, **Mercy** shall be built up for ever: thy faithfulness shalt thou establish in the very heavens. ☐

Psalms 89:28, My **mercy** will I keep for him for evermore, and my covenant shall stand fast with him. ☐

Psalms 90:14, O satisfy us early with thy **mercy**; that we may rejoice and be glad all our days. ☐

Psalms 94:18, When I said, My foot slippeth; thy **mercy**, O LORD, held me up. ☐

Isaiah 50:4, The Lord GOD hath given me the **tongue** of the learned, that I should know how to speak a word in season to him that is weary: he wakeneth morning by morning, he wakeneth mine ear to hear as the learned. ☐

Isaiah 54:17, No weapon that is formed against thee shall prosper; and every **tongue** that shall rise against thee in judgment thou shalt condemn. This is the heritage of the servants of the LORD, and their righteousness is of me, saith the LORD. ☐

Acts 2:26, Therefore did my heart rejoice, and my **tongue** was glad; moreover also my flesh shall rest in hope. ☐

1 Corinthians 14:2, For he that speaketh in an unknown **tongue** speaketh not unto men, but unto God: for no man understandeth him; howbeit in the spirit he speaketh mysteries. ☐

1 Corinthians 14:4, He that speaketh in an unknown **tongue** edifieth himself; but he that prophesieth edifieth the church. ☐

Philippians 2:11, And that every **tongue** should confess that Jesus Christ is Lord, to the glory of God the Father. ☐

James 1:26, If any man among you seem to be religious, and bridleth not his **tongue**, but deceiveth his own heart, this man's religion is vain. ☐

James 3:5, Even so the **tongue** is a little member, and boasteth great things. Behold, how great a matter a little fire kindleth! ☐

James 3:6, And the **tongue** is a fire, a world of iniquity: so is the **tongue** among our members, that it defileth the whole body, and setteth on fire the course of nature; and it is set on fire of hell. ☐

CAST YOUR CARES UPON ON JESUS

In God We Trust

Matthew 7:11, If ye then, being evil, know how to give **good** gifts unto your children, how much more shall your Father which is in heaven give **good** things to them that ask him? □

Matthew 14:27, But straightway Jesus spake unto them, saying, Be of **good** cheer; it is I; be not afraid. □

Matthew 25:21, His lord said unto him, Well done, thou **good** and faithful servant: thou hast been faithful over a few things, I will make thee ruler over many things: enter thou into the joy of thy lord. □

1 Corinthians 15:33, Be not deceived: evil communications corrupt **good** manners. □

2 Corinthians 9:8, And God is able to make all grace abound toward you; that ye, always having all sufficiency in all things, may abound to every **good** work. □

2 Corinthians 13:11, Finally, brethren, farewell. Be perfect, be of **good** comfort, be of one mind, live in peace; and the God of love and peace shall be with you. □

Galatians 5:22, But the fruit of the Spirit is love, joy, peace, longsuffering, gentleness, **goodness**, faith. □

Galatians 6:10, As we have therefore opportunity, let us do **good** unto all men, especially unto them who are of the household of faith. □

Ephesians 2:10, For we are his workmanship, created in Christ Jesus unto **good** works, which God hath before ordained that we should walk in them. □

Ephesians 4:29, Let no corrupt communication proceed out of your mouth, but that which is **good** to the use of edifying, that it may minister grace unto the hearers. □

Ephesians 5:9, For the fruit of the Spirit is in all **goodness** and righteousness and truth. □

Matthew 26:39, And he went a little further, and fell on his face, and prayed, saying, O my Father, if it be possible, let this cup pass from me: nevertheless not as I will, but as thou wilt. □

Matthew 27:63, Saying, Sir, we remember that that deceiver said, while he was yet alive, After three days I will rise again. □

Mark 6:23, And he sware unto her, Whatsoever thou shalt ask of me, I will give it thee, unto the half of my kingdom. □

Mark 11:29, And Jesus answered and said unto them, I will also ask of you one question, and answer me, and I will tell you by what authority I do these things. □

Mark 14:31, But he spake the more vehemently, If I should die with thee, I will not deny thee in any wise. Likewise also said they all. □

Mark 14:58, We heard him say, I will destroy this temple that is made with hands, and within three days I will build another made without hands. □

Luke 4:6, And the devil said unto him, All this power will I give thee, and the glory of them: for that is delivered unto me; and to whomsoever I will I give it. □

Luke 5:5, And Simon answering said unto him, Master, we have toiled all the night, and have taken nothing: nevertheless at thy word I will let down the net. □

Luke 6:47, Whosoever cometh to me, and heareth my sayings, and doeth them, I will shew you to whom he is like. □

Luke 11:24, When the unclean spirit is gone out of a man, he walketh through dry places, seeking rest; and finding none, he saith, I will return unto my house whence I came out. □

Luke 12:5, But I will forewarn you whom ye shall fear: Fear him, which after he hath killed hath power to cast into hell; yea, I say unto you, Fear him. □

Proverbs 14:21, He that despiseth his neighbour sinneth: but he that hath mercy on the poor, **happy** is he. ☐

Proverbs 16:20, He that handleth a matter wisely shall find good: and whoso trusteth in the LORD, **happy** is he. ☐

Proverbs 29:18, Where there is no vision, the people perish: but he that keepeth the law, **happy** is he. ☐

Proverbs 28:14, **Happy** is the man that feareth alway: but he that hardeneth his heart shall fall into mischief. ☐

John 13:17, If ye know these things, **happy** are ye if ye do them. ☐

1 Corinthians 7:40, But she is **happier** if she so abide, after my judgment: and I think also that I have the Spirit of God. ☐

Romans 14:22, Hast thou faith? have it to thyself before God. **Happy** is he that condemneth not himself in that thing which he alloweth. ☐

James 5:11, Behold, we count them **happy** which endure. Ye have heard of the patience of Job, and have seen the end of the Lord; that the Lord is very pitiful, and of tender mercy. ☐

1 Peter 3:14, But and if ye suffer for righteousness' sake, **happy** are ye: and be not afraid of their terror, neither be troubled. ☐

1 Peter 4:14, If ye be reproached for the name of Christ, **happy** are ye; for the spirit of glory and of God resteth upon you: on their part he is evil spoken of, but on your part he is glorified. ☐

In God We Trust

Deuteronomy 6:13, Thou shalt fear the LORD thy God, and **serve** him, and shalt swear by his name. ☐

Deuteronomy 10:20, Thou shalt fear the LORD thy God; him shalt thou **serve**, and to him shalt thou cleave, and swear by his name. ☐

Deuteronomy 11:16, Take heed to yourselves, that your heart be not deceived, and ye turn aside, and **serve** other gods, and worship them. ☐

Deuteronomy 13:4, Ye shall walk after the LORD your God, and fear him, and keep his commandments, and obey his voice, and ye shall **serve** him, and cleave unto him. ☐

Joshua 24:16, And the people answered and said, God forbid that we should forsake the LORD, to **serve** other gods. ☐

1 Samuel 12:14, If ye will fear the LORD, and **serve** him, and obey his voice, and not rebel against the commandment of the LORD, then shall both ye and also the king that reigneth over you continue following the LORD your God. ☐

Psalms 72:11, Yea, all kings shall fall down before him: all nations shall **serve** him. ☐

Isaiah 14:3, And it shall come to pass in the day that the LORD shall give thee rest from thy sorrow, and from thy fear, and from the hard bondage wherein thou wast made to **serve**. ☐

Matthew 4:10, Then saith Jesus unto him, Get thee hence, Satan: for it is written, Thou shalt worship the Lord thy God, and him only shalt thou **serve**. ☐

Matthew 6:24, No man can **serve** two masters: for either he will hate the one, and love the other; or else he will hold to the one, and despise the other. Ye cannot **serve** God and mammon. ☐

Psalms 119:12, Blessed art thou, O LORD: **teach** me thy statutes. ☐

Psalms 119:26, I have declared my ways, and thou heardest me: **teach** me thy statutes. ☐

Psalms 119:33, **Teach** me, O LORD, the way of thy statutes; and I shall keep it unto the end. ☐

Psalms 119:64, The earth, O LORD, is full of thy mercy: **teach** me thy statutes. ☐

Psalms 119:66, **Teach** me good judgment and knowledge: for I have believed thy commandments. ☐

Psalms 119:68, Thou art good, and doest good; **teach** me thy statutes. ☐

Psalms 119:108, Accept, I beseech thee, the freewill offerings of my mouth, O LORD, and **teach** me thy judgments. ☐

Psalms 119:124, Deal with thy servant according unto thy mercy, and **teach** me thy statutes. ☐

Psalms 143:10, **Teach** me to do thy will; for thou art my God: thy spirit is good; lead me into the land of uprightness. ☐

Proverbs 9:9, Give instruction to a wise man, and he will be yet wiser: **teach** a just man, and he will increase in learning. ☐

Isaiah 28:26, For his God doth instruct him to discretion, and doth **teach** him. ☐

Matthew 5:19, Whosoever therefore shall break one of these least commandments, and shall **teach** men so, he shall be called the least in the kingdom of heaven: but whosoever shall do and **teach** them, the same shall be called great in the kingdom of heaven. ☐

Matthew 28:19, Go ye therefore, and **teach** all nations, baptizing them in the name of the Father, and of the Son, and of the Holy Ghost. ☐

Psalms 8:4, What is man, that thou art mindful of him? and the **son of man**, that thou visitest him? □

Psalms 80:17, Let thy hand be upon the man of thy right hand, upon the **son of man** whom thou madest strong for thyself. □

Psalms 144:3, LORD, what is man, that thou takest knowledge of him! or the **son of man**, that thou makest account of him! □

Isaiah 56:2, Blessed is the man that doeth this, and the **son of man** that layeth hold on it; that keepeth the sabbath from polluting it, and keepeth his hand from doing any evil. □

Matthew 8:20, And Jesus saith unto him, The foxes have holes, and the birds of the air have nests; but the **Son of man** hath not where to lay his head. □

Matthew 9:6, But that ye may know that the **Son of man** hath power on earth to forgive sins, (then saith he to the sick of the palsy,) Arise, take up thy bed, and go unto thine house. □

Matthew 11:19, The **Son of man** came eating and drinking, and they say, Behold a man gluttonous, and a winebibber, a friend of publicans and sinners. But wisdom is justified of her children. □

Matthew 12:32, And whosoever speaketh a word against the **Son of man**, it shall be forgiven him: but whosoever speaketh against the Holy Ghost, it shall not be forgiven him, neither in this world, neither in the world to come. □

Matthew 12:40, For as Jonah was three days and three nights in the whale's belly; so shall the **Son of man** be three days and three nights in the heart of the earth. □

Matthew 13:37, He answered and said unto them, He that soweth the good seed is the **Son of man**. □

BE FRUITFUL
30, 60, 100 FOLD

Hebrews 8:6, But now hath he obtained a more excellent ministry, by how much also **he is** the mediator of a better covenant, which was established upon better promises. □

Hebrews 11:6, But without faith it is impossible to please him: for he that cometh to God must believe that **he is**, and that **he is** a rewarder of them that diligently seek him. □

James 1:12, Blessed is the man that endureth temptation: for when **he is** tried, he shall receive the crown of life, which the Lord hath promised to them that love him. □

James 1:13, Let no man say when **he is** tempted, I am tempted of God: for God cannot be tempted with evil, neither tempteth he any man. □

James 1:14, But every man is tempted, when **he is** drawn away of his own lust, and enticed. □

1 John 1:9, If we confess our sins, **he is** faithful and just to forgive us our sins, and to cleanse us from all unrighteousness. □

1 John 2:2, And **he is** the propitiation for our sins: and not for ours only, but also for the sins of the whole world. □

1 John 3:2, Beloved, now are we the sons of God, and it doth not yet appear what we shall be: but we know that, when he shall appear, we shall be like him; for we shall see him as **he is**. □

1 John 3:3, And every man that hath this hope in him purifieth himself, even as **he is** pure. □

1 John 3:7, Little children, let no man deceive you: he that doeth righteousness is righteous, even as **he is** righteous. □

1 John 4:20, If a man say, I love God, and hateth his brother, **he is** a liar: for he that loveth not his brother whom he hath seen, how can he love God whom he hath not seen? □

Galatians 5:6, For in Jesus Christ neither circumcision availeth any thing, nor uncircumcision; but **faith** which worketh by love. ☐

Galatians 5:22, But the fruit of the Spirit is love, joy, peace, longsuffering, gentleness, goodness, **faith**. ☐

Galatians 6:10, As we have therefore opportunity, let us do good unto all men, especially unto them who are of the household of **faith**. ☐

Ephesians 1:15, Wherefore I also, after I heard of your **faith** in the Lord Jesus, and love unto all the saints. ☐

Ephesians 2:8, For by grace are ye saved through **faith**; and that not of yourselves: it is the gift of God. ☐

Ephesians 3:12, In whom we have boldness and access with confidence by the **faith** of him. ☐

Ephesians 3:17, That Christ may dwell in your hearts by **faith**; that ye, being rooted and grounded in love. ☐

Ephesians 4:13, Till we all come in the unity of the **faith**, and of the knowledge of the Son of God, unto a perfect man, unto the measure of the stature of the fulness of Christ. ☐

Ephesians 6:16, Above all, taking the shield of **faith**, wherewith ye shall be able to quench all the fiery darts of the wicked. ☐

Philippians 3:9, And be found in him, not having mine own righteousness, which is of the law, but that which is through the **faith** of Christ, the righteousness which is of God by **faith**. ☐

Colossians 1:4, Since we heard of your **faith** in Christ Jesus, and of the love which ye have to all the saints. ☐

Colossians 1:23, If ye continue in the **faith** grounded and settled, and be not moved away from the hope of the gospel, which ye have heard, and which was preached to every creature which is under heaven; whereof I Paul am made a minister. ☐

Mark 9:1, And he said unto them, Verily **I say** unto you, That there be some of them that stand here, which shall not taste of death, till they have seen the kingdom of God come with power. ☐

Mark 9:41, For whosoever shall give you a cup of water to drink in my name, because ye belong to Christ, verily **I say** unto you, he shall not lose his reward. ☐

Mark 10:15, Verily **I say** unto you, Whosoever shall not receive the kingdom of God as a little child, he shall not enter therein. ☐

Mark 10:29, And Jesus answered and said, Verily **I say** unto you, There is no man that hath left house, or brethren, or sisters, or father, or mother, or wife, or children, or lands, for my sake, and the gospel's. ☐

Mark 11:23, For verily **I say** unto you, That whosoever shall say unto this mountain, Be thou removed, and be thou cast into the sea; and shall not doubt in his heart, but shall believe that those things which he saith shall come to pass; he shall have whatsoever he saith. ☐

Mark 11:24, Therefore **I say** unto you, What things soever ye desire, when ye pray, believe that ye receive them, and ye shall have them. ☐

Mark 13:37, And what **I say** unto you **I say** unto all, Watch. ☐

Mark 14:9, Verily **I say** unto you, Wheresoever this gospel shall be preached throughout the whole world, this also that she hath done shall be spoken of for a memorial of her. ☐

Luke 4:24, And he said, Verily **I say** unto you, No prophet is accepted in his own country. ☐

Luke 6:46, And why call ye me, Lord, Lord, and do not the things **I say**? ☐

Luke 7:14, And he came and touched the bier: and they that bare him stood still. And he said, Young man, **I say** unto thee, Arise. ☐

Deuteronomy 6:3, Hear therefore, O Israel, and observe to do it; that it may be well with thee, and that ye may **increase** mightily, as the LORD God of thy fathers hath promised thee, in the land that floweth with milk and honey. □

Deuteronomy 14:22, Thou shalt truly tithe all the **increase** of thy seed, that the field bringeth forth year by year. □

2 Chronicles 32:28, Storehouses also for the **increase** of corn, and wine, and oil; and stalls for all manner of beasts, and cotes for flocks. □

Job 8:7, Though thy beginning was small, yet thy latter end should greatly **increase**. □

Psalms 62:10, Trust not in oppression, and become not vain in robbery: if riches **increase**, set not your heart upon them. □

Psalms 67:6, Then shall the earth yield her **increase**; and God, even our own God, shall bless us. □

Psalms 71:21, Thou shalt **increase** my greatness, and comfort me on every side. □

Psalms 78:46, He gave also their **increase** unto the caterpiller, and their labour unto the locust. □

Psalms 85:12, Yea, the LORD shall give that which is good; and our land shall yield her **increase**. □

Psalms 107:37, And sow the fields, and plant vineyards, which may yield fruits of **increase**. □

Psalms 115:14, The LORD shall **increase** you more and more, you and your children. □

Proverbs 1:5, A wise man will hear, and will **increase** learning; and a man of understanding shall attain unto wise counsels. □

Matthew 13:58, And he did not many mighty works there because of their **unbelief**. ☐

Matthew 17:20, And Jesus said unto them, Because of your **unbelief**: for verily I say unto you, If ye have faith as a grain of mustard seed, ye shall say unto this mountain, Remove hence to yonder place; and it shall remove; and nothing shall be impossible unto you. ☐

Mark 6:6, And he marvelled because of their **unbelief**. And he went round about the villages, teaching. ☐

Mark 9:24, And straightway the father of the child cried out, and said with tears, Lord, I **believe**; help thou mine **unbelief**. ☐

Mark 16:14, Afterward he appeared unto the eleven as they sat at meat, and upbraided them with their **unbelief** and hardness of heart, because they **believed** not them which had seen him after he was risen. ☐

Romans 3:3, For what if some did not **believe**? shall their **unbelief** make the faith of God without effect? ☐

Romans 3:22, Even the righteousness of God which is by faith of Jesus Christ unto all and upon all them that **believe**: for there is no difference. ☐

Romans 4:20, He staggered not at the promise of God through **unbelief**; but was strong in faith, giving glory to God. ☐

Romans 11:20, Well; because of **unbelief** they were broken off, and thou standest by faith. Be not highminded, but fear. ☐

Romans 11:23, And they also, if they abide not still in **unbelief**, shall be grafted in: for God is able to graft them in again. ☐

Romans 11:30, For as ye in times past have not **believed** God, yet have now obtained mercy through their **unbelief**. ☐

Romans 11:32, For God hath concluded them all in **unbelief**, that he might have mercy upon all. ☐

Romans 11:20, Well; because of unbelief they were broken off, and thou standest by **faith**. Be not highminded, but fear. ☐

1 Corinthians 2:5, That your **faith** should not stand in the wisdom of men, but in the power of God. ☐

1 Corinthians 12:9, To another **faith** by the same Spirit; to another the gifts of healing by the same Spirit. ☐

1 Corinthians 13:2, And though I have the gift of prophecy, and understand all mysteries, and all knowledge; and though I have all **faith**, so that I could remove mountains, and have not charity, I am nothing. ☐

1 Corinthians 13:13, And now abideth **faith**, hope, charity, these three; but the greatest of these is charity. ☐

1 Corinthians 15:14, And if Christ be not risen, then is our preaching vain, and your **faith** is also vain. ☐

1 Corinthians 16:13, Watch ye, stand fast in the **faith**, quit you like men, be strong. ☐

2 Corinthians 1:24, Not for that we have dominion over your **faith**, but are helpers of your joy: for by **faith** ye stand. ☐

2 Corinthians 4:13, We having the same spirit of **faith**, according as it is written, I believed, and therefore have I spoken; we also believe, and therefore speak. ☐

2 Corinthians 5:7, For we walk by **faith**, not by sight. ☐

2 Corinthians 8:7, Therefore, as ye abound in every thing, in **faith**, and utterance, and knowledge, and in all diligence, and in your love to us, see that ye abound in this grace also. ☐

2 Corinthians 10:15, Not boasting of things without our measure, that is, of other men's labours; but having hope, when your **faith** is increased, that we shall be enlarged by you according to our rule abundantly. ☐

In God We Trust

Romans 3:24, Being justified freely by his grace through the redemption that is **in Christ Jesus.** ☐

Romans 8:1, There is therefore now no condemnation to them which are **in Christ Jesus**, who walk not after the flesh, but after the Spirit. ☐

Romans 8:2, For the law of the Spirit of life **in Christ Jesus** hath made me free from the law of sin and death. ☐

Romans 8:39, Nor height, nor depth, nor any other creature, shall be able to separate us from the love of God, which is **in Christ Jesus** our Lord. ☐

Romans 9:1, I say the truth **in Christ**, I lie not, my conscience also bearing me witness in the Holy Ghost. ☐

Romans 12:5, So we, being many, are one body **in Christ**, and every one members one of another. ☐

Romans 16:3, Greet Priscilla and Aquila my helpers **in Christ Jesus.** ☐

1 Corinthians 1:30, But of him are ye **in Christ Jesus**, who of God is made unto us wisdom, and righteousness, and sanctification, and redemption: ☐

1 Corinthians 4:10, We are fools for Christ's sake, but ye are wise **in Christ**; we are weak, but ye are strong; ye are honourable, but we are despised. ☐

1 Corinthians 15:22, For as in Adam all die, even so **in Christ** shall all be made alive. ☐

1 Corinthians 15:31, I protest by your rejoicing which I have **in Christ Jesus** our Lord, I die daily. ☐

1 Corinthians 16:24, My love be with you all **in Christ Jesus.** Amen. ☐

2 Corinthians 1:21, Now he which stablisheth us with you **in Christ**, and hath anointed us, is God. ☐

Acts 15:7 And when there had been much disputing, Peter rose up, and said unto them, Men and brethren, ye know how that a good while ago God made choice among us, that the Gentiles by my mouth should hear the word of the gospel, and **believe**. □

Acts 16:31, And they said, **Believe** on the Lord Jesus Christ, and thou shalt be saved, and thy house. □

Acts 19:4, Then said Paul, John verily baptized with the baptism of repentance, saying unto the people, that they should **believe** on him which should come after him, that is, on Christ Jesus. □

Romans 6:8, Now if we be dead with Christ, we **believe** that we shall also live with him. □

Romans 10:9, That if thou shalt confess with thy mouth the Lord Jesus, and shalt **believe** in thine heart that God hath raised him from the dead, thou shalt be saved. □

1 Corinthians 1:21, For after that in the wisdom of God the world by wisdom knew not God, it pleased God by the foolishness of preaching to save them that **believe**. □

1 Corinthians 14:22, Wherefore tongues are for a sign, not to them that **believe**, but to them that **believe** not: but prophesying serveth not for them that **believe** not, but for them which **believe**. □

2 Corinthians 4:4, In whom the god of this world hath blinded the minds of them which **believe** not, lest the light of the glorious gospel of Christ, who is the image of God, should shine unto them. □

2 Corinthians 4:13, We having the same spirit of faith, according as it is written, I **believed**, and therefore have I spoken; we also **believe**, and therefore speak. □

Galatians 3:22, But the scripture hath concluded all under sin, that the promise by faith of Jesus Christ might be given to them that **believe**. □

Ephesians 1:19, And what is the exceeding greatness of his power to us-ward who **believe**, according to the working of his mighty power. □

In God We Trust
197

2 Corinthians 4:17, For our light affliction, which is but for a moment, worketh **for us** a far more exceeding and eternal weight of glory. ☐

2 Corinthians 5:21, For he hath made him to be sin **for us**, who knew no sin; that we might be made the righteousness of God in him. ☐

Galatians 3:13, Christ hath redeemed us from the curse of the law, being made a curse **for us**: for it is written, Cursed is every one that hangeth on a tree. ☐

Ephesians 5:2, And walk in love, as Christ also hath loved us, and hath given himself **for us** an offering and a sacrifice to God for a sweetsmelling savour. ☐

2 Thessalonians 3:1, Finally, brethren, pray **for us**, that the word of the Lord may have free course, and be glorified, even as it is with you. ☐

Titus 2:14, Who gave himself **for us**, that he might redeem us from all iniquity, and purify unto himself a peculiar people, zealous of good works. ☐

Hebrews 13:18, Pray **for us**: for we trust we have a good conscience, in all things willing to live honestly. ☐

1 Peter 2:21, For even hereunto were ye called: because Christ also suffered **for us**, leaving us an example, that ye should follow his steps. ☐

1 Peter 4:1, Forasmuch then as Christ hath suffered **for us** in the flesh, arm yourselves likewise with the same mind: for he that hath suffered in the flesh hath ceased from sin. ☐

In God We Trust

Psalms 43:5, Why art thou cast down, O **my soul**? and why art thou disquieted within me? hope in God: for I shall yet praise him, who is the health of my countenance, and my God. ☐

Psalms 49:15, But God will redeem **my soul** from the power of the grave: for he shall receive me. Selah. ☐

Psalms 55:18, He hath delivered **my soul** in peace from the battle that was against me: for there were many with me. ☐

Psalms 56:6, They gather themselves together, they hide themselves, they mark my steps, when they wait for **my soul**. ☐

Psalms 56:13, For thou hast delivered **my soul** from death: wilt not thou deliver my feet from falling, that I may walk before God in the light of the living? ☐

Psalms 57:1, Be merciful unto me, O God, be merciful unto me: for **my soul** trusteth in thee: yea, in the shadow of thy wings will I make my refuge, until these calamities be overpast. ☐

Psalms 62:1, Truly **my soul** waiteth upon God: from him cometh my salvation. ☐

Psalms 62:5, **My soul**, wait thou only upon God; for my expectation is from him. ☐

Psalms 63:1, O God, thou art my God; early will I seek thee: **my soul** thirsteth for thee, my flesh longeth for thee in a dry and thirsty land, where no water is. ☐

Psalms 63:5, **My soul** shall be satisfied as with marrow and fatness; and my mouth shall praise thee with joyful lips. ☐

Psalms 63:8, **My soul** followeth hard after thee: thy right hand upholdeth me. ☐

Psalms 69:18, Draw nigh unto **my soul**, and redeem it: deliver me because of mine enemies. ☐

Proverbs 18:2, A fool hath no delight in **understanding**, but that his heart may discover itself. ☐

Proverbs 19:8, He that getteth wisdom loveth his own soul: he that keepeth **understanding** shall find good. ☐

Proverbs 20:5, Counsel in the heart of man is like deep water; but a man of **understanding** will draw it out. ☐

Proverbs 21:16, The man that wandereth out of the way of **understanding** shall remain in the congregation of the dead. ☐

Proverbs 21:30, There is no wisdom nor **understanding** nor counsel against the LORD. ☐

Proverbs 23:23, Buy the truth, and sell it not; also wisdom, and instruction, and **understanding**. ☐

Proverbs 24:30, I went by the field of the slothful, and by the vineyard of the man void of **understanding**. ☐

Proverbs 28:11, The rich man is wise in his own conceit; but the poor that hath **understanding** searcheth him out. ☐

Isaiah 11:2, And the spirit of the LORD shall rest upon him, the spirit of wisdom and **understanding**, the spirit of counsel and might, the spirit of knowledge and of the fear of the LORD. ☐

Daniel 2:21, And he changeth the times and the seasons: he removeth kings, and setteth up kings: he giveth wisdom unto the wise, and knowledge to them that know **understanding**. ☐

1 Corinthians 14:14, For if I pray in an unknown tongue, my spirit prayeth, but my **understanding** is unfruitful. ☐

BE STRONG, FULL OF COURAGE, DO IT!

In God We Trust

1 Timothy 5:8, But if any provide not for his own, and specially for those of his own house, he hath denied the **faith**, and is worse than an infidel. ☐

1 Timothy 6:11, But thou, O man of God, flee these things; and follow after righteousness, godliness, **faith**, love, patience, meekness. ☐

1 Timothy 6:12, Fight the good fight of **faith**, lay hold on eternal life, whereunto thou art also called, and hast professed a good profession before many witnesses. ☐

1 Timothy 6:21, Which some professing have erred concerning the **faith**. Grace be with thee. Amen. ☐

2 Timothy 1:13, Hold fast the form of sound words, which thou hast heard of me, in **faith** and love which is in Christ Jesus. ☐

2 Timothy 4:7, I have fought a good fight, I have finished my course, I have kept the **faith**: ☐

Titus 1:1, Paul, a servant of God, and an apostle of Jesus Christ, according to the **faith** of God's elect, and the acknowledging of the truth which is after godliness. ☐

Titus 1:4, To Titus, mine own son after the common **faith**: Grace, mercy, and peace, from God the Father and the Lord Jesus Christ our Saviour. ☐

Titus 1:13, This witness is true. Wherefore rebuke them sharply, that they may be sound in the **faith**. ☐

Titus 2:2, That the aged men be sober, grave, temperate, sound in **faith**, in charity, in patience. ☐

Philemon 1:5, Hearing of thy love and **faith**, which thou hast toward the Lord Jesus, and toward all saints. ☐

Philemon 1:6, That the communication of thy **faith** may become effectual by the acknowledging of every good thing which is in you in Christ Jesus. ☐

Psalms 63:1, O God, thou art my God; early will I **seek** thee: my soul thirsteth for thee, my flesh longeth for thee in a dry and thirsty land, where no water is. ☐

Psalms 63:9, But those that **seek** my soul, to destroy it, shall go into the lower parts of the earth. ☐

Psalms 69:32, The humble shall see this, and be glad: and your heart shall live that **seek** God. ☐

Psalms 70:4, Let all those that **seek** thee rejoice and be glad in thee: and let such as love thy salvation say continually, Let God be magnified. ☐

Psalms 71:24, My tongue also shall talk of thy righteousness all the day long: for they are confounded, for they are brought unto shame, that **seek** my hurt. ☐

Psalms 105:4, **Seek** the LORD, and his strength: **seek** his face evermore. ▮

Psalms 119:2, Blessed are they that keep his testimonies, and that **seek** him with the whole heart. ☐

Psalms 119:45, And I will walk at liberty: for I **seek** thy precepts. ☐

Psalms 119:155, Salvation is far from the wicked: for they **seek** not thy statutes. ☐

Psalms 122:9, Because of the house of the LORD our God I will **seek** thy good. ☐

Proverbs 1:28, Then shall they call upon me, but I will not answer; they shall **seek** me early, but they shall not find me. ☐

Proverbs 7:15, Therefore came I forth to meet thee, diligently to **seek** thy face, and I have found thee. ☐

Proverbs 8:17, I love them that love me; and those that **seek** me early shall find me. ☐

Psalms 27:14, Wait on the LORD: be of **good** courage, and he shall strengthen thine heart: wait, I say, on the LORD. ☐

Psalms 31:24, Be of **good** courage, and he shall strengthen your heart, all ye that hope in the LORD. ☐

Psalms 34:8, O taste and see that the LORD is **good**: blessed is the man that trusteth in him. ☐

Psalms 34:10, The young lions do lack, and suffer hunger: but they that seek the LORD shall not want any **good** thing. ☐

Psalms 34:12, What man is he that desireth life, and loveth many days, that he may see **good**? ☐

Psalms 34:14, Depart from evil, and do **good**; seek peace, and pursue it. ☐

Psalms 37:3, Trust in the LORD, and do **good**; so shalt thou dwell in the land, and verily thou shalt be fed. ☐

Psalms 37:23, The steps of a **good** man are ordered by the LORD: and he delighteth in his way. ☐

Psalms 37:27, Depart from evil, and do **good**; and dwell for evermore. ☐

Psalms 38:20, They also that render evil for **good** are mine adversaries; because I follow the thing that **good** is. ☐

Psalms 45:1, My heart is inditing a **good** matter: I speak of the things which I have made touching the king: my tongue is the pen of a ready writer. ☐

Psalms 52:3, Thou lovest evil more than **good**; and lying rather than to speak righteousness. Selah. ☐

Psalms 54:6, I will freely sacrifice unto thee: I will praise thy name, O LORD; for it is **good**. ☐

Matthew 5:10, **Blessed** are they which are persecuted for righteousness' sake: for theirs is the kingdom of heaven. ☐

Matthew 5:11, **Blessed** are ye, when men shall revile you, and persecute you, and shall say all manner of evil against you falsely, for my sake. ☐

Mark 11:9, And they that went before, and they that followed, cried, saying, Hosanna; **Blessed** is he that cometh in the name of the Lord. ☐

Mark 11:10, **Blessed** be the kingdom of our father David, that cometh in the name of the Lord: Hosanna in the highest. ☐

Mark 14:22, And as they did eat, Jesus took bread, and **blessed**, and brake it, and gave to them, and said, Take, eat: this is my body. ☐

Mark 14:61, But he held his peace, and answered nothing. Again the high priest asked him, and said unto him, Art thou the Christ, the Son of the **Blessed**? ☐

Luke 1:68, **Blessed** be the Lord God of Israel; for he hath visited and redeemed his people. ☐

Acts 20:35, I have shewed you all things, how that so labouring ye ought to support the weak, and to remember the words of the Lord Jesus, how he said, It is more **blessed** to give than to receive. ☐

Romans 4:7, Saying, **Blessed** are they whose iniquities are forgiven, and whose sins are covered. ☐

Romans 15:29, And I am sure that, when I come unto you, I shall come in the fullness of the **blessing** of the gospel of Christ. ☐

Galatians 3:14, That the **blessing** of Abraham might come on the Gentiles through Jesus Christ; that we might receive the promise of the Spirit through faith. ☐

Ephesians 1:3, **Blessed** be the God and Father of our Lord Jesus Christ, who hath **blessed** us with all spiritual **blessings** in heavenly places in Christ. ☐

Proverbs 14:20, The poor is hated even of his own neighbour: but the rich hath many **friends**. ☐

Proverbs 16:28, A froward man soweth strife: and a whisperer separateth chief **friends**. ☐

Proverbs 19:4, Wealth maketh many **friends**; but the poor is separated from his neighbour. ☐

Proverbs 19:7, All the brethren of the poor do hate him: how much more do his **friends** go far from him? he pursueth them with words, yet they are wanting to him. ☐

Mark 5:19, Howbeit Jesus suffered him not, but saith unto him, Go home to thy **friends**, and tell them how great things the Lord hath done for thee, and hath had compassion on thee. ☐

Luke 11:5, And he said unto them, Which of you shall have a **friend**, and shall go unto him at midnight, and say unto him, **Friend**, lend me three loaves. ☐

Luke 12:4, And I say unto you my **friends**, Be not afraid of them that kill the body, and after that have no more that they can do. ☐

John 11:11, These things said he: and after that he saith unto them, Our **friend** Lazarus sleepeth; but I go, that I may awake him out of sleep. ☐

John 15:13, Greater love hath no man than this, that a man lay down his life for his **friends**. ☐

John 15:14, Ye are my **friends**, if ye do whatsoever I command you. ☐

James 2:23, And the scripture was fulfilled which saith, Abraham believed God, and it was imputed unto him for righteousness: and he was called the **Friend** of God. ☐

James 4:4, Ye adulterers and adulteresses, know ye not that the **friendship** of the world is enmity with God? whosoever therefore will be a **friend** of the world is the enemy of God. ☐

In God We Trust

2 Corinthians 12:9, And he said unto me, My **grace** is sufficient for thee: for my strength is made perfect in weakness. Most gladly therefore will I rather glory in my infirmities, that the power of Christ may rest upon me. ☐

2 Corinthians 13:14, The **grace** of the Lord Jesus Christ, and the love of God, and the communion of the Holy Ghost, be with you all. Amen. ☐

Ephesians 2:7, That in the ages to come he might shew the exceeding riches of his **grace** in his kindness toward us through Christ Jesus. ☐

Ephesians 2:8, For by **grace** are ye saved through faith; and that not of yourselves: it is the gift of God. ☐

Ephesians 3:7, Whereof I was made a minister, according to the gift of the **grace** of God given unto me by the effectual working of his power. ☐

Ephesians 6:24, **Grace** be with all them that love our Lord Jesus Christ in sincerity. Amen. ☐

Colossians 4:6, Let your speech be alway with **grace**, seasoned with salt, that ye may know how ye ought to answer every man. ☐

1 Timothy 1:14, And the **grace** of our Lord was exceeding abundant with faith and love which is in Christ Jesus. ☐

2 Timothy 2:1, Thou therefore, my son, be strong in the **grace** that is in Christ Jesus. ☐

2 Timothy 4:22, The Lord Jesus Christ be with thy spirit. **Grace** be with you. Amen. ☐

Titus 3:7, That being justified by his **grace**, we should be made heirs according to the hope of eternal life. ☐

Hebrews 4:16, Let us therefore come boldly unto the throne of **grace**, that we may obtain mercy, and find **grace** to help in time of need. ☐

Psalms 132:15, I will abundantly bless her provision: I will satisfy her **poor** with bread. ☐

Psalms 140:12, I know that the LORD will maintain the cause of the afflicted, and the right of the **poor**. ☐

Proverbs 18:23, The **poor** useth intreaties; but the **rich** answereth roughly. ☐

Proverbs 19:1, Better is the **poor** that walketh in his integrity, than he that is perverse in his lips, and is a fool. ☐

Proverbs 19:17, He that hath pity upon the **poor** lendeth unto the LORD; and that which he hath given will he pay him again. ☐

Proverbs 19:22, The desire of a man is his kindness: and a **poor** man is better than a liar. ☐

Proverbs 21:13, Whoso stoppeth his ears at the cry of the **poor**, he also shall cry himself, but shall not be heard. ☐

Proverbs 22:2, The **rich** and **poor** meet together: the LORD is the maker of them all. ☐

Proverbs 28:3, A **poor** man that oppresseth the **poor** is like a sweeping rain which leaveth no food. ☐

Proverbs 28:6, Better is the **poor** that walketh in his uprightness, than he that is perverse in his ways, though he be **rich**. ☐

Proverbs 28:8, He that by usury and unjust gain increaseth his substance, he shall gather it for him that will pity the **poor**. ☐

Proverbs 28:11, The **rich** man is wise in his own conceit; but the **poor** that hath understanding searcheth him out. ☐

Proverbs 28:15, As a roaring lion, and a ranging bear; so is a wicked ruler over the **poor** people. ☐

RECEIVE HIS WORD WITH GLADNESS

In God We Trust
207

I BELIEVE
BIGGER
BETTER
BOLDER
BLESSINGS

GOOD *

70 DAY
MORNING
90 DAY CHALLENGE

Psalms 69:16, Hear me, O LORD; for thy lovingkindness is **good**: turn unto me according to the multitude of thy tender mercies. ☐

Psalms 73:1, Truly God is **good** to Israel, even to such as are of a clean heart. ☐

Psalms 73:28, But it is **good** for me to draw near to God: I have put my trust in the Lord GOD, that I may declare all thy works. ☐

Psalms 84:11, For the LORD God is a sun and shield: the LORD will give grace and glory: no **good** thing will he withhold from them that walk uprightly. ☐

Psalms 85:12, Yea, the LORD shall give that which is **good**; and our land shall yield her increase. ☐

Psalms 100:5, For the LORD is **good**; his mercy is everlasting; and his truth endureth to all generations. ☐

Psalms 109:21, But do thou for me, O GOD the Lord, for thy name's sake: because thy mercy is **good**, deliver thou me. ☐

Psalms 112:5, A **good** man sheweth favour, and lendeth: he will guide his affairs with discretion. ☐

Psalms 119:122, Be surety for thy servant for **good**: let not the proud oppress me. ☐

Psalms 143:10, Teach me to do thy will; for thou art my God: thy spirit is **good**; lead me into the land of uprightness. ☐

Psalms 145:9, The LORD is **good** to all: and his tender mercies are over all his works. ☐

Proverbs 3:4, So shalt thou find favour and **good** understanding in the sight of God and man. ☐

Proverbs 3:27, Withhold not **good** from them to whom it is due, when it is in the power of thine hand to do it. ☐

Psalms 22:2, O **my God**, I cry in the daytime, but thou hearest not; and in the night season, and am not silent. ☐

Psalms 25:2, O **my God**, I trust in thee: let me not be ashamed, let not mine enemies triumph over me. ☐

Psalms 30:2, O LORD **my God**, I cried unto thee, and thou hast healed me. ☐

Psalms 30:12, To the end that my glory may sing praise to thee, and not be silent. O LORD **my God**, I will give thanks unto thee for ever. ☐

Psalms 31:14, But I trusted in thee, O LORD: I said, Thou art **my God**. ☐

Psalms 35:23, Stir up thyself, and awake to my judgment, even unto my cause, **my God** and my Lord. ☐

Psalms 35:24, Judge me, O LORD **my God**, according to thy righteousness; and let them not rejoice over me. ☐

Psalms 38:15, For in thee, O LORD, do I hope: thou wilt hear, O Lord **my God**. ☐

Psalms 38:21, Forsake me not, O LORD: O **my God**, be not far from me. ☐

Psalms 40:5, Many, O LORD **my God**, are thy wonderful works which thou hast done, and thy thoughts which are to us-ward: they cannot be reckoned up in order unto thee: if I would declare and speak of them, they are more than can be numbered. ☐

Psalms 40:8, I delight to do thy will, O **my God**: yea, thy law is within my heart. ☐

Psalms 40:17, But I am poor and needy; yet the Lord thinketh upon me: thou art my help and my deliverer; make no tarrying, O **my God**. ☐

Psalms 42:6, O **my God**, my soul is cast down within me: therefore will I remember thee from the land of Jordan, and of the Hermonites, from the hill Mizar. ☐

Psalms 4:5, Offer the sacrifices of righteousness, and put your **trust in the LORD**. ☐

Psalms 5:11, But let all those that put their **trust in** thee rejoice: let them ever shout for joy, because thou defendest them: let them also that love thy name be joyful in thee. ☐

Psalms 9:10, And they that know thy name will put their **trust in** thee: for thou, LORD, hast not forsaken them that seek thee. ☐

Psalms 18:30, As for God, his way is perfect: the word of the LORD is tried: he is a buckler to all those that **trust in** him. ☐

Psalms 25:2, O my God, I **trust in** thee: let me not be ashamed, let not mine enemies triumph over me. ☐

Psalms 25:20, O keep my soul, and deliver me: let me not be ashamed; for I put my **trust in** thee. ☐

Psalms 31:6, I have hated them that regard lying vanities: but I **trust in the LORD**. ☐

Psalms 31:19, Oh how great is thy goodness, which thou hast laid up for them that fear thee; which thou hast wrought for them that **trust in** thee before the sons of men! ☐

Psalms 34:22, The LORD redeemeth the soul of his servants: and none of them that **trust in** him shall be desolate. ☐

Psalms 37:3, **Trust in the LORD**, and do good; so shalt thou dwell in the land, and verily thou shalt be fed. ☐

Psalms 37:40, And the LORD shall help them, and deliver them: he shall deliver them from the wicked, and save them, because they **trust in** him. ☐

Psalms 40:3, And he hath put a new song in my mouth, even praise unto our God: many shall see it, and fear, and shall **trust in the LORD**. ☐

Psalms 44:6, For I will not **trust in** my bow, neither shall my sword save me.☐

Numbers 13:30, And Caleb stilled the people before Moses, and said, Let us go up at once, and possess it; for we are well able to **overcome** it. ☐

John 16:33, These things I have spoken unto you, that in me ye might have peace. In the world ye shall have tribulation: but be of good cheer; I have **overcome** the world. ☐

Romans 12:21, Be not **overcome** of evil, but **overcome** evil with good. ☐

1 John 2:13, I write unto you, fathers, because ye have known him that is from the beginning. I write unto you, young men, because ye have **overcome** the wicked one. I write unto you, little children, because ye have known the Father. ☐

1 John 2:14, I have written unto you, fathers, because ye have known him that is from the beginning. I have written unto you, young men, because ye are strong, and the word of God abideth in you, and ye have **overcome** the wicked one. ☐

1 John 5:4, For whatsoever is born of God **overcometh** the world: and this is the victory that **overcometh** the world, even our faith. ☐

1 John 5:5, Who is he that **overcometh** the world, but he that believeth that Jesus is the Son of God? ☐

Revelation 2:7, He that hath an ear, let him hear what the Spirit saith unto the churches; To him that **overcometh** will I give to eat of the tree of life, which is in the midst of the paradise of God. ☐

Revelation 2:11, He that hath an ear, let him hear what the Spirit saith unto the churches; He that **overcometh** shall not be hurt of the second death. ☐

Revelation 2:26, And he that **overcometh**, and keepeth my works unto the end, to him will I give power over the nations. ☐

Revelation 3:21, To him that **overcometh** will I grant to sit with me in my throne, even as I also overcame, and am set down with my Father in his throne. ☐

In God We Trust

Proverbs 14:16, A wise man feareth, and departeth from evil: but the **fool** rageth, and is confident. ☐

Proverbs 14:24, The crown of the wise is their riches: but the **foolishness** of **fools** is folly. ☐

Proverbs 15:2, The tongue of the wise useth knowledge aright: but the mouth of **fools** poureth out **foolishness.** ☐

Proverbs 15:5, A **fool** despiseth his father's instruction: but he that regardeth reproof is prudent. ☐

Proverbs 15:7, The lips of the wise disperse knowledge: but the heart of the **foolish** doeth not so. ☐

Proverbs 15:14, The heart of him that hath understanding seeketh knowledge: but the mouth of **fool** feedeth on **foolishness.** ☐

Proverbs 15:20, A wise son maketh a glad father: but a **foolish** man despiseth his mother. ☐

Proverbs 17:7, Excellent speech becometh not a **fool**: much less do lying lips a prince. ☐

Proverbs 17:10, A reproof entereth more into a wise man than an hundred stripes into a **fool**. ☐

Proverbs 17:12, Let a bear robbed of her whelps meet a man, rather than a **fool** in his folly. ☐

Proverbs 17:16, Wherefore is there a price in the hand of a **fool** to get wisdom, seeing he hath no heart to it? ☐

Proverbs 17:21, He that begetteth a **fool** doeth it to his sorrow: and the father of a **fool** hath no joy. ☐

Proverbs 17:24, Wisdom is before him that hath understanding; but the eyes of a **fool** are in the ends of the earth. ☐

Romans 12:18, If it be possible, as much as lieth **in you**, live peaceably with all men. ☐

1 Corinthians 1:6, Even as the testimony of Christ was confirmed **in you**.☐

1 Corinthians 3:16, Know ye not that ye are the temple of God, and that the Spirit of God dwelleth **in you**? ☐

1 Corinthians 6:19, What? know ye not that your body is the temple of the Holy Ghost which is **in you**, which ye have of God, and ye are not your own? ☐

1 Corinthians 14:25, And thus are the secrets of his heart made manifest; and so falling down on his face he will worship God, and report that God is **in you** of a truth. ☐

2 Corinthians 2:3, And I wrote this same unto you, lest, when I came, I should have sorrow from them of whom I ought to rejoice; having confidence **in you** all, that my joy is the joy of you all. ☐

2 Corinthians 4:12, So then death worketh in us, but life **in you**. ☐

2 Corinthians 7:7, And not by his coming only, but by the consolation wherewith he was comforted **in you**, when he told us your earnest desire, your mourning, your fervent mind toward me; so that I rejoiced the more. ☐

2 Corinthians 7:16, I rejoice therefore that I have confidence **in you** in all things. ☐

2 Corinthians 8:6, Insomuch that we desired Titus, that as he had begun, so he would also finish **in you** the same grace also. ☐

2 Corinthians 8:22, And we have sent with them our brother, whom we have oftentimes proved diligent in many things, but now much more diligent, upon the great confidence which I have **in you**. ☐

2 Corinthians 9:14, And by their prayer for you, which long after you for the exceeding grace of God **in you**. ☐

Psalms 71:2, Deliver me in thy **righteousness**, and cause me to escape: incline thine ear unto me, and save me. ☐

Psalms 71:15, My mouth shall shew forth thy **righteousness** and thy salvation all the day; for I know not the numbers thereof. ☐

Psalms 71:16, I will go in the strength of the Lord GOD: I will make mention of thy **righteousness**, even of thine only. ☐

Psalms 71:19, Thy **righteousness** also, O God, is very high, who hast done great things: O God, who is like unto thee! ☐

Psalms 71:24, My tongue also shall talk of thy **righteousness** all the day long: for they are confounded, for they are brought unto shame, that seek my hurt. ☐

Psalms 85:10, Mercy and truth are met together; **righteousness** and peace have kissed each other. ☐

Psalms 85:11, Truth shall spring out of the earth; and **righteousness** shall look down from heaven. ☐

Psalms 103:6, The LORD executeth **righteousness** and judgment for all that are oppressed. ☐

Psalms 106:3, Blessed are they that keep judgment, and he that doeth **righteousness** at all times. ☐

Psalms 106:31, And that was counted unto him for **righteousness** unto all generations for evermore. ☐

Psalms 111:3, His work is honourable and glorious: and his **righteousness** endureth forever. ☐

Psalms 112:3, Wealth and riches shall be in his house: and his **righteousness** endureth forever. ☐

Psalms 112:9, He hath dispersed, he hath given to the poor; his **righteousness** endureth for ever; his horn shall be exalted with honour. ☐

In God We Trust

1 Kings 3:11, And God said unto him, Because thou hast asked this thing, and hast not asked for thyself long life; neither hast asked riches for thyself, nor hast asked the life of thine enemies; but hast asked for thyself **understanding** to discern judgment. ☐

Job 38:36, Who hath put wisdom in the inward parts? or who hath given **understanding** to the heart? ☐

Psalms 47:7, For God is the King of all the earth: sing ye praises with **understanding**. ☐

Psalms 49:3, My mouth shall speak of wisdom; and the meditation of my heart shall be of **understanding**. ☐

Psalms 111:10, The fear of the LORD is the beginning of wisdom: a good **understanding** have all they that do his commandments: his praise endureth forever. ☐

Psalms 119:34, Give me **understanding**, and I shall keep thy law; yea, I shall observe it with my whole heart. ☐

Psalms 119:73, Thy hands have made me and fashioned me: give me **understanding**, that I may learn thy commandments. ☐

Psalms 119:99, I have more **understanding** than all my teachers: for thy testimonies are my meditation. ☐

Psalms 119:104, Through thy precepts I get **understanding**: therefore I hate every false way. ☐

Psalms 119:125, I am thy servant; give me **understanding**, that I may know thy testimonies. ☐

Psalms 119:130, The entrance of thy words giveth light; it giveth **understanding** unto the simple. ☐

Psalms 147:5, Great is our Lord, and of great power: his **understanding** is infinite. ☐

In God We Trust
215

MY SOUL *

Psalms 71:23, My lips shall greatly rejoice when I sing unto thee; and **my soul**, which thou hast redeemed. ☐

Psalms 84:2, **My soul** longeth, yea, even fainteth for the courts of the LORD: my heart and my flesh crieth out for the living God. ☐

Psalms 86:2, Preserve **my soul**; for I am holy: O thou my God, save thy servant that trusteth in thee. ☐

Psalms 86:13, For great is thy mercy toward me: and thou hast delivered **my soul** from the lowest hell. ☐

Psalms 103:1, Bless the LORD, O **my soul**: and all that is within me, bless his holy name. ☐

Psalms 103:2, Bless the LORD, O **my soul**, and forget not all his benefits.☐

Psalms 104:1, Bless the LORD, O **my soul**. O LORD my God, thou art very great; thou art clothed with honour and majesty. ☐

Psalms 116:4, Then called I upon the name of the LORD; O LORD, I beseech thee, deliver **my soul**. ☐

Psalms 116:7, Return unto thy rest, O **my soul**; for the LORD hath dealt bountifully with thee. ☐

Psalms 120:2, Deliver **my soul**, O LORD, from lying lips, and from a deceitful tongue. ☐

Psalms 130:5, I wait for the LORD, **my soul** doth wait, and in his word do I hope. ☐

Psalms 23:3, He restoreth **my soul**: he leadeth me in the paths of righteousness for his name's sake. ☐

Psalms 25:1, Unto thee, O LORD, do I lift up **my soul**. ☐

Psalms 25:20, O keep **my soul**, and deliver me: let me not be ashamed; for I put my trust in thee. ☐

Exodus 23:27, I will send my fear before thee, and will destroy all the people to whom thou shalt come, and I will make all thine **enemies** turn their backs unto thee. ☐

Leviticus 26:7, And ye shall chase your **enemies**, and they shall fall before you by the sword. ☐

Leviticus 26:8, And five of you shall chase an hundred, and an hundred of you shall put ten thousand to flight: and your **enemies** shall fall before you by the sword. ☐

Numbers 10:35, And it came to pass, when the ark set forward, that Moses said, Rise up, LORD, and let thine **enemies** be scattered; and let them that hate thee flee before thee. ☐

Deuteronomy 6:19, To cast out all thine **enemies** from before thee, as the LORD hath spoken. ☐

Deuteronomy 12:10, But when ye go over Jordan, and dwell in the land which the LORD your God giveth you to inherit, and when he giveth you rest from all your **enemies** round about, so that ye dwell in safety. ☐

Deuteronomy 20:4, For the LORD your God is he that goeth with you, to fight for you against your **enemies**, to save you. ☐

Deuteronomy 33:29, Happy art thou, O Israel: who is like unto thee, O people saved by the LORD, the shield of thy help, and who is the sword of thy excellency! and thine **enemies** shall be found liars unto thee; and thou shalt tread upon their high places. ☐

Psalms 5:8, Lead me, O LORD, in thy righteousness because of mine **enemies**; make thy way straight before my face. ☐

Psalms 6:10, Let all mine **enemies** be ashamed and sore vexed: let them return and be ashamed suddenly. ☐

Psalms 9:3, When mine **enemies** are turned back, they shall fall and perish at thy presence. ☐

1 Chronicles 16:27, Glory and **honour** are in his presence; strength and gladness are in his place. ☐

1 Chronicles 29:12, Both riches and **honour** come of thee, and thou reignest over all; and in thine hand is power and might; and in thine hand it is to make great, and to give strength unto all. ☐

1 Chronicles 29:28, And he died in a good old age, full of days, riches, and **honour**: and Solomon his son reigned in his stead. ☐

2 Chronicles 1:12, Wisdom and knowledge is granted unto thee; and I will give thee riches, and wealth, and **honour**, such as none of the kings have had that have been before thee, neither shall there any after thee have the like. ☐

2 Chronicles 32:27, And Hezekiah had exceeding much riches and **honour**: and he made himself treasuries for silver, and for gold, and for precious stones, and for spices, and for shields, and for all manner of pleasant jewels. ☐

Psalms 111:3, His work is **honourable** and glorious: and his righteousness endureth forever. ☐

Isaiah 42:21, The LORD is well pleased for his righteousness' sake; he will magnify the law, and make it **honourable**. ☐

Isaiah 43:4, Since thou wast precious in my sight, thou hast been **honourable**, and I have loved thee: therefore will I give men for thee, and people for thy life. ☐

1 Corinthians 4:10, We are fools for Christ's sake, but ye are wise in Christ; we are weak, but ye are strong; ye are **honourable**, but we are despised. ☐

Hebrews 13:4, Marriage is **honourable** in all, and the bed undefiled: but whoremongers and adulterers God will judge. ☐

In God We Trust

Deuteronomy 32:4, **He is** the Rock, his work is perfect: for all his ways are judgment: a God of truth and without iniquity, just and right is he. ☐

1 Chronicles 16:34, O give thanks unto the LORD; for **he is** good; for his mercy endureth forever. ☐

Psalms 37:26, **He is** ever merciful, and lendeth; and his seed is blessed.☐

Psalms 37:39, But the salvation of the righteous is of the LORD: **he is** their strength in the time of trouble. ☐

Psalms 58:11, So that a man shall say, Verily there is a reward for the righteous: verily **he is** a God that judgeth in the earth. ☐

Psalms 62:6, He only is my rock and my salvation: **he is** my defence; I shall not be moved. ☐

Psalms 91:2, I will say of the LORD, **He is** my refuge and my fortress: my God; in him will I trust. ☐

Psalms 92:15, To shew that the LORD is upright: **he is** my rock, and there is no unrighteousness in him. ☐

Psalms 106:1, Praise ye the LORD. O give thanks unto the LORD; for **he is** good: for his mercy endureth forever. ☐

Psalms 112:4, Unto the upright there ariseth light in the darkness: **he is** gracious, and full of compassion, and righteous. ☐

Psalms 118:1, O give thanks unto the LORD; for **he is** good: because his mercy endureth forever. ☐

Proverbs 22:6, Train up a child in the way he should go: and when **he is** old, he will not depart from it. ☐

Isaiah 55:6, Seek ye the LORD while he may be found, call ye upon him while **he is** near. ☐

Psalms 74:22, Arise, O God, plead thine own cause: remember how the foolish man reproacheth thee daily. ☐

Proverbs 7:22, He goeth after her straightway, as an ox goeth to the slaughter, or as a fool to the correction of the stocks. ☐

Proverbs 9:6, Forsake the foolish, and live; and go in the way of understanding. ☐

Proverbs 9:13, A foolish woman is clamorous: she is simple, and knoweth nothing. ☐

Proverbs 10:1, The proverbs of Solomon. A wise son maketh a glad father: but a foolish son is the heaviness of his mother. ☐

Proverbs 10:8, The wise in heart will receive commandments: but a prating fool shall fall. ☐

Proverbs 10:10, He that winketh with the eye causeth sorrow: but a prating fool shall fall. ☐

Proverbs 10:14, Wise men lay up knowledge: but the mouth of the foolish is near destruction. ☐

Proverbs 10:18, He that hideth hatred with lying lips, and he that uttereth a slander, is a fool. ☐

Proverbs 12:15, The way of a fool is right in his own eyes: but he that hearkeneth unto counsel is wise. ☐

Proverbs 13:16, Every prudent man dealeth with knowledge: but a fool layeth open his folly. ☐

Proverbs 14:3, In the mouth of the foolish is a rod of pride: but the lips of the wise shall preserve them. ☐

Proverbs 14:7, Go from the presence of a foolish man, when thou perceivest not in him the lips of knowledge. ☐

John 16:24, Hitherto have ye asked nothing in my name: ask, and ye shall receive, that your **joy** may be full. □

John 17:13, And now come I to thee; and these things I speak in the world, that they might have my **joy** fulfilled in themselves. □

Acts 8:8, And there was great **joy** in that city. □

Acts 20:24, But none of these things move me, neither count I my life dear unto myself, so that I might finish my course with **joy**, and the ministry, which I have received of the Lord Jesus, to testify the gospel of the grace of God. □

Romans 5:11, And not only so, but we also **joy** in God through our Lord Jesus Christ, by whom we have now received the atonement. □

Romans 14:17, For the kingdom of God is not meat and drink; but righteousness, and peace, and **joy** in the Holy Ghost. □

Romans 15:13, Now the God of hope fill you with all **joy** and peace in believing, that ye may abound in hope, through the power of the Holy Ghost. □

Romans 15:32, That I may come unto you with **joy** by the will of God, and may with you be refreshed. □

2 Corinthians 1:24, Not for that we have dominion over your faith, but are helpers of your **joy**: for by faith ye stand. □

Philippians 1:4, Always in every prayer of mine for you all making request with **joy**. □

Philippians 1:25, And having this confidence, I know that I shall abide and continue with you all for your furtherance and **joy** of faith. □

Philippians 2:2, Fulfil ye my **joy**, that ye be likeminded, having the same love, being of one accord, of one mind. □

Matthew 5:16, Let your light so shine before men, that they may see your **good works**, and glorify your Father which is in heaven. ☐

John 10:32, Jesus answered them, Many **good works** have I shewed you from my Father; for which of those works do ye stone me?☐

Ephesians 2:10, For we are his workmanship, created in Christ Jesus unto **good works**, which God hath before ordained that we should walk in them. ☐

1 Timothy 2:10, But which becometh women professing godliness with **good works**. ☐

1 Timothy 5:10, Well reported of for **good works**; if she have brought up children, if she have lodged strangers, if she have washed the saints' feet, if she have relieved the afflicted, if she have diligently followed every **good work**. ☐

1 Timothy 5:25, Likewise also the **good works** of some are manifest beforehand; and they that are otherwise cannot be hid. ☐

1 Timothy 6:18, That they do good, that they be rich in **good works**, ready to distribute, willing to communicate. ☐

Titus 1:16, They profess that they know God; but in works they deny him, being abominable, and disobedient, and unto every **good work** reprobate. ☐

Titus 3:8, This is a faithful saying, and these things I will that thou affirm constantly, that they which have believed in God might be careful to maintain **good works**. These things are good and profitable unto men. ☐

Titus 3:14, And let ours also learn to maintain **good works** for necessary uses, that they be not unfruitful. ☐

Hebrews 10:24, And let us consider one another to provoke unto love and to **good works**. ☐

In God We Trust
222

Psalms 35:27, Let them shout for joy, and be glad, that favour my righteous cause: yea, let them say continually, Let the LORD be magnified, which hath pleasure in the **prosperity** of his servant. ☐

Psalms 73:3, For I was envious at the foolish, when I saw the **prosperity** of the wicked. ☐

Psalms 118:25, Save now, I beseech thee, O LORD: O LORD, I beseech thee, send now **prosperity**. ☐

Psalms 122:6, Pray for the peace of Jerusalem: they shall **prosper** that love thee. ☐

Psalms 122:7, Peace be within thy walls, and **prosperity** within thy palaces. ☐

Proverbs 28:13, He that covereth his sins shall not **prosper**: but whoso confesseth and forsaketh them shall have mercy. ☐

Proverbs 1:32, For the turning away of the simple shall slay them, and the **prosperity** of fools shall destroy them. ☐

Ecclesiastes 7:14, In the day of **prosperity** be joyful, but in the day of adversity consider: God also hath set the one over against the other, to the end that man should find nothing after him. ☐

Isaiah 53:10, Yet it pleased the LORD to bruise him; he hath put him to grief: when thou shalt make his soul an offering for sin, he shall see his seed, he shall prolong his days, and the pleasure of the LORD shall **prosper** in his hand. ☐

Isaiah 54:17, No weapon that is formed against thee shall **prosper**; and every tongue that shall rise against thee in judgment thou shalt condemn. This is the heritage of the servants of the LORD, and their righteousness is of me, saith the LORD. ☐

Isaiah 55:11, So shall my word be that goeth forth out of my mouth: it shall not return unto me void, but it shall accomplish that which I please, and it shall **prosper** in the thing whereto I sent it. ☐

Matthew 4:4, But he answered and said, **It is written**, Man shall not live by bread alone, but by every word that proceedeth out of the mouth of God. ☐

Matthew 4:6, And saith unto him, If thou be the Son of God, cast thyself down: for **it is written**, He shall give his angels charge concerning thee: and in their hands they shall bear thee up, lest at any time thou dash thy foot against a stone. ☐

Matthew 4:7, Jesus said unto him, **It is written** again, Thou shalt not tempt the Lord thy God. ☐

Matthew 4:10, Then saith Jesus unto him, Get thee hence, Satan: for **it is written**, Thou shalt worship the Lord thy God, and him only shalt thou serve. ☐

Matthew 11:10, For this is he, of whom **it is written**, Behold, I send my messenger before thy face, which shall prepare thy way before thee. ☐

Matthew 21:13, And said unto them, **It is written**, My house shall be called the house of prayer; but ye have made it a den of thieves. ☐

Mark 1:2, As **it is written** in the prophets, Behold, I send my messenger before thy face, which shall prepare thy way before thee. ☐

Mark 9:12, And he answered and told them, Elias verily cometh first, and restoreth all things; and how **it is written** of the Son of man, that he must suffer many things, and be set at nought. ☐

Luke 3:4, As **it is written** in the book of the words of Esaias the prophet, saying, The voice of one crying in the wilderness, Prepare ye the way of the Lord, make his paths straight. ☐

Luke 4:4, And Jesus answered him, saying, **It is written**, That man shall not live by bread alone, but by every word of God. ☐

Luke 4:10, For **it is written**, He shall give his angels charge over thee, to keep thee. ☐

1 Chronicles 16:34, O **give thanks** unto the LORD; for he is good; for his mercy endureth forever. ☐

Psalms 75:1, Unto thee, O God, do we **give thanks**, unto thee do we **give thanks**: for that thy name is near thy wondrous works declare. ☐

Psalms 92:1, It is a good thing to **give thanks** unto the LORD, and to sing praises unto thy name, O most High. ☐

Psalms 105:1, O **give thanks** unto the LORD; call upon his name: make known his deeds among the people. ☐

Psalms 106:1, Praise ye the LORD. O **give thanks** unto the LORD; for he is good: for his mercy endureth forever. ☐

Psalms 106:47, Save us, O LORD our God, and gather us from among the heathen, to **give thanks** unto thy holy name, and to triumph in thy praise. ☐

Psalms 119:62, At midnight I will rise to **give thanks** unto thee because of thy righteous judgments. ☐

Psalms 122:4, Whither the tribes go up, the tribes of the LORD, unto the testimony of Israel, to **give thanks** unto the name of the LORD. ☐

Psalms 136:2, O **give thanks** unto the God of gods: for his mercy endureth forever. ☐

Psalms 136:3, O **give thanks** to the Lord of lords: for his mercy endureth forever. ☐

Psalms 140:13, Surely the righteous shall **give thanks** unto thy name: the upright shall dwell in thy presence. ☐

Hebrews 13:15, By him therefore let us offer the sacrifice of praise to God continually, that is, the fruit of our lips **giving thanks** to his name. ☐

In God We Trust

Psalms 42:11, Why art thou cast down, O my soul? and why art thou disquieted within me? hope thou in God: for I shall yet praise him, who is the health of my countenance, and **my God**. ☐

Psalms 43:4, Then will I go unto the altar of God, unto God my exceeding joy: yea, upon the harp will I praise thee, O God **my God**. ☐

Psalms 59:1, Deliver me from mine enemies, O **my God**: defend me from them that rise up against me. ☐

Psalms 63:1, O God, thou art **my God**; early will I seek thee: my soul thirsteth for thee, my flesh longeth for thee in a dry and thirsty land, where no water is. ☐

Psalms 71:4, Deliver me, O **my God**, out of the hand of the wicked, out of the hand of the unrighteous and cruel man. ☐

Psalms 71:12, O God, be not far from me: O **my God**, make haste for my help. ☐

Psalms 71:22, I will also praise thee with the psaltery, even thy truth, O **my God**: unto thee will I sing with the harp, O thou Holy One of Israel. ☐

Psalms 86:2, Preserve my soul; for I am holy: O thou **my God**, save thy servant that trusteth in thee. ☐

Psalms 86:12, I will praise thee, O Lord **my God**, with all my heart: and I will glorify thy name for evermore. ☐

Psalms 89:26, He shall cry unto me, Thou art my father, **my God**, and the rock of my salvation. ☐

Psalms 91:2, I will say of the LORD, He is my refuge and my fortress: **my God**; in him will I trust. ☐

LEARN TO VALUE
THE WORD OF GOD

Psalms 10:7, His mouth is full of cursing and deceit and fraud: under his **tongue** is mischief and vanity. ☐

Psalms 12:3, The LORD shall cut off all flattering lips, and the **tongue** that speaketh proud things. ☐

Psalms 34:13, Keep thy **tongue** from evil, and thy lips from speaking guile. ☐

Psalms 37:30, The mouth of the righteous speaketh wisdom, and his **tongue** talketh of judgment. ☐

Psalms 52:2, Thy **tongue** deviseth mischiefs; like a sharp razor, working deceitfully. ☐

Psalms 52:4, Thou lovest all devouring words, O thou deceitful **tongue**. ☐

Psalms 64:3, Who whet their **tongue** like a sword, and bend their bows to shoot their arrows, even bitter words. ☐

Psalms 64:8, So they shall make their own **tongue** to fall upon themselves: all that see them shall flee away. ☐

Psalms 109:2, For the mouth of the wicked and the mouth of the deceitful are opened against me: they have spoken against me with a lying **tongue**. ☐

Psalms 120:2, Deliver my soul, O LORD, from lying lips, and from a deceitful **tongue**. ☐

Proverbs 6:24, To keep thee from the evil woman, from the flattery of the **tongue** of a strange woman. ☐

Proverbs 6:17, A proud look, a lying **tongue**, and hands that shed innocent blood. ☐

Proverbs 10:20, The **tongue** of the just is as choice silver: the heart of the wicked is little worth. ☐

SEEK *
SEEKETH
SEEKING

76 DAY
EVENING
90 DAY CHALLENGE

Lamentations 3:25, The LORD is good unto them that wait for him, to the soul that **seeketh** him. ☐

Daniel 9:3, And I set my face unto the Lord God, to **seek** by prayer and supplications, with fasting, and sackcloth, and ashes. ☐

Amos 5:4, For thus saith the LORD unto the house of Israel, **Seek** ye me, and ye shall live. ☐

Amos 5:14, **Seek** good, and not evil, that ye may live: and so the LORD, the God of hosts, shall be with you, as ye have spoken. ☐

Zephaniah 2:3, **Seek** ye the LORD, all ye meek of the earth, which have wrought his judgment; **seek** righteousness, **seek** meekness: it may be ye shall be hid in the day of the LORD'S anger. ☐

Matthew 6:33, But **seek** ye first the kingdom of God, and his righteousness; and all these things shall be added unto you. ☐

Matthew 7:7, Ask, and it shall be given you; **seek**, and ye shall find; knock, and it shall be opened unto you. ☐

Matthew 7:8, For every one that asketh receiveth; and he that **seeketh** findeth; and to him that knocketh it shall be opened. ☐

Matthew 13:45, Again, the kingdom of heaven is like unto a merchant man, **seeking** goodly pearls. ☐

Luke 11:9, And I say unto you, Ask, and it shall be given you; **seek**, and ye shall find; knock, and it shall be opened unto you. ☐

Luke 19:10, For the Son of man is come to **seek** and to save that which was lost. ☐

1 Peter 3:11, Let him eschew evil, and do good; let him **seek** peace, and ensue it. ☐

In God We Trust
228

Romans 16:20, And the God of peace shall bruise Satan under your feet shortly. The **grace** of our Lord Jesus Christ be with you. Amen. ☐

Romans 16:24, The **grace** of our Lord Jesus Christ be with you all. Amen. ☐

1 Corinthians 1:3, **Grace** be unto you, and peace, from God our Father, and from the Lord Jesus Christ. ☐

1 Corinthians 1:4, I thank my God always on your behalf, for the **grace** of God which is given you by Jesus Christ. ☐

1 Corinthians 3:10, According to the **grace** of God which is given unto me, as a wise masterbuilder, I have laid the foundation, and another buildeth thereon. But let every man take heed how he buildeth thereupon. ☐

1 Corinthians 15:10, But by the **grace** of God I am what I am: and his **grace** which was bestowed upon me was not in vain; but I laboured more abundantly than they all: yet not I, but the **grace** of God which was with me. ☐

1 Corinthians 16:23, The **grace** of our Lord Jesus Christ be with you. ☐

2 Corinthians 4:15, For all things are for your sakes, that the abundant **grace** might through the thanksgiving of many redound to the glory of God. ☐

2 Corinthians 8:9, For ye know the **grace** of our Lord Jesus Christ, that, though he was rich, yet for your sakes he became poor, that ye through his poverty might be rich. ☐

2 Corinthians 9:8, And God is able to make all **grace** abound toward you; that ye, always having all sufficiency in all things, may abound to every good work. ☐

2 Corinthians 9:14, And by their prayer for you, which long after you for the exceeding **grace** of God in you. ☐

Psalms 68:22, The Lord said, **I will** bring again from Bashan, **I will** bring my people again from the depths of the sea. ☐

Psalms 69:30, **I will** praise the name of God with a song, and will magnify him with thanksgiving. ☐

Psalms 71:14, But **I will** hope continually, and will yet praise thee more and more. ☐

Psalms 71:16, **I will** go in the strength of the Lord GOD: **I will** make mention of thy righteousness, even of thine only. ☐

Psalms 75:9, But **I will** declare forever; **I will** sing praises to the God of Jacob. ☐

Psalms 77:10, And I said, This is my infirmity: but **I will** remember the years of the right hand of the most High. ☐

Psalms 77:11, **I will** remember the works of the LORD: surely **I will** remember thy wonders of old. ☐

Psalms 77:12, **I will** meditate also of all thy work, and talk of thy doings. ☐

Psalms 78:2, **I will** open my mouth in a parable: **I will** utter dark sayings of old. ☐

Psalms 81:8, Hear, O my people, and **I will** testify unto thee: O Israel, if thou wilt hearken unto me. ☐

Psalms 81:10, I am the LORD thy God, which brought thee out of the land of Egypt: open thy mouth wide, and **I will** fill it. ☐

Psalms 85:8, **I will** hear what God the LORD will speak: for he will speak peace unto his people, and to his saints: but let them not turn again to folly. ☐

Psalms 86:7, In the day of my trouble **I will** call upon thee: for thou wilt answer me. ☐

Genesis 18:18, Seeing that Abraham shall surely become a great and mighty nation, and all the nations of the earth shall be blessed **in him**? ☐

Job 13:15, Though he slay me, yet will I trust **in him**: but I will maintain mine own ways before him. ☐

Psalms 18:30, As for God, his way is perfect: the word of the LORD is tried: he is a buckler to all those that trust **in him**. ☐

Psalms 22:8, He trusted on the LORD that he would deliver him: let him deliver him, seeing he delighted **in him**. ☐

Psalms 28:7, The LORD is my strength and my shield; my heart trusted **in him** and I am helped: therefore my heart greatly rejoiceth; and with my song will I praise him. ☐

Psalms 33:21, For our heart shall rejoice **in him**, because we have trusted in his holy name. ☐

Psalms 34:8, O taste and see that the LORD is good: blessed is the man that trusteth **in him**. ☐

Psalms 34:22, The LORD redeemeth the soul of his servants: and none of them that trust **in him** shall be desolate. ☐

Psalms 37:5, Commit thy way unto the LORD; trust also **in him**; and he shall bring it to pass. ☐

Psalms 37:40, And the LORD shall help them, and deliver them: he shall deliver them from the wicked, and save them, because they trust **in him**. ☐

Psalms 62:8, Trust **in him** at all times; ye people, pour out your heart before him: God is a refuge for us. Selah. ☐

Psalms 64:10, The righteous shall be glad in the LORD, and shall trust **in him**; and all the upright in heart shall glory. ☐

John 1:51, And he saith unto him, **Verily**, **verily**, I say unto you, Hereafter ye shall see heaven open, and the angels of God ascending and descending upon the Son of man. ☐

John 3:5, Jesus answered, **Verily**, **verily**, I say unto thee, Except a man be born of water and of the Spirit, he cannot enter into the kingdom of God. ☐

John 3:3, Jesus answered and said unto him, **Verily**, **verily**, I say unto thee, Except a man be born again, he cannot see the kingdom of God. ☐

John 3:11, **Verily**, **verily**, I say unto thee, We speak that we do know, and testify that we have seen; and ye receive not our witness. ☐

John 6:47, **Verily**, **verily**, I say unto you, He that believeth on me hath everlasting life. ☐

John 6:53, Then Jesus said unto them, **Verily**, **verily**, I say unto you, Except ye eat the flesh of the Son of man, and drink his blood, ye have no life in you. ☐

John 8:34, Jesus answered them, **Verily**, **verily**, I say unto you, Whosoever committeth sin is the servant of sin. ☐

John 10:1, **Verily**, **verily**, I say unto you, He that entereth not by the door into the sheepfold, but climbeth up some other way, the same is a thief and a robber. ☐

John 10:7, Then said Jesus unto them again, **Verily**, **verily**, I say unto you, I am the door of the sheep. ☐

John 12:24, **Verily**, **verily**, I say unto you, Except a corn of wheat fall into the ground and die, it abideth alone: but if it die, it bringeth forth much fruit. ☐

John 13:20, **Verily**, **verily**, I say unto you, He that receiveth whomsoever I send receiveth me; and he that receiveth me receiveth him that sent me. ☐

I BELIEVE
BIGGER
BETTER
BOLDER
BLESSINGS

LOVE*
LOVED

78 DAY
AFTERNOON
90 DAY CHALLENGE

Psalms 5:11, But let all those that put their trust in thee rejoice: let them ever shout for joy, because thou defendest them: let them also that **love** thy name be joyful in thee. ☐

Psalms 18:1, I will **love** thee, O LORD, my strength. ☐

Psalms 31:23, O **love** the LORD, all ye his saints: for the LORD preserveth the faithful, and plentifully rewardeth the proud doer. ☐

Psalms 40:16, Let all those that seek thee rejoice and be glad in thee: let such as **love** thy salvation say continually, The LORD be magnified. ☐

Psalms 69:36, The seed also of his servants shall inherit it: and they that **love** his name shall dwell therein. ☐

Psalms 70:4, Let all those that seek thee rejoice and be glad in thee: and let such as **love** thy salvation say continually, Let God be magnified. ☐

Psalms 91:14, Because he hath set his **love** upon me, therefore will I deliver him: I will set him on high, because he hath known my name. ☐

Psalms 97:10, Ye that **love** the LORD, hate evil: he preserveth the souls of his saints; he delivereth them out of the hand of the wicked. ☐

Psalms 116:1, I **love** the LORD, because he hath heard my voice and my supplications. ☐

Psalms 119:97, O how **love** I thy law! it is my meditation all the day. ☐

Psalms 119:127, Therefore I **love** thy commandments above gold; yea, above fine gold. ☐

Psalms 119:132, Look thou upon me, and be merciful unto me, as thou usest to do unto those that **love** thy name. ☐

REMEMBER:
IT ONLY TAKES . . .
PAGE XXV

1 John 4:19, We **love** him, because he first **loved** us. ☐

Psalms 30:2, O LORD my God, I cried unto thee, and thou hast **healed** me. ☐

Matthew 8:8, The centurion answered and said, Lord, I am not worthy that thou shouldest come under my roof: but speak the word only, and my servant shall be **healed**. ☐

Matthew 8:13, And Jesus said unto the centurion, Go thy way; and as thou hast believed, so be it done unto thee. And his servant was **healed** in the selfsame hour. ☐

Matthew 8:16, When the even was come, they brought unto him many that were possessed with devils: and he cast out the spirits with his word, and **healed** all that were sick. ☐

Matthew 12:15, But when Jesus knew it, he withdrew himself from thence: and great multitudes followed him, and he **healed** them all. ☐

Matthew 14:14, And Jesus went forth, and saw a great multitude, and was moved with compassion toward them, and he **healed** their sick. ☐

Matthew 15:30, And great multitudes came unto him, having with them those that were lame, blind, dumb, maimed, and many others, and cast them down at Jesus' feet; and he **healed** them. ☐

Matthew 21:14, And the blind and the lame came to him in the temple; and he **healed** them. ☐

Mark 1:34, And he **healed** many that were sick of divers diseases, and cast out many devils; and suffered not the devils to speak, because they knew him. ☐

Mark 3:10, For he had **healed** many; insomuch that they pressed upon him for to touch him, as many as had plagues. ☐

Mark 6:5, And he could there do no mighty work, save that he laid his hands upon a few sick folk, and **healed** them. ☐

Mark 6:13, And they cast out many devils, and anointed with oil many that were sick, and **healed** them. ☐

BE GRATEFUL ALWAYS

In God We Trust

Psalms 4:2, O ye sons of men, how long will ye turn my glory into shame? how long will ye love vanity, and **seek** after leasing? Selah. ☐

Psalms 9:10, And they that know thy name will put their trust in thee: for thou, LORD, hast not forsaken them that **seek** thee. ☐

Psalms 10:4, The wicked, through the pride of his countenance, will not **seek** after God: God is not in all his thoughts. ☐

Psalms 10:15, Break thou the arm of the wicked and the evil man: **seek** out his wickedness till thou find none. ☐

Psalms 14:2, The LORD looked down from heaven upon the children of men, to see if there were any that did understand, and **seek** God. ☐

Psalms 22:26, The meek shall eat and be satisfied: they shall praise the LORD that **seek** him: your heart shall live forever. ☐

Psalms 24:6, This is the generation of them that **seek** him, that **seek** thy face, O Jacob. Selah. ☐

Psalms 27:4, One thing have I desired of the LORD, that will I **seek** after; that I may dwell in the house of the LORD all the days of my life, to behold the beauty of the LORD, and to enquire in his temple. ☐

Psalms 27:8, When thou saidst, **Seek** ye my face; my heart said unto thee, Thy face, LORD, will I **seek**. ☐

Psalms 34:10, The young lions do lack, and suffer hunger: but they that **seek** the LORD shall not want any good thing. ☐

Psalms 34:14, Depart from evil, and do good; **seek** peace, and pursue it. ☐

Psalms 40:16, Let all those that **seek** thee rejoice and be glad in thee: let such as love thy salvation say continually, The LORD be magnified. ☐

Psalms 53:2, God looked down from heaven upon the children of men, to see if there were any that did understand, that did **seek** God. ☐

Psalms 67:4, O let the nations be glad and sing for **joy**: for thou shalt judge the people righteously, and govern the nations upon earth. Selah. ☐

Proverbs 23:24, The father of the righteous shall greatly rejoice: and he that begetteth a wise child shall have **joy** of him. ☐

Isaiah 52:9, Break forth into **joy**, sing together, ye waste places of Jerusalem: for the LORD hath comforted his people, he hath re-deemed Jerusalem. ☐

Jeremiah 33:11, The voice of **joy**, and the voice of gladness, the voice of the bridegroom, and the voice of the bride, the voice of them that shall say, Praise the LORD of hosts: for the LORD is good; for his mercy endureth for ever: and of them that shall bring the sacrifice of praise into the house of the LORD. For I will cause to return the captivity of the land, as at the first, saith the LORD. ☐

Lamentations 5:15, The **joy** of our heart is ceased; our dance is turned into mourning. ☐

Matthew 13:20, But he that received the seed into stony places, the same is he that heareth the word, and anon with **joy** receiveth it. ☐

Matthew 25:21, His lord said unto him, Well done, thou good and faithful servant: thou hast been faithful over a few things, I will make thee ruler over many things: enter thou into the **joy** of thy lord. ☐

Matthew 25:23, His lord said unto him, Well done, good and faithful servant; thou hast been faithful over a few things, I will make thee ruler over many things: enter thou into the **joy** of thy lord. ☐

Luke 1:14, And thou shalt have **joy** and gladness; and many shall rejoice at his birth. ☐

Luke 2:10, And the angel said unto them, Fear not: for, behold, I bring you good tidings of great **joy**, which shall be to all people. ☐

Jeremiah 36:6, Therefore go thou, and read in the roll, which thou hast written from my mouth, the words of the LORD in the **ears** of the people in the LORD'S house upon the fasting day: and also thou shalt read them in the **ears** of all Judah that come out of their cities. □

Matthew 11:15, He that hath **ears** to hear, let him hear. □

Matthew 13:15, For this people's heart is waxed gross, and their **ears** are dull of hearing, and their eyes they have closed; lest at any time they should see with their eyes, and hear with their **ears**, and should understand with their heart, and should be converted, and I should heal them. □

Matthew 13:16, But blessed are your eyes, for they see: and your **ears**, for they hear. □

Matthew 13:43, Then shall the righteous shine forth as the sun in the kingdom of their Father. Who hath **ears** to hear, let him hear. □

Mark 7:16, If any man have **ears** to hear, let him hear. □

Luke 4:21, And he began to say unto them, This day is this scripture fulfilled in your **ears**. □

Luke 9:44, Let these sayings sink down into your **ears**: for the Son of man shall be delivered into the hands of men. □

2 Timothy 4:3, For the time will come when they will not endure sound doctrine; but after their own lusts shall they heap to themselves teachers, having itching **ears**. □

2 Timothy 4:4, And they shall turn away their **ears** from the truth, and shall be turned unto fables. □

In God We Trust

Colossians 2:7, Rooted and built up in him, and stablished in the **faith**, as ye have been taught, abounding therein with thanksgiving. ☐

Colossians 2:12, Buried with him in baptism, wherein also ye are risen with him through the **faith** of the operation of God, who hath raised him from the dead. ☐

1 Thessalonians 1:3, Remembering without ceasing your work of **faith**, and labour of love, and patience of hope in our Lord Jesus Christ, in the sight of God and our Father. ☐

1 Thessalonians 3:7, Therefore, brethren, we were comforted over you in all our affliction and distress by your **faith**. ☐

1 Thessalonians 3:10, Night and day praying exceedingly that we might see your face, and might perfect that which is lacking in your **faith**? ☐

1 Thessalonians 5:8, But let us, who are of the day, be sober, putting on the breastplate of **faith** and love; and for an helmet, the hope of salvation. ☐

2 Thessalonians 1:3, We are bound to thank God always for you, brethren, as it is meet, because that your **faith** groweth exceedingly, and the charity of every one of you all toward each other aboundeth. ☐

2 Thessalonians 1:11, Wherefore also we pray always for you, that our God would count you worthy of this calling, and fulfil all the good pleasure of his goodness, and the work of **faith** with power. ☐

2 Thessalonians 3:2, And that we may be delivered from unreasonable and wicked men: for all men have not **faith**. ☐

1 Timothy 1:19, Holding **faith**, and a good conscience; which some having put away concerning **faith** have made shipwreck. ☐

1 Timothy 2:15, Notwithstanding she shall be saved in childbearing, if they continue in **faith** and charity and holiness with sobriety. ☐

1 Timothy 3:9, Holding the mystery of the **faith** in a pure conscience. ☐

Matthew 18:3, And said, Verily **I say** unto you, Except ye be converted, and become as little children, ye shall not enter into the kingdom of heaven. □

Matthew 18:10, Take heed that ye despise not one of these little ones; for **I say** unto you, That in heaven their angels do always behold the face of my Father which is in heaven. □

Matthew 18:13, And if so be that he find it, verily **I say** unto you, he rejoiceth more of that sheep, than of the ninety and nine which went not astray. □

Matthew 18:18, Verily **I say** unto you, Whatsoever ye shall bind on earth shall be bound in heaven: and whatsoever ye shall loose on earth shall be loosed in heaven. □

Matthew 18:19, Again **I say** unto you, That if two of you shall agree on earth as touching any thing that they shall ask, it shall be done for them of my Father which is in heaven. □

Matthew 18:22, Jesus saith unto him, **I say** not unto thee, Until seven times: but, Until seventy times seven. □

Matthew 19:24, And again **I say** unto you, It is easier for a camel to go through the eye of a needle, than for a rich man to enter into the kingdom of God. □

Matthew 23:39, For **I say** unto you, Ye shall not see me henceforth, till ye shall say, Blessed is he that cometh in the name of the Lord. □

Matthew 24:47, Verily **I say** unto you, That he shall make him ruler over all his goods. □

Mark 2:11, **I say** unto thee, Arise, and take up thy bed, and go thy way into thine house. □

In God We Trust

239

Psalms 119:144, The righteousness of thy testimonies is everlasting: give me **understanding**, and I shall live. ☐

Psalms 119:169, Let my cry come near before thee, O LORD: give me **understanding** according to thy word. ☐

Proverbs 1:2, To know wisdom and instruction; to perceive the words of **understanding**. ☐

Proverbs 1:5, A wise man will hear, and will increase learning; and a man of **understanding** shall attain unto wise counsels. ☐

Proverbs 2:2, So that thou incline thine ear unto wisdom, and apply thine heart to **understanding**. ☐

Proverbs 2:3, Yea, if thou criest after knowledge, and liftest up thy voice for **understanding**. ☐

Proverbs 2:6, For the LORD giveth wisdom: out of his mouth cometh knowledge and **understanding**. ☐

Proverbs 2:11, Discretion shall preserve thee, **understanding** shall keep thee. ☐

Proverbs 3:4, So shalt thou find favour and good **understanding** in the sight of God and man. ☐

Proverbs 3:5, Trust in the LORD with all thine heart; and lean not unto thine own **understanding**. ☐

Proverbs 3:13, Happy is the man that findeth wisdom, and the man that getteth **understanding**. ☐

Proverbs 3:19, The LORD by wisdom hath founded the earth; by **understanding** hath he established the heavens. ☐

Proverbs 4:1, Hear, ye children, the instruction of a father, and attend to know **understanding**. ☐

Deuteronomy 6:5, And thou shalt love the Lord thy God with all **thine heart**, and with all thy soul, and with all thy might. ☐

2 Chronicles 1:11, And God said to Solomon, Because this was in **thine heart**, and thou hast not asked riches, wealth, or honour, nor the life of thine enemies, neither yet hast asked long life; but hast asked wisdom and knowledge for thyself, that thou mayest judge my people, over whom I have made thee king: ☐

Psalm 27:14, Wait on the Lord: be of good courage, and he shall strengthen **thine heart**: wait, I say, on the Lord. ☐

Psalm 37:4, Delight thyself also in the Lord: and he shall give thee the desires of **thine heart**. ☐

Proverbs 2:2, So that thou incline thine ear unto wisdom, and apply **thine heart** to understanding; ☐

Proverbs 2:10, When wisdom entereth into **thine heart**, and knowledge is pleasant unto thy soul; ☐

Proverbs 3:3, Let not mercy and truth forsake thee: bind them about thy neck; write them upon the table of **thine heart**: ☐

Proverbs 3:5, Trust in the Lord with all **thine heart**; and lean not unto thine own understanding. ☐

Proverbs 4:4, He taught me also, and said unto me, Let **thine heart** retain my words: keep my commandments, and live. ☐

Proverbs 6:21, Bind them continually upon **thine heart**, and tie them about thy neck. ☐

Proverbs 23:12, Apply **thine heart** unto instruction, and thine ears to the words of knowledge. ☐

Proverbs 23:17, Let not **thine heart** envy sinners: but be thou in the fear of the Lord all the day long. ☐

Proverbs 24:17, Rejoice not when thine enemy falleth, and let not **thine heart** be glad when he stumbleth: ☐

Psalms 119:98, Thou through thy commandments hast made me wiser than mine **enemies**: for they are ever with me. ☐

Psalms 119:139, My zeal hath consumed me, because mine **enemies** have forgotten thy words. ☐

Psalms 119:157, Many are my persecutors and mine **enemies**; yet do I not decline from thy testimonies. ☐

Psalms 132:18, His **enemies** will I clothe with shame: but upon himself shall his crown flourish. ☐

Psalms 136:24, And hath redeemed us from our **enemies**: for his mercy endureth forever. ☐

Psalms 139:20, For they speak against thee wickedly, and thine **enemies** take thy name in vain. ☐

Psalms 139:22, I hate them with perfect hatred: I count them mine **enemies**. ☐

Psalms 143:9, Deliver me, O LORD, from mine **enemies**: I flee unto thee to hide me. ☐

Psalms 143:12, And of thy mercy cut off mine **enemies**, and destroy all them that afflict my soul: for I am thy servant. ☐

Proverbs 16:7, When a man's ways please the LORD, he maketh even his **enemies** to be at peace with him. ☐

Matthew 5:44, But I say unto you, Love your **enemies**, bless them that curse you, do good to them that hate you, and pray for them which despitefully use you, and persecute you. ☐

Matthew 22:44, The LORD said unto my Lord, Sit thou on my right hand, till I make thine **enemies** thy footstool? ☐

Luke 1:71, That we should be saved from our **enemies**, and from the hand of all that hate us. ☐

Matthew 19:2, And great multitudes followed him; and he **healed** them there. ☐

Luke 5:15, But so much the more went there a fame abroad of him: and great multitudes came together to hear, and to be **healed** by him of their infirmities. ☐

Luke 6:19, And the whole multitude sought to touch him: for there went virtue out of him, and **healed** them all. ☐

Luke 7:7, Wherefore neither thought I myself worthy to come unto thee: but say in a word, and my servant shall be **healed**. ☐

Luke 8:36, They also which saw it told them by what means he that was possessed of the devils was **healed**. ☐

Luke 14:4, And they held their peace. And he took him, and **healed** him, and let him go. ☐

Acts 14:9, The same heard Paul speak: who stedfastly beholding him, and perceiving that he had faith to be **healed**. ☐

James 5:16, Confess your faults one to another, and pray one for another, that ye may be **healed**. The effectual fervent prayer of a righteous man availeth much. ☐

1 Peter 2:24, Who his own self bare our sins in his own body on the tree, that we, being dead to sins, should live unto righteousness: by whose stripes ye were **healed**. ☐

In God We Trust

FOOL *
FOOLISH *
FOOLISHNESS *

DAY
MORNING
90 DAY CHALLENGE

Proverbs 17:25, A **foolish** son is a grief to his father, and bitterness to her that bare him. ☐

Proverbs 17:28, Even a **fool**, when he holdeth his peace, is counted wise: and he that shutteth his lips is esteemed a man of understanding. ☐

Proverbs 18:2, A **fool** hath no delight in understanding, but that his heart may discover itself. ☐

Proverbs 19:1, Better is the poor that walketh in his integrity, than he that is perverse in his lips, and is a **fool**. ☐

Proverbs 19:3, The **foolishness** of man perverteth his way: and his heart fretteth against the LORD. ☐

Proverbs 19:10, Delight is not seemly for a **fool**; much less for a servant to have rule over princes. ☐

Proverbs 19:13, A **foolish** son is the calamity of his father: and the contentions of a wife are a continual dropping. ☐

Proverbs 20:3, It is an honour for a man to cease from strife: but every **fool** will be meddling. ☐

Proverbs 21:20, There is treasure to be desired and oil in the dwelling of the wise; but a **foolish** man spendeth it up. ☐

Proverbs 22:15, **Foolishness** is bound in the heart of a child; but the rod of correction shall drive it far from him. ☐

Proverbs 23:9, Speak not in the ears of a **fool**: for he will despise the wisdom of thy words. ☐

Proverbs 24:7, Wisdom is too high for a **fool**: he openeth not his mouth in the gate. ☐

Proverbs 24:9, The thought of **foolishness** is sin: and the scorner is an abomination to men. ☐

Proverbs 11:23, The desire of the righteous is only **good**: but the expectation of the wicked is wrath. ☐

Proverbs 12:14, A man shall be satisfied with **good** by the fruit of his mouth: and the recompence of a man's hands shall be rendered unto him. ☐

Proverbs 12:25, Heaviness in the heart of man maketh it stoop: but a **good** word maketh it glad. ☐

Proverbs 13:2, A man shall eat **good** by the fruit of his mouth: but the soul of the transgressors shall eat violence. ☐

Proverbs 13:21, Evil pursueth sinners: but to the righteous **good** shall be repayed. ☐

Proverbs 15:23, A man hath joy by the answer of his mouth: and a word spoken in due season, how **good** is it! ☐

Proverbs 15:30, The light of the eyes rejoiceth the heart: and a **good** report maketh the bones fat. ☐

Proverbs 16:20, He that handleth a matter wisely shall find **good**: and whoso trusteth in the LORD, happy is he. ☐

Proverbs 17:20, He that hath a froward heart findeth no **good**: and he that hath a perverse tongue falleth into mischief. ☐

Proverbs 22:1, A **good** name is rather to be chosen than great riches, and loving favour rather than silver and gold. ☐

Proverbs 24:23, These things also belong to the wise. It is not **good** to have respect of persons in judgment. ☐

Proverbs 31:12, She will do him **good** and not evil all the days of her life. ☐

Ecclesiastes 2:24, There is nothing better for a man, than that he should eat and drink, and that he should make his soul enjoy **good** in his labour. This also I saw, that it was from the hand of God. ☐

Luke 19:46, Saying unto them, **It is written**, My house is the house of prayer: but ye have made it a den of thieves. ☐

Luke 24:46, And said unto them, Thus **it is written**, and thus it behoved Christ to suffer, and to rise from the dead the third day. ☐

John 6:31, Our fathers did eat manna in the desert; as **it is written**, He gave them bread from heaven to eat. ☐

Acts 23:5, Then said Paul, I wist not, brethren, that he was the high priest: for **it is written**, Thou shalt not speak evil of the ruler of thy people. ☐

Romans 1:17, For therein is the righteousness of God revealed from faith to faith: as **it is written**, The just shall live by faith. ☐

Romans 3:10, As **it is written**, There is none righteous, no, not one. ☐

Romans 4:17, (As **it is written**, I have made thee a father of many nations,) before him whom he believed, even God, who quickeneth the dead, and calleth those things which be not as though they were. ☐

Romans 8:36, As **it is written**, For thy sake we are killed all the day long; we are accounted as sheep for the slaughter. ☐

Romans 9:13, As **it is written**, Jacob have I loved, but Esau have I hated. ☐

Romans 10:15, And how shall they preach, except they be sent? as **it is written**, How beautiful are the feet of them that preach the gospel of peace, and bring glad tidings of good things! ☐

Romans 12:19, Dearly beloved, avenge not yourselves, but rather give place unto wrath: for **it is written**, Vengeance is mine; I will repay, saith the Lord. ☐

Romans 14:11, For **it is written**, As I live, saith the Lord, every knee shall bow to me, and every tongue shall confess to God. ☐

Romans 15:13, Now the God of hope fill you with all **joy** and peace in believing, that ye may abound in hope, through the power of the Holy Ghost. ☐

Romans 15:32, That I may come unto you with **joy** by the will of God, and may with you be refreshed. ☐

2 Corinthians 8:2, How that in a great trial of affliction the abundance of their **joy** and their deep poverty abounded unto the riches of their liberality. ☐

Galatians 5:22, But the fruit of the Spirit is love, **joy**, peace, longsuffering, gentleness, goodness, faith. ☐

Philippians 1:4, Always in every prayer of mine for you all making request with **joy**. ☐

Philippians 1:25, And having this confidence, I know that I shall abide and continue with you all for your furtherance and **joy** of faith. ☐

Philippians 2:2, Fulfil ye my **joy**, that ye be likeminded, having the same love, being of one accord, of one mind. ☐

Philippians 2:17, Yea, and if I be offered upon the sacrifice and service of your faith, I **joy**, and rejoice with you all. ☐

Philippians 2:18, For the same cause also do ye **joy**, and rejoice with me. ☐

Philippians 4:1, Therefore, my brethren dearly beloved and longed for, my **joy** and crown, so stand fast in the Lord, my dearly beloved. ☐

James 4:9, Be afflicted, and mourn, and weep: let your laughter be turned to mourning, and your **joy** to heaviness. ☐

1 Peter 4:13, But rejoice, inasmuch as ye are partakers of Christ's sufferings; that, when his glory shall be revealed, ye may be glad also with exceeding **joy**. ☐

1 John 1:4, And these things write we unto you, that your **joy** may be full. ☐

Romans 5:2, By whom also we have access by faith into this **grace** wherein we stand, and rejoice in hope of the glory of God. ☐

Romans 5:15, But not as the offence, so also is the free gift. For if through the offence of one many be dead, much more the **grace** of God, and the gift by **grace**, which is by one man, Jesus Christ, hath abounded unto many. ☐

Romans 5:17, For if by one man's offence death reigned by one; much more they which receive abundance of **grace** and of the gift of righteousness shall reign in life by one, Jesus Christ. ☐

Romans 5:20, Moreover the law entered, that the offence might abound. But where sin abounded, **grace** did much more abound. ☐

Romans 5:21, That as sin hath reigned unto death, even so might **grace** reign through righteousness unto eternal life by Jesus Christ our Lord. ☐

Romans 6:14, For sin shall not have dominion over you: for ye are not under the law, but under **grace**. ☐

Romans 6:15, What then? shall we sin, because we are not under the law, but under **grace**? God forbid. ☐

Romans 11:6, And if by **grace**, then is it no more of works: otherwise **grace** is no more **grace**. But if it be of works, then is it no more **grace**: otherwise work is no more work. ☐

Romans 12:3, For I say, through the **grace** given unto me, to every man that is among you, not to think of himself more highly than he ought to think; but to think soberly, according as God hath dealt to every man the measure of faith. ☐

Romans 15:15, Nevertheless, brethren, I have written the more boldly unto you in some sort, as putting you in mind, because of the **grace** that is given to me of God. ☐

Colossians 2:7, Rooted and built up **in him**, and stablished in the faith, as ye have been taught, abounding therein with thanksgiving. ☐

Colossians 2:9, For **in him** dwelleth all the fulness of the Godhead bodily. ☐

Colossians 2:10, And ye are complete **in him**, which is the head of all principality and power. ☐

1 John 1:5, This then is the message which we have heard of him, and declare unto you, that God is light, and **in him** is no darkness at all. ☐

1 John 2:5, But whoso keepeth his word, **in him** verily is the love of God perfected: hereby know we that we are **in him**. ☐

1 John 2:6, He that saith he abideth **in him** ought himself also so to walk, even as he walked. ☐

1 John 2:8, Again, a new commandment I write unto you, which thing is true **in him** and in you: because the darkness is past, and the true light now shineth. ☐

1 John 2:28, And now, little children, abide **in him**; that, when he shall appear, we may have confidence, and not be ashamed before him at his coming. ☐

1 John 3:5, And ye know that he was manifested to take away our sins; and **in him** is no sin. ☐

1 John 3:6, Whosoever abideth **in him** sinneth not: whosoever sinneth hath not seen him, neither known him. ☐

1 John 4:13, Hereby know we that we dwell **in him**, and he in us, because he hath given us of his Spirit. ☐

1 John 4:15, Whosoever shall confess that Jesus is the Son of God, God dwelleth **in him**, and he in God. ☐

In God We Trust
249

Psalms 18:49, Therefore will I **give thanks** unto thee, O LORD, among the heathen, and sing praises unto thy name. □

Psalms 30:4, Sing unto the LORD, O ye saints of his, and **give thanks** at the remembrance of his holiness. □

Psalms 30:12, To the end that my glory may sing praise to thee, and not be silent. O LORD my God, I will **give thanks** unto thee forever. □

Psalms 118:1, O **give thanks** unto the LORD; for he is good: because his mercy endureth forever. □

Matthew 15:36, And he took the seven loaves and the fishes, and gave **thanks**, and brake them, and gave to his disciples, and the disciples to the multitude. □

Matthew 26:27, And he took the cup, and gave **thanks**, and gave it to them, saying, Drink ye all of it. □

1 Corinthians 10:30, For if I by grace be a partaker, why am I evil spoken of for that for which I **give thanks**? □

1 Corinthians 11:24, And when he had given **thanks**, he brake it, and said, Take, eat: this is my body, which is broken for you: this do in remembrance of me. □

2 Corinthians 2:14, Now **thanks** be unto God, which always causeth us to triumph in Christ, and maketh manifest the savour of his knowledge by us in every place. □

2 Corinthians 8:16, But **thanks** be to God, which put the same earnest care into the heart of Titus for you. □

2 Corinthians 9:15, **Thanks** be unto God for his unspeakable gift. □

Ephesians 5:4, Neither filthiness, nor foolish talking, nor jesting, which are not convenient: but rather giving of **thanks**. □

BLESSED *
BLESSING *
BLESS

DAY
AFTERNOON
90 DAY CHALLENGE

Genesis 12:2, And I will make of thee a great nation, and I will **bless** thee, and make thy name great; and thou shalt be a **blessing**. ☐

Genesis 22:17, That in **blessing** I will **bless** thee, and in multiplying I will multiply thy seed as the stars of the heaven, and as the sand which is upon the sea shore; and thy seed shall possess the gate of his enemies. ☐

Genesis 39:5, And it came to pass from the time that he had made him overseer in his house, and over all that he had, that the LORD **blessed** the Egyptian's house for Joseph's sake; and the **blessing** of the LORD was upon all that he had in the house, and in the field. ☐

Genesis 49:28, All these are the twelve tribes of Israel: and this is it that their father spake unto them, and **blessed** them; every one according to his **blessing** he **blessed** them. ☐

Exodus 32:29, For Moses had said, Consecrate yourselves to day to the LORD, even every man upon his son, and upon his brother; that he may bestow upon you a **blessing** this day. ☐

Deuteronomy 11:27, A **blessing**, if ye obey the commandments of the LORD your God, which I command you this day. ☐

Deuteronomy 16:17, Every man shall give as he is able, according to the **blessing** of the LORD thy God which he hath given thee. ☐

Deuteronomy 28:3, **Blessed** shalt thou be in the city, and **blessed** shalt thou be in the field. ☐

Deuteronomy 28:4, **Blessed** shall be the fruit of thy body, and the fruit of thy ground, and the fruit of thy cattle, the increase of thy kine, and the flocks of thy sheep. ☐

Deuteronomy 28:5, **Blessed** shall be thy basket and thy store. ☐

Deuteronomy 28:8, The LORD shall command the **blessing** upon thee in thy storehouses, and in all that thou settest thine hand unto; and he shall **bless** thee in the land which the LORD thy God giveth thee. ☐

Psalms 35:9, And my soul shall be **joyful** in the LORD: it shall rejoice in his salvation. ☐

Psalms 63:5, My soul shall be satisfied as with marrow and fatness; and my mouth shall praise thee with **joyful** lips. ☐

Psalms 81:1, Sing aloud unto God our strength: make a **joyful** noise unto the God of Jacob. ☐

Psalms 89:15, Blessed is the people that know the **joyful** sound: they shall walk, O LORD, in the light of thy countenance. ☐

Psalms 95:1, O come, let us sing unto the LORD: let us make a **joyful** noise to the rock of our salvation. ☐

Psalms 95:2, Let us come before his presence with thanksgiving, and make a **joyful** noise unto him with psalms. ☐

Psalms 96:12, Let the field be **joyful**, and all that is therein: then shall all the trees of the wood rejoice. ☐

Habakkuk 3:18, Yet I will rejoice in the LORD, I will **joy** in the God of my salvation. ☐

1 Thessalonians 1:6, And ye became followers of us, and of the Lord, having received the word in much affliction, with **joy** of the Holy Ghost. ☐

2 Timothy 1:4, Greatly desiring to see thee, being mindful of thy tears, that I may be filled with **joy**. ☐

Philemon 1:7, For we have great **joy** and consolation in thy love, because the bowels of the saints are refreshed by thee, brother. ☐

James 1:2, My brethren, count it all **joy** when ye fall into divers temptations. ☐

3 John 1:4, I have no greater **joy** than to hear that my children walk in truth. ☐

Psalms 94:22, But the LORD is my defence; and **my God** is the rock of my refuge. ☐

Psalms 102:24, I said, O **my God**, take me not away in the midst of my days: thy years are throughout all generations. ☐

Psalms 104:1, Bless the LORD, O my soul. O LORD **my God**, thou art very great; thou art clothed with honour and majesty. ☐

Psalms 104:33, I will sing unto the LORD as long as I live: I will sing praise to **my God** while I have my being. ☐

Psalms 109:26, Help me, O LORD **my God**: O save me according to thy mercy. ☐

Psalms 118:28, Thou art **my God**, and I will praise thee: thou art my God, I will exalt thee. ☐

Psalms 119:115, Depart from me, ye evildoers: for I will keep the commandments of **my God**. ☐

Psalms 140:6, I said unto the LORD, Thou art **my God**: hear the voice of my supplications, O LORD. ☐

Psalms 143:10, Teach me to do thy will; for thou art **my God**: thy spirit is good; lead me into the land of uprightness. ☐

Psalms 145:1, I will extol thee, **my God**, O king; and I will bless thy name for ever and ever. ☐

Psalms 146:2, While I live will I praise the LORD: I will sing praises unto **my God** while I have any being. ☐

Isaiah 25:1, O LORD, thou art **my God**; I will exalt thee, I will praise thy name; for thou hast done wonderful things; thy counsels of old are faithfulness and truth. ☐

In God We Trust
253

John 13:34, A new commandment I give unto you, That ye **love** one another; as I have **loved** you, that ye also **love** one another. ☐

John 15:9, As the Father hath **loved** me, so have I **loved** you: continue ye in my **love**. ☐

John 15:12, This is my commandment, That ye **love** one another, as I have **loved** you. ☐

Romans 8:37, Nay, in all these things we are more than conquerors through him that **loved** us. ☐

Galatians 2:20, I am crucified with Christ: nevertheless I live; yet not I, but Christ liveth in me: and the life which I now live in the flesh I live by the faith of the Son of God, who **loved** me, and gave himself for me. ☐

Ephesians 2:4, But God, who is rich in mercy, for his great **love** wherewith he **loved** us. ☐

Ephesians 5:2, And walk in **love**, as Christ also hath **loved** us, and hath given himself for us an offering and a sacrifice to God for a sweetsmelling savour. ☐

Ephesians 5:25, Husbands, **love** your wives, even as Christ also **loved** the church, and gave himself for it. ☐

2 Thessalonians 2:16, Now our Lord Jesus Christ himself, and God, even our Father, which hath **loved** us, and hath given us everlasting consolation and good hope through grace. ☐

Hebrews 1:9, Thou hast **loved** righteousness, and hated iniquity; therefore God, even thy God, hath anointed thee with the oil of gladness above thy fellows. ☐

1 John 4:10, Herein is **love**, not that we **loved** God, but that he **loved** us, and sent his Son to be the propitiation for our sins. ☐

1 John 4:11, Beloved, if God so **loved** us, we ought also to **love** one another. ☐

In God We Trust
254

Luke 6:23, Rejoice ye in that day, and leap for joy: for, behold, your reward is great in heaven: for in the like manner did their fathers unto the prophets. □

Luke 8:13, They on the rock are they, which, when they hear, receive the word with joy; and these have no root, which for a while believe, and in time of temptation fall away. □

Luke 15:10, Likewise, I say unto you, there is joy in the presence of the angels of God over one sinner that repenteth. □

John 15:11, These things have I spoken unto you, that my joy might remain in you, and that your joy might be full. □

John 16:20, Verily, verily, I say unto you, That ye shall weep and lament, but the world shall rejoice: and ye shall be sorrowful, but your sorrow shall be turned into joy. □

John 16:22, And ye now therefore have sorrow: but I will see you again, and your heart shall rejoice, and your joy no man taketh from you. □

John 16:24, Hitherto have ye asked nothing in my name: ask, and ye shall receive, that your joy may be full. □

John 17:13, And now come I to thee; and these things I speak in the world, that they might have my joy fulfilled in themselves. □

Acts 8:8, And there was great joy in that city. □

Acts 20:24, But none of these things move me, neither count I my life dear unto myself, so that I might finish my course with joy, and the ministry, which I have received of the Lord Jesus, to testify the gospel of the grace of God. □

Romans 14:17, For the kingdom of God is not meat and drink; but righteousness, and peace, and joy in the Holy Ghost. □

Psalms 119:13, With **my lips** have I declared all the judgments of thy mouth ☐

Psalms 119:108, Accept, I beseech thee, the freewill offerings of **my mouth**, O LORD, and teach me thy judgments. ☐

Psalms 145:21, **My mouth** shall speak the praise of the LORD: and let all flesh bless his holy name for ever and ever. ☐

Proverbs 4:5, Get wisdom, get understanding: forget it not; neither decline from the words of **my mouth**. ☐

Proverbs 5:7, Hear me now therefore, O ye children, and depart not from the words of **my mouth**. ☐

Isaiah 55:11, So shall my word be that goeth forth out of **my mouth**: it shall not return unto me void, but it shall accomplish that which I please, and it shall prosper in the thing whereto I sent it. ☐

Jeremiah 1:9, Then the LORD put forth his hand, and touched **my mouth**. And the LORD said unto me, Behold, I have put my words in thy mouth. ☐

Matthew 13:35, That it might be fulfilled which was spoken by the prophet, saying, I will open **my mouth** in parables; I will utter things which have been kept secret from the foundation of the world. ☐

Ephesians 6:19, And for me, that utterance may be given unto me, that I may open **my mouth** boldly, to make known the mystery of the gospel. ☐

In God We Trust
256

Psalms 119:2, **Blessed** are they that keep his testimonies, and that seek him with the whole heart. ☐

Psalms 119:12, **Blessed** art thou, O LORD: teach me thy statutes. ☐

Psalms 128:1, **Blessed** is every one that feareth the LORD; that walketh in his ways. ☐

Proverbs 10:7, The memory of the just is **blessed**: but the name of the wicked shall rot. ☐

Proverbs 10:22, The **blessing** of the LORD, it maketh rich, and he addeth no sorrow with it. ☐

Proverbs 11:11, By the **blessing** of the upright the city is exalted: but it is overthrown by the mouth of the wicked. ☐

Proverbs 11:26, He that withholdeth corn, the people shall curse him: but **blessing** shall be upon the head of him that selleth it. ☐

Proverbs 20:7, The just man walketh in his integrity: his children are **blessed** after him. ☐

Proverbs 22:9, He that hath a bountiful eye shall be **blessed**; for he giveth of his bread to the poor. ☐

Proverbs 24:25, But to them that rebuke him shall be delight, and a good **blessing** shall come upon them. ☐

Proverbs 31:28, Her children arise up, and call her **blessed**; her husband also, and he praiseth her. ☐

Isaiah 44:3, For I will pour water upon him that is thirsty, and floods upon the dry ground: I will pour my spirit upon thy seed, and my **blessing** upon thine offspring. ☐

Isaiah 56:2, **Blessed** is the man that doeth this, and the son of man that layeth hold on it; that keepeth the sabbath from polluting it, and keepeth his hand from doing any evil. ☐

Job 22:29, When men are cast down, then thou shalt say, There is lifting up; and he shall save the **humble** person. ☐

Proverbs 15:33, The fear of the LORD is the instruction of wisdom; and before honour is **humility**. ☐

Proverbs 18:12, Before destruction the heart of man is haughty, and before honour is **humility**. ☐

Proverbs 22:4, By **humility** and the fear of the LORD are riches, and honour, and life. ☐

Isaiah 57:15, For thus saith the high and lofty One that inhabiteth eternity, whose name is Holy; I dwell in the high and holy place, with him also that is of a contrite and **humble** spirit, to revive the spirit of the **humble**, and to revive the heart of the contrite ones. ☐

Matthew 18:4, Whosoever therefore shall **humble** himself as this little child, the same is greatest in the kingdom of heaven. ☐

Matthew 23:12, And whosoever shall exalt himself shall be abased; and he that shall **humble** himself shall be exalted. ☐

Acts 20:19, Serving the Lord with all **humility** of mind, and with many tears, and temptations, which befell me by the lying in wait of the Jews. ☐

James 4:6, But he giveth more grace. Wherefore he saith, God resisteth the proud, but giveth grace unto the **humble**. ☐

James 4:10, **Humble** yourselves in the sight of the Lord, and he shall lift you up. ☐

1 Peter 5:5, Likewise, ye younger, submit yourselves unto the elder. Yea, all of you be subject one to another, and be clothed with **humility**: for God resisteth the proud, and giveth grace to the **humble**. ☐

1 Peter 5:6, **Humble** yourselves therefore under the mighty hand of God, that he may exalt you in due time. ☐

In God We Trust

John 5:19, Then answered Jesus and said unto them, **Verily, verily**, I say unto you, The Son can do nothing of himself, but what he seeth the Father do: for what things soever he doeth, these also doeth the Son likewise. ☐

John 5:24, **Verily, verily**, I say unto you, He that heareth my word, and believeth on him that sent me, hath everlasting life, and shall not come into condemnation; but is passed from death unto life. ☐

John 5:25, **Verily, verily**, I say unto you, The hour is coming, and now is, when the dead shall hear the voice of the Son of God: and they that hear shall live. ☐

John 6:32, Then Jesus said unto them, **Verily, verily**, I say unto you, Moses gave you not that bread from heaven; but my Father giveth you the true bread from heaven. ☐

John 8:51, **Verily, verily**, I say unto you, If a man keep my saying, he shall never see death. ☐

John 8:58, Jesus said unto them, **Verily, verily**, I say unto you, Before Abraham was, I am. ☐

John 13:16, **Verily, verily**, I say unto you, The servant is not greater than his lord; neither he that is sent greater than he that sent him. ☐

John 13:38, Jesus answered him, Wilt thou lay down thy life for my sake? **Verily, verily**, I say unto thee, The cock shall not crow, till thou hast denied me thrice. ☐

John 14:12, **Verily, verily**, I say unto you, He that believeth on me, the works that I do shall he do also; and greater works than these shall he do; because I go unto my Father. ☐

John 16:23, And in that day ye shall ask me nothing. **Verily, verily**, I say unto you, Whatsoever ye shall ask the Father in my name, he will give it you. ☐

Proverbs 22:17, Bow down thine ear, and hear the words of the wise, and apply thine heart unto my **knowledge**. ☐

Proverbs 22:20, Have not I written to thee excellent things in counsels and **knowledge**, ☐

Proverbs 23:12, Apply thine heart unto instruction, and thine ears to the words of **knowledge**. ☐

Proverbs 24:4, And by **knowledge** shall the chambers be filled with all precious and pleasant riches. ☐

Proverbs 24:5, A wise man is strong; yea, a man of **knowledge** increaseth strength. ☐

Proverbs 24:14 So shall the **knowledge** of wisdom be unto thy soul: when thou hast found it, then there shall be a reward, and thy expectation shall not be cut off. ☐

Proverbs 28:2 For the transgression of a land many are the princes thereof: but by a man of understanding and **knowledge** the state thereof shall be prolonged. ☐

Ecclesiastes 1:16, I communed with mine own heart, saying, Lo, I am come to great estate, and have gotten more wisdom than all they that have been before me in Jerusalem: yea, my heart had great experience of wisdom and **knowledge**. ☐

Ecclesiastes 1:18, For in much wisdom is much grief: and he that increaseth **knowledge** increaseth sorrow. ☐

Ecclesiastes 2:26, For God giveth to a man that is good in his sight wisdom, and **knowledge**, and joy: but to the sinner he giveth travail, to gather and to heap up, that he may give to him that is good before God. This also is vanity and vexation of spirit. ☐

Ecclesiastes 7:12, For wisdom is a defence, and money is a defence: but the excellency of **knowledge** is, that wisdom giveth life to them that have it. ☐

In God We Trust
260

POOR *
RICH *
RICHES

87 DAY

EVENING
90 DAY CHALLENGE

Psalms 86:1, Bow down thine ear, O LORD, hear me: for I am **poor** and needy. □

Psalms 107:41, Yet setteth he the **poor** on high from affliction, and maketh him families like a flock. □

Psalms 109:16, Because that he remembered not to shew mercy, but persecuted the **poor** and needy man, that he might even slay the broken in heart. □

Psalms 109:22, For I am **poor** and needy, and my heart is wounded within me. □

Proverbs 10:4, He becometh **poor** that dealeth with a slack hand: but the hand of the diligent maketh **rich**. □

Proverbs 10:15, The **rich** man's wealth is his strong city: the destruction of the **poor** is their poverty. □

Proverbs 13:7, There is that maketh himself **rich**, yet hath nothing: there is that maketh himself **poor**, yet hath great **riches**. □

Proverbs 14:20, The **poor** is hated even of his own neighbour: but the **rich** hath many friends. □

Proverbs 14:21, He that despiseth his neighbour sinneth: but he that hath mercy on the **poor**, happy is he. □

Proverbs 14:31, He that oppresseth the **poor** reproacheth his Maker: but he that honoureth him hath mercy on the **poor**. □

Proverbs 18:23, The **poor** useth entreaties; but the **rich** answereth roughly. □

Proverbs 21:17, He that loveth pleasure shall be a **poor** man: he that loveth wine and oil shall not be **rich**. □

Proverbs 22:2, The **rich** and **poor** meet together: the LORD is the maker of them all. □

In God We Trust

Psalms 34:1, I will bless the LORD at all times: his praise shall continually be in my mouth. ☐

Psalms 34:11, Come, ye children, hearken unto me: I will teach you the fear of the LORD. ☐

Psalms 35:18, I will give thee thanks in the great congregation: I will praise thee among much people. ☐

Psalms 38:18, For I will declare mine iniquity; I will be sorry for my sin. ☐

Psalms 39:1, I said, I will take heed to my ways, that I sin not with my tongue: I will keep my mouth with a bridle, while the wicked is before me. ☐

Psalms 42:9, I will say unto God my rock, Why hast thou forgotten me? why go I mourning because of the oppression of the enemy? ☐

Psalms 44:6, For I will not trust in my bow, neither shall my sword save me. ☐

Psalms 45:17, I will make thy name to be remembered in all generations: therefore shall the people praise thee for ever and ever. ☐

Psalms 46:10, Be still, and know that I am God: I will be exalted among the heathen, I will be exalted in the earth. ☐

Psalms 49:4, I will incline mine ear to a parable: I will open my dark saying upon the harp. ☐

Psalms 50:7, Hear, O my people, and I will speak; O Israel, and I will testify against thee: I am God, even thy God. ☐

Psalms 50:8, I will not reprove thee for thy sacrifices or thy burnt offerings, to have been continually before me. ☐

Psalms 50:15, And call upon me in the day of trouble: I will deliver thee, and thou shalt glorify me. ☐

Deuteronomy 28:6, **Blessed** shalt thou be when thou comest in, and **blessed** shalt thou be when thou goest out. ☐

Judges 13:24, And the woman bare a son, and called his name Samson: and the child grew, and the LORD **blessed** him. ☐

Psalms 1:1, **Blessed** is the man that walketh not in the counsel of the ungodly, nor standeth in the way of sinners, nor sitteth in the seat of the scornful. ☐

Psalms 2:12, Kiss the Son, lest he be angry, and ye perish from the way, when his wrath is kindled but a little. **Blessed** are all they that put their trust in him. ☐

Psalms 3:8, Salvation belongeth unto the LORD: thy **blessing** is upon thy people. Selah. ☐

Psalms 18:46, The LORD liveth; and **blessed** be my rock; and let the God of my salvation be exalted. ☐

Psalms 21:6, For thou hast made him most **blessed** for ever: thou hast made him exceeding glad with thy countenance. ☐

Psalms 24:5, He shall receive the **blessing** from the LORD, and righteousness from the God of his salvation. ☐

Psalms 28:6, **Blessed** be the LORD, because he hath heard the voice of my supplications. ☐

Psalms 31:21, **Blessed** be the LORD: for he hath shewed me his marvellous kindness in a strong city. ☐

Psalms 32:1, **Blessed** is he whose transgression is forgiven, whose sin is covered. ☐

Psalms 32:2, **Blessed** is the man unto whom the LORD imputeth not iniquity, and in whose spirit there is no guile. ☐

Psalms 118:19, Open to me the gates of righteousness: **I will** go into them, and **I will** praise the LORD. ☐

Psalms 118:21, **I will** praise thee: for thou hast heard me, and art become my salvation. ☐

Psalms 118:28, Thou art my God, and **I will** praise thee: thou art my God, **I will** exalt thee. ☐

Psalms 119:7, **I will** praise thee with uprightness of heart, when I shall have learned thy righteous judgments. ☐

Psalms 119:8, **I will** keep thy statutes: O forsake me not utterly. ☐

Psalms 119:15, **I will** meditate in thy precepts, and have respect unto thy ways. ☐

Psalms 119:16, **I will** delight myself in thy statutes: **I will** not forget thy word. ☐

Psalms 119:32, **I will** run the way of thy commandments, when thou shalt enlarge my heart. ☐

Psalms 119:45, And **I will** walk at liberty: for I seek thy precepts. ☐

Psalms 119:46, **I will** speak of thy testimonies also before kings, and will not be ashamed. ☐

Psalms 119:47, And **I will** delight myself in thy commandments, which I have loved. ☐

Psalms 119:48, My hands also will I lift up unto thy commandments, which I have loved; and **I will** meditate in thy statutes. ☐

Psalms 119:62, At midnight **I will** rise to give thanks unto thee because of thy righteous judgments. ☐

Psalms 119:69, The proud have forged a lie against me: but **I will** keep thy precepts with my whole heart. ☐

Proverbs 16:19, **Better** it is to be of an humble spirit with the lowly, than to divide the spoil with the proud. ☐

Proverbs 16:32, He that is slow to anger is **better** than the mighty; and he that ruleth his spirit than he that taketh a city. ☐

Proverbs 17:1, **Better** is a dry morsel, and quietness therewith, than an house full of sacrifices with strife. ☐

Proverbs 19:1, **Better** is the poor that walketh in his integrity, than he that is perverse in his lips, and is a fool. ☐

Proverbs 19:22, The desire of a man is his kindness: and a poor man is **better** than a liar. ☐

Proverbs 27:5, Open rebuke is **better** than secret love. ☐

Proverbs 28:6, **Better** is the poor that walketh in his uprightness, than he that is perverse in his ways, though he be rich. ☐

Ecclesiastes 7:3, Sorrow is **better** than laughter: for by the sadness of the countenance the heart is made **better**. ☐

Ecclesiastes 7:5, It is **better** to hear the rebuke of the wise, than for a man to hear the song of fools. ☐

1 Peter 3:17, For it is **better**, if the will of God be so, that ye suffer for well doing, than for evil doing. ☐

MORE SEED,
MORE FAITH

In God We Trust
265

Psalm 119:66, Teach me good judgment and **knowledge**: for I have believed thy commandments. ☐

Psalm 139:6, Such **knowledge** is too wonderful for me; it is high, I cannot attain unto it. ☐

Proverbs 1:4, To give subtilty to the simple, to the young man **knowledge** and discretion. ☐

Proverbs 1:22, How long, ye simple ones, will ye love simplicity? and the scorners delight in their scorning, and fools hate **knowledge?** ☐

Proverbs 2:3, Yea, if thou criest after **knowledge**, and liftest up thy voice for understanding; ☐

Proverbs 2:5, Then shalt thou understand the fear of the Lord, and find the **knowledge** of God. ☐

Proverbs 2:6, For the Lord giveth wisdom: out of his mouth cometh **knowledge** and understanding. ☐

Proverbs 2:10, When wisdom entereth into thine heart, and **knowledge** is pleasant unto thy soul; ☐

Proverbs 5:2, That thou mayest regard discretion, and that thy lips may keep **knowledge.** ☐

Proverbs 8:9, They are all plain to him that understandeth, and right to them that find **knowledge.** ☐

Proverbs 8:10, Receive my instruction, and not silver; and **knowledge** rather than choice gold. ☐

Proverbs 8:12, I wisdom dwell with prudence, and find out **knowledge** of witty inventions. ☐

Proverbs 10:14, Wise men lay up **knowledge**: but the mouth of the foolish is near destruction. ☐

Deuteronomy 10:12, And now, Israel, what doth the LORD thy God require of thee, but to fear the LORD thy God, to walk in all his ways, and to love him, and to **serve the LORD** thy God with all thy heart and with all thy soul. ☐

Joshua 24:15, And if it seem evil unto you to serve the LORD, choose you this day whom ye will serve; whether the gods which your fathers served that were on the other side of the flood, or the gods of the Amorites, in whose land ye dwell: but as for me and my house, we will **serve the LORD**. ☐

Joshua 24:21, And the people said unto Joshua, Nay; but we will **serve the LORD**. ☐

1 Samuel 12:20, And Samuel said unto the people, Fear not: ye have done all this wickedness: yet turn not aside from following the LORD, but **serve the Lord** with all your heart. ☐

Psalms 2:11, **Serve the LORD** with fear, and rejoice with trembling. ☐

Psalms 100:2, **Serve the LORD** with gladness: come before his presence with singing. ☐

Psalms 102:22, When the people are gathered together, and the kingdoms, to **serve the LORD**. ☐

Jeremiah 30:9, But they shall **serve the LORD** their God, and David their king, whom I will raise up unto them. ☐

Colossians 3:24, Knowing that of the Lord ye shall receive the reward of the inheritance: for ye **serve the Lord** Christ. ☐

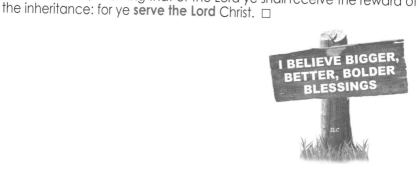

In God We Trust

Psalm 73:22, So foolish was I, and **ignorant**: I was as a beast before thee. ☐

Act 4:13, Now when they saw the boldness of Peter and John, and perceived that they were unlearned and **ignorant** men, they marvelled; and they took knowledge of them, that they had been with Jesus. ☐

Romans: 1:13, Now I would not have you **ignorant**, brethren, that oftentimes I purposed to come unto you, (but was let hitherto,) that I might have some fruit among you also, even as among other Gentiles. ☐

Romans: 10:3, For they being **ignorant** of God's righteousness, and going about to establish their own righteousness, have not submitted themselves unto the righteousness of God. ☐

Romans 11:25; For I would not, brethren, that ye should be **ignorant** of this mystery, lest ye should be wise in your own conceits; that blindness in part is happened to Israel, until the fulness of the Gentiles be come in. ☐

1 Corinthians 12:1, Now concerning spiritual gifts, brethren, I would not have you **ignorant**. ☐

2 Corinthians 2:11, Lest Satan should get an advantage of us: for we are not **ignorant** of his devices. ☐

1 Thessalonians 4:13, But I would not have you to be **ignorant**, brethren, concerning them which are asleep, that ye sorrow not, even as others which have no hope. ☐

1 Peter 1:14, As obedient children, not fashioning yourselves according to the former lusts in your **ignorance**: ☐

1 Peter 2:15, For so is the will of God, that with well doing ye may put to silence the **ignorance** of foolish men: ☐

READ
PSALM 119:11

In God We Trust

Proverbs 12:1, Whoso loveth instruction loveth **knowledge:** but he that hateth reproof is brutish. ☐

Proverbs 12:23, A prudent man concealeth **knowledge:** but the heart of fools proclaimeth foolishness. ☐

Proverbs 13:16, Every prudent man dealeth with **knowledge:** but a fool layeth open his folly. ☐

Proverbs 14:18, The simple inherit folly: but the prudent are crowned with **knowledge.** ☐

Proverbs 15:2, The tongue of the wise useth **knowledge** aright: but the mouth of fools poureth out foolishness. ☐

Proverbs 15:7, The lips of the wise disperse **knowledge:** but the heart of the foolish doeth not so. ☐

Proverbs 15:14, The heart of him that hath understanding seeketh **knowledge:** but the mouth of fools feedeth on foolishness. ☐

Proverbs 17:27, He that hath **knowledge** spareth his words: and a man of understanding is of an excellent spirit. ☐

Proverbs 18:15, The heart of the prudent getteth **knowledge**; and the ear of the wise seeketh **knowledge.** ☐

Proverbs 19:2, Also, that the soul be without **knowledge**, it is not good; and he that hasteth with his feet sinneth. ☐

Proverbs 19:27, Cease, my son, to hear the instruction that causeth to err from the words of **knowledge.** ☐

Proverbs 20:15, There is gold, and a multitude of rubies: but the lips of **knowledge** are a precious jewel. ☐

Proverbs 22:12, The eyes of the Lord preserve **knowledge**, and he overthroweth the words of the transgressor. ☐

Daniel 9:9, To the Lord our God belong mercies and **forgivenesses**, though we have rebelled against him. ☐

Acts 5:31, Him hath God exalted with his right hand to be a Prince and a Saviour, for to give repentance to Israel, and **forgiveness** of sins. ☐

Acts 13:38, Be it known unto you therefore, men and brethren, that through this man is preached unto you the **forgiveness** of sins. ☐

Colossians 1:14, In whom we have redemption through his blood, even the **forgiveness** of sins. ☐

Colossians 2:13, And you, being dead in your sins and the uncircumcision of your flesh, hath he quickened together with him, having **forgiven** you all trespasses. ☐

James 5:15, And the prayer of faith shall save the sick, and the Lord shall raise him up; and if he have committed sins, they shall be **forgiven** him. ☐

1 John 2:12, I write unto you, little children, because your sins are **forgiven** you for his name's sake. ☐

In God We Trust

NOAH WEBSTER

Webster's American Dictionary of the
English Language, 1828 Edition

"The Bible must be considered as the great source
of all the truth by which men are to be guided in
government as well as in all social transactions."

NOAH WEBSTER

"Education is useless without the Bible. The Bible was
America's basic text book in all fields. God's Word,
contained in the Bible, has furnished all neccesary
rules to direct our conduct. "

NOAH WEBSTER

WWW.WEBSTERDICTIONARY1828.COM

Believe

BELIE'VE, verb transitive To credit upon the authority or testimony of another; to be persuaded of the truth of something upon the declaration of another, or upon evidence furnished by reasons, arguments, and deductions of the mind, or by other circumstances, than personal knowledge. When we believe upon the authority of another, we always put confidence in his veracity.

When we believe upon the authority of reasoning, arguments, or a concurrence of facts and circumstances, we rest our conclusions upon their strength or probability, their agreement with our own experience, etc.

2. To expect or hope with confidence; to trust. I had fainted, unless I had believed to see the goodness of the Lord in the land of the living. Psalms 27:13.

BELIE'VE, verb intransitive To have a firm persuasion of any thing.

In some cases, to have full persuasion, approaching to certainty; in others, more doubt is implied. It is often followed by in or on, especially in the scriptures. To believe in, is to hold as the object of faith. 'Ye believe in God, believe also in me.' John 14:1. To believe on, is to trust, to place full confidence in, to rest upon with faith. 'To them gave he power to become the sons of God, even to them that

believe on his name.' John 1:7. Johnson. But there is no ground for much distinction.

In theology, to believe sometimes expresses a mere assent of the understanding to the truths of the gospel; as in the case of Simon. Acts 8:37. In others, the word implies, with this assent of the mind, a yielding of the will and affections, accompanied with a humble reliance on Christ for salvation .John 1:12. John 3:15.

In popular use and familiar discourse, to believe often expresses an opinion in a vague manner, without a very exact estimate of evidence, noting a mere preponderance of opinion, and is nearly equivalent to think or suppose.

Better

BET'TER, a comparative of bet. See Best.

1. Having good qualities in a greater degree than another; applied to physical, acquired or moral qualities; as a better soil, a better man, a better physician, a better house, a better air, a better harvest.

2. More advantageous. Were it not better for us to return to Egypt: Exodus 14:12.

3. More acceptable. To obey is better than sacrifice. 1 Samuel 15:22.

4. More safe. It is better to trust in the Lord, than to put confidence in man. Psalms 118:8.

5. Improved in health; less affected with disease; as, the patient is better

6. To be better off, to be in a better

ondition. Beddoes, Hygeia. This is a very common phrase; but ought
ot off, to be of? It is not elegant.

To have the better is to have the advantage or superiority, followed
y of before him or that over which the advantage is enjoyed; as, the
nglish had the better of the Spaniards.

To get or gain the better is to obtain the advantage, superiority or
ctory; as, to get the better of an enemy.

For the better is for the advantage or improvement.

ET'TER, adverb In a more excellent manner; with more skill and wisdom,
rtue, advantage or success; as, to perform work better; to plan a
cheme better; land better cultivated; laws better executed;
overnment better
dministered.

More correctly, or fully; as, to understand a subject better than another.

With superior excellence; as, to write or speak better than another.

With more affection; in a higher degree; as, to love one better than
nother.

is not easy to specify and exemplify the various applications of better
general, it implies what is more excellent, advantageous, useful, or
rtuous, than something else.

ET'TER, verb transitive

To improve; to meliorate; to increase the good qualities of; as, manure
etters land; discipline may better the morals.

To surpass; to exceed.

he works of nature do always aim at that which cannot be bettered.
u., is not the sense, made better:

To advance; to support; to give advantage to; as, to better a party; to
etter a cause.

ET'TER, noun A superior; one who has a claim to precedence on
ccount of his rank, age, or office; as, give place to your betters. It is
enerally or always used in the plural.

essed

LESS'ED, participle passive Made happy or prosperous; extolled;
ronounced happy.

LESS'ED, adjective Happy; prosperous in
orldly affairs; enjoying spiritual happiness and the favor of God;
njoying heavenly felicity.

essed-Thistle. A plant of the genus Cnicus, sometimes used in
ecoctions, for a bitter.

essed

LESS'ED, participle passive Made happy or prosperous; extolled;
ronounced happy.

LESS'ED, adjective Happy; prosperous in worldly affairs; enjoying spiritual

happiness and the favor of God; enjoying heavenly felicity.
Blessed-Thistle. A plant of the genus Cnicus, sometimes used in decoctions, for a bitter.

Blessing
BLESS'ING, participle present tense Making happy; wishing happiness to; praising or extolling; consecrating by prayer.
BLESS'ING,noun Benediction; a wish of happiness pronounced; a prayer imploring happiness upon another.
1. A solemn prophetic benediction, in which happiness is desired, invoked or foretold.
This is the blessing wherewith Moses--blessed the children of Israel. Deuteronomy 33:1.
2. Any means of happiness; a gift, benefit or advantage; that which promotes temporal prosperity and welfare, or secures immortal felicity.
A just and pious magistrate is a public blessing The divine favor is the greatest blessing
3. Among the Jews, a present; a gift; either because it was attended with kind wishes for the welfare of the giver, or because it was the means of increasing happiness.
Take, I pray thee, my blessing that is brought to thee. Genesis 33:11.

Cheerful
CHEERFUL, adjective
1. Lively; animated; having good spirits; moderately joyful. This is the most usual signification of the word, expressing a degree of animation less than mirth and jollity.
2. Full of life; gay; animated; mirthful; musical; as the cheerful birds.
3. Expressive of good spirits or joy; lively; animated.
A merry heart maketh a cheerful countenance. Proverbs 15:13.

Cheerfulness
CHEERFULNESS, noun Life; animation; good spirits; a state of moderate joy or gayety; alacrity.
He that showeth mercy, with cheerfulness Romans 12:8.

Christ
CHRIST, noun THE ANOINTED; an appellation given to the Savior of the World, and synonymous with the Hebrew Messiah. It was a custom of antiquity to consecrate persons to the sacerdotal and regal offices by anointing them with oil.

compassion

COMPASSION, noun

. A suffering with another; painful sympathy; a sensation of sorrow excited
y the distress or misfortunes of another; pity; commiseration. compassion is
 mixed passion, compounded of love and sorrow; at least some portion of
ove generally attends the pain or regret, or is excited by it. Extreme distress
f an enemy even changes enmity into at least temporary affection.
e being full of compassion forgave their iniquity. Psalms 78:38.
is father had compassion and ran, and fell on his neck, and kissed him.
Luke 15:20. COMPASSION, verb transitive To pity.

correct

CORRECT, adjective [Latin , to set right; right, straight. See Right.] Literally,
et right, or made straight. Hence, right; conformable to truth, rectitude
r propriety, or conformable to a just standard; not faulty; free from error.
correct edition of a book is exactly according to the original copy.
orrect manners correspond with the rules of morality and received
otions of decorum. correct principles coincide with the truth. correct
anguage is agreeable to established usage.

ORRECT, verb transitive

. To make right; to rectify; to bring to the standard of truth, justice, or
ropriety; as, to correct manners or principles. Hence,

. To amend; to remove or retrench faults or errors; to set right; as, to
orrect a book; to correct a copy for the press; or in printing, to correct
e press, or errors of the press.

. To bring back or attempt to bring back to
ropriety in morals; to punish for faults or deviations from moral rectitude;
o chastise; to discipline; as, a child should be corrected for lying.
ORRECT thy son, and he shall give thee rest. Proverbs 29:17.

. To obviate or remove whatever is wrong or inconvenient; to reduce
r change the qualities of any thing by mixture, or other application;
o counteract whatever is injurious; as, to correct the acidity of the
omach by alkaline preparations; to correct the relaxing quality of water
y

correction

CORRECTION, noun [Latin]

. The act of correcting; the act of bringing back, from error or deviation, to
 just standard, as to truth, rectitude, justice or propriety; as the correction
f opinions or manners. All scripture is profitable for correction 2 Timothy 3:16.

. Retrenchment of faults or errors; amendment; as the correction of a
ook, or of the press. 3. That which is substituted in the place of what is
rong; as the corrections of a copy are numerous; set the corrections in

Correction continue . . .

the margin of a proof-sheet.

4. That which is intended to rectify, or to cure faults; punishment; discipline; chastisement; that which corrects.

Withhold not correction from the child. Proverbs 23:13.

5. In scriptural language, whatever tends to correct the moral conduct, and bring back from error or sin, as afflictions.

They have refused to receive correction Jeremiah 5:3.

My son, despise not the chastening of the Lord, nor be weary of his correction Proverbs 3:11.

6. Critical notice; animadversion.

7. Abatement of noxious qualities; the counteraction of what is inconvenient or hurtful in its effects; as the correction of acidity in the stomach.

House of correction a house where disorderly persons are confined; a bridewell.

Covenant

COVENANT, noun [L, to come; a coming together; a meeting or agreement of minds.]

1. A mutual consent or agreement of two or more persons, to do or to forbear some act or thing; a contract; stipulation. A covenant is created by deed in writing, sealed and executed; or it may be implied in the contract.

2. A writing containing the terms of agreement or contract between parties; or the clause of agreement in a deed containing the covenant

3. In theology, the covenant of works, is that implied in the commands, prohibitions, and promises of God; the promise of God to man, that mans perfect obedience should entitle him to happiness. This do, and live; that do, and die. The covenant of redemption, is the mutual agreement between the Father and Son, respecting the redemption of sinners by Christ The covenant of grace, is that by which God engages to bestow salvation on man, upon the condition that man shall believe in Christ and yield obedience to the terms of the gospel.

4. In church affairs, a solemn agreement between the members of a church, that they will walk together according to the precepts of the gospel, in brotherly affection.

COVENANT, verb intransitive To enter into a formal agreement; to stipulate; to bind ones self by contract. A covenants with B to convey to him a certain estate. When the terms are expressed ti has for before the thing or price.

They covenanted with him for thirty pieces of silver. Matthew 26:15.

COVENANT, verb transitive To grant or promise by covenant

eclare

DECLA'RE, verb transitive [Latin to make clear.]

. To clear; to free from obscurity; to make plain.

. To make known; to tell explicitly; to manifest or communicate plainly to thers by words. I will declare what he hath done for my soul. Psalms 66:16.

. To make known; to show to the eye or to the understanding; to exhibit; o manifest by other means than words. The heavens declare the glory of God. Psalms 19:1.

. To publish; to proclaim. Declare his glory among the heathen. Chronicles 16:24. Declaring the conversion of the Gentiles. Acts 15:4.

. To assert; to affirm; as, he declares the story to be false.

o declare one's self, to throw off reserve and avow one's opinion; to show penly what one thinks, or which side he espouses.

DECLA'RE, verb intransitive

. To make a declaration; to proclaim or avow some opinion or resolution n favor or in opposition; to make known explicitly some determination; with for or against; as, the prince declared for the allies; the allied powers eclared against France. Like fawning courtiers, for success they wait; nd then come smiling, and declare for fate.

. In law, to recite the causes of complaint against the defendant; as, he plaintiff declares in debt or trespass.

. To show or manifest the issue or event; to decide in favor of; as, victory ad not declared for either party.

ominion

DOMINION, noun [Latin See Dominant.]

. Sovereign or supreme authority; the power of governing and controlling. he dominion of the Most High is an everlasting dominion Daniel 4:3.

. Power to direct, control, use and dispose of at pleasure; right of possession nd use without being accountable; as the private dominion of individuals.

. Territory under a government; region; country; district governed, or within he limits of the authority of a prince or state; as the British dominions.

. Government; right of governing. Jamaica is under the dominion of reat Britain.

. Predominance; ascendant.

. An order of angels. Whether they be thrones, or dominions, or principalities, or powers. olossians 1:16.

. Persons governed. Judah was his sanctuary; Israel his dominion salms 114:2.

nemy

N'EMY, noun [Latin inimicus.]

. A foe; an adversary. A private enemy is one who hates another and

Enemy continue . . .

wishes him injury, or attempts to do him injury to gratify his own malice or ill will. A public enemy or foe, is one who belongs to a nation or party, at war with another.

I way to you, love your enemies. Matthew 5:43.

Enemies in war; in peace friends.

2. One who hates or dislikes; as an enemy to truth or falsehood.

3. In theology, and by way of eminence, the enemy is the Devil; the archfiend.

4. In military affairs, the opposing army or naval force in war, is called the enemy

Excellent

EX'CELLENT, adjective Being of great virtue or worth; eminent or distinguished for what is amiable, valuable or laudable; as an excellent man or citizen; an excellent judge or magistrate.

1. Being of great value or use, applied to things; remarkable for good properties; as excellent timber; an excellent farm; an excellent horse; excellent fruit.

2. Distinguished for superior attainments; as an excellent artist.

3. Consummate; complete; in an ill sense.

Elizabeth was an excellent hypocrite.

Faith

FAITH, noun [Latin fides, fido, to trust; Gr. to persuade, to draw towards any thing, to conciliate; to believe, to obey. In the Greek. Lexicon of Hederic it is said, the primitive signification of the verb is to bind and draw or lead, as signifies a rope or cable. But this remark is a little incorrect. The sense of the verb, from which that of rope and binding is derived, is to strain, to draw, and thus to bind or make fast. A rope or cable is that which makes fast. Heb.

1. Belief; the assent of the mind to the truth of what is declared by another, resting on his authority and veracity, without other evidence; the judgment that what another states or testifies is the truth. I have strong faith or no faithin the testimony of a witness, or in what a historian narrates.

2. The assent of the mind to the truth of a proposition advanced by another; belief, or probable evidence of any kind.

3. In theology, the assent of the mind or understanding to the truth of what God has revealed. Simple belief of the scriptures, of the being and perfections of God, and of the existence, character and doctrines of Christ, founded on the testimony of the sacred writers, is called historical or speculative faith; afaith little distinguished from the belief of the existence and achievements of Alexander or of Cesar.

4. Evangelical, justifying, or saving faith is the assent of the mind to the truth of divine revelation, on the authority of God's testimony, accompanied with

a cordial assent of the will or approbation of the heart; an entire confidence or trust in God's character and declarations, and in the character and doctrines of Christ, with an unreserved surrender of the will to his guidance, and dependence on his merits for salvation. In other words, that firm belief of God's testimony, and of the truth of the gospel, which influences the will, and leads to an entire reliance on Christ for salvation. Being justified by faith Romans 5:1. Without faith it is impossible to please God. Hebrews 11:1. For we walk by faith and not by sight. 2 Corinthians 5:7. With the heart man believeth to righteousness. Romans 10:6. The faith of the gospel is that emotion of the mind, which is called trust or confidence, exercised towards the moral character of God, and particularly of the Savior.

FAITH is an affectionate practical confidence in the testimony of God. FAITH is a firm, cordial belief in the veracity of God, in all the declarations of his word; or a full and affectionate confidence in the certainty of those things which God has declared, and because he has declared them.

5. The object of belief; a doctrine or system of doctrines believed; a system of revealed truths received by christians. They heard only, that he who persecuted us in times past, now preacheth the faith which once he destroyed. Galatians 1:23.

6. The promises of God, or his truth and faithfulness. shall their unbelief make the faith of God without effect? Rom 3.

7. An open profession of gospel truth. Your faith is spoken of throughout the whole world. Rom 1.

8. A persuasion or belief of the lawfulness of things indifferent. Hast thou faith? Have it to thyself before God. Rom 14.

9. Faithfulness; fidelity; a strict adherence to duty and fulfillment of promises. Her failing, while her faith to me remains, I would conceal.

Follow

FOL'LOW, verb transitive

1. To go after or behind; to walk, ride or move behind, but in the same direction. Soldiers will usually follow a brave officer.

2. To pursue; to chase; as an enemy, or as game.

3. To accompany; to attend in a journey. And Rebekah arose, and her damsels, and they rode on the camels, and followed the man. Genesis 24:5.

4. To accompany; to be of the same company; to attend, for any purpose. Luke 5:27.

5. To succeed in order of time; to come after; as a storm is followed by a calm. Signs following signs lead on the mighty year.

6. To be consequential; to result from, as effect from a cause. Intemperance is often followed by disease or poverty, or by both.

Follow continue . . .

7. To result from, as an inference or deduction. It follows from these facts that the accused is guilty.

8. To pursue with the eye; to keep the eyes fixed on a moving body. He followed or his eyes followed the ship, till it was beyond sight. He followed with his eyes the fleeting shade.

9. To imitate; to copy; as, to follow a pattern or model; to follow fashion.

10. To embrace; to adopt and maintain; to have or entertain like opinions; to think or believe like another; as, to follow the opinions and tenets of a philsophic sect; to follow Plato.

11. To obey; to observe; to practice; to act in conformity to. It is our duty to follow the commands of Christ. Good soldiers follow the orders of their general; good servants follow the directions of their master.

12. To pursue as an object of desire; to endeavor to obtain. Follow peace with all men. Hebrews 12:14.

13. To use; to practice; to make the chief business; as, to follow the trade of a carpenter; to follow the profession of law.

14. To adhere to; to side with. The house of Judah followed David. 2 Samuel 2:10.

15. To adhere to; to honor; to worship; to serve. If the Lord be God, follow him. 1 Kings 18:21.

16. To be led or guided by. Wo to the foolish prophets, who follow their own spirit, and have seen nothing. Ezekiel 13:3.

17. To move on in the same course or direction; to be guided by; as, to follow a track or course. FOL'LOW, verb intransitive

1. To come after another.
The famine - shall follow close after you. Jeremiah 42:16.

2. To attend; to accompany.

3. To be posterior in time; as following ages.

4. To be consequential, as effect to cause. From such measures, great mischiefs must follow

5. To result, as an inference. The facts may be admitted, but the inference drawn from them does not follow. To follow on, to continue pursuit or endeavor; to persevere. Then shall we know, if we follow on to know the Lord. Hosea 6.

Fool

FOOL, noun [Heb.]

1. One who is destitute of reason, or the common powers of understanding; an idiot. Some persons are born fools, and are called natural fools; others may become fools by some injury done to the brain.

2. In common language, a person who is somewhat deficient in intellect, but not an idiot; or a person who acts absurdly; one who does not exercise his reason; one who pursues a course contrary to the dictates of wisdom.

Fool continue . . .

Experience keeps a dear school, but fools will learn in no other.

3. In scripture, fool is often used for a wicked or depraved person; one who acts contrary to sound wisdom in his moral deportment; one who follows his own inclinations, who prefers trifling and temporary pleasures to the service of God and eternal happiness. The fool hath said in his heart, there is no God. Psalms 14:1.

4. A weak christian; a godly person who has much remaining sin and unbelief. O fools, and slow of heart to believe all the prophets have written. Luke 24:25. Also, one who is accounted or called a fool by ungodly men. 1 Corinthians 4:10.

5. A term of indignity and reproach. To be thought knowing, you must first put the fool upon all mankind.

6. One who counterfeits folly; a buffoon; as a king's fool I scorn, although their drudge, to be their fool or jester.

1. To play the fool to act the buffoon; to jest; to make sport.

2. To act like one void of understanding. To put the fool on, to impose on; to delude. To make a fool of, to frustrate; to defeat; to disappoint.

FOOL, verb intransitive To trifle; to toy; to spend time in idleness, sport or mirth. Is this a time for fooling?

FOOL, verb transitive

1. To treat with contempt; to disappoint; to defeat; to frustrate; to deceive; to impose on.

When I consider life, 'tis all a cheat; for fooled with hope, men favor the deceit.

2. To infatuate; to make foolish.

3. To cheat; as, to fool one out of his money.

1. To fool away, to spend in trifles, idleness, folly, or without advantage; as, to fool away time.

2. To spend for things of no value or use; to expend improvidently; as, to fool away money.

FOOL, noun A liquid made of gooseberries scalded and pounded, with cream.

Foolish

FOOL'ISH, adjective

1. Void of understanding or sound judgment; weak in intellect; applied to general character.

2. Unwise; imprudent; acting without judgment or discretion in particular things.

3. Proceeding from folly, or marked with folly; silly; vain; trifling. But foolish questions avoid. 2 Timothy 2:23.

4. Ridiculous; despicable. A foolish figure he must make.

5. In scripture, wicked; sinful; acting without regard to the divine law and

glory, or to one's own eternal happiness. O foolish Galatians - Galatians 3:1.
6. Proceeding from depravity; sinful; as foolish lusts. 1 Timothy 6:9.

Foolishness
FOOL'ISHNESS, noun
1. Folly; want of understanding.
2. Foolish practice; want of wisdom or good judgment.
3. In a scriptural sense, absurdity; folly. The preaching of the cross is to them that perish foolishness 1 Corinthians 1:18.

Forgive
FORGIVE, verb transitive for giv'. preterit tense forgave; participle passive forgiven. [Latin remitto. See Give.]
1. To pardon; to remit, as an offense or debt; to overlook an offense, and treat the offender as not guilty. The original and proper phrase is to forgive the offense, to send it away, to reject it, that is, not to impute it, [put it to] the offender. But by an easy transition, we also use the phrase, to forgive the person offending.
FORGIVE us our debts.
If we forgive men their trespasses, your heavenly father will also forgive you. Matthew 6:12.
As savages never forget a favor, so they never forgive an injury.
It is to be noted that pardon, like forgive may be followed by the name or person, and by the offense; but remit can be followed by the offense only. We forgive or pardon the man, but we do not remit him.
2. To remit as a debt, fine or penalty.

Friendship
FRIEND'SHIP, noun frend'ship.
1. An attachment to a person, proceeding from intimate acquaintance, and a reciprocation of kind offices, or from a favorable opinion of the amiable and respectable qualities of his mind. friendship differs from benevolence, which is good will to mankind in general, and from that love which springs from animal appetite. True friendship is a noble and virtuous attachment, springing from a pure source, a respect for worth or amiable qualities. False friendship may subsist between bad men, as between thieves and pirates. This is a temporary attachment springing from interest, and may change in a moment to enmity and rancor.
There can be no friendship without confidence, and no confidence without integrity. There is little friendship in the world. The first law of friendship is sincerity.
2. Mutual attachment; intimacy. If not in friendship live at least in peace.
3. Favor; personal kindness.

Friendship continue . . .

His friendships, still a few confined, were always of the middling kind.
4. Friendly aid; help; assistance.
5. Conformity; affinity; correspondence; aptness to unite.
We know those colors which have a friendship with each other.
[Not common and hardly legitimate.]

Fruit

FRUIT, noun [Latin fructus. The Latin word is the participle of fruor,
contracted from frugor, or frucor, to use, to take the profit of.]
1. In a general sense, whatever the earth produces for the nourishment of
animals, or for clothing or profit. Among the fruits of the earth are included
not only corn of all kinds, but grass, cotton, flax, grapes and all cultivated
plants. In this comprehensive sense, the word is generally used in the plural.
2. In a more limited sense, the produce of a tree or other plant; the last
production for the propagation or multiplication of its kind; the seed of
plants, or the part that contains the seeds; as wheat, rye, oats, apples,
quinces, pears, cherries, acorns, melons, etc.
3. In botany, the seed of a plant, or the seed with the pericarp.
4. Production; that which is produced.
The fruit of the spirit is in all goodness, and righteousness, and truth .
Ephesians 5:9.
5. The produce of animals; offspring; young; as the fruit of the womb,
of the loins, of the body.
6. Effect or consequence. They shall eat the fruit of their doings. Isaiah 3:10.
7. Advantage; profit; good derived.
What fruit had ye then in those things whereof ye are now ashamed?
Romans 6:21.
8. Production, effect or consequence; in an ill sense; as the fruits of sin;
the fruits of intemperance.
FRUIT, verb intransitive To produce fruit [Not well authorized.]

God

GOD, noun
1. The Supreme Being; Jehovah; the eternal and infinite spirit, the creator,
and the sovereign of the universe.
GOD is a spirit; and they that worship him, must worship him in spirit and in
truth. John 4:24.
2. A false god; a heathen deity; an idol. Fear not the gods of the Amorites.
Judges 6:10.
3. A prince; a ruler; a magistrate or judge; an angel. Thou shalt not revile
the gods, nor curse the ruler of thy people. Exodus 22:28. Psalms 97:7.
Gods here is a bad translation.]
4. Any person or thing exalted too much in estimation, or deified and

honored as the chief good. Whose god is their belly. Philippians 3:19.
GOD, verb transitive To deify.

Good
GOOD, adjective
1. Valid; legally firm; not weak or defective; having strength adequate to its support; as a good title; a good deed; a good claim.
2. Valid; sound; not weak, false or fallacious; as a good argument.
3. Complete or sufficiently perfect in its kind; having the physical qualities best adapted to its design and use; opposed to bad, imperfect, corrupted, impaired. We say, good timber, good cloth, a good soil, a good color. And God saw every thing that he had made, and behold, it was very good Genesis 1:4.
4. Having moral qualities best adapted to its design and use, or the qualities which God's law requires; virtuous; pious; religious; applied to persons, and opposed to bad, vitious, wicked, evil.
Yet peradventure for a good man some would even dare to die. Romans 5:7.
5. Conformable to the moral law; virtuous; applied to actions.
In all things showing thyself a pattern of good works.
Titus 2:3.
6. Proper; fit; convenient; seasonable; well adapted to the end. It was a good time to commence operations. He arrived in good time.
7. Convenient; useful; expedient; conducive to happiness.
It is not good that the man should be alone. Genesis 2:9.
8. Sound; perfect; uncorrupted; undamaged. This fruit will keep good the whole year.
9. Suitable to the taste or to health; wholesome; salubrious; palatable; not disagreeable or noxious; as fruit good to eat; a tree good for food. Genesis 2:9
10. Suited to produce a salutary effect; adapted to abate or cure; medicinal; salutary; beneficial; as, fresh vegetables are good for scorbutic diseases.
11. Suited to strengthen or assist the healthful functions; as, a little wine is good for a weak stomach.
12. Pleasant to the taste; as a good apple.
My son, eat thou honey, because it is good and the honeycomb, which is sweet to thy taste. Proverbs 24:13.
13. Full; complete.
The protestant subjects of the abbey make up a good third of its people.
14. Useful; valuable; having qualities or a tendency to produce a good effect.
All quality, that is good for any thing, is originally founded on merit.
15. Equal; adequate; competent. His security is good for the amount of the debt; applied to persons able to fulfill contracts.

Good continue . . .

Antonio is a good man.

6. Favorable; convenient for any purpose; as a good stand for business; a good station for a camp.

7. Convenient; suitable; safe; as a good harbor for ships.

8. Well qualified; able; skillful; or performing duties with skill and fidelity; as a good prince; a good commander; a good officer; a good physician.

9. Ready; dexterous.

Those are generally good at flattering who are good for nothing else.

20. Kind; benevolent; affectionate; as a good father; good will.

21. Kind; affectionate; faithful; as a good friend.

22. Promotive of happiness; pleasant; agreeable; cheering; gratifying.

Behold, how good and how pleasant it is for brethren to dwell together in unity. Psalms 133:1.

23. Pleasant or prosperous; as, good morrow, Sir; good morning.

24. Honorable; fair; unblemished; unimpeached; as a man of good fame or report.

A good name is better than precious ointment. Ecclesiastes 7:1.

25. Cheerful; favorable to happiness. Be of good comfort.

26. Great or considerable; not small nor very great; as a good while ago; he is a good way off, or at a good distance; he has a good deal of leisure; I had a good share of the trouble. Here we see the primary sense of extending, advancing.

27. Elegant; polite; as good breeding.

28. Real; serious; not feigned.

Love not in good earnest.

29. Kind; favorable; benevolent; humane.

The men were very good to us. 1 Samuel 25:3.

30. Benevolent; merciful; gracious.

Truly God is good to Israel, even to such as are of a clean heart. Psalms 73:1.

31. Seasonable; commendable; proper.

Why trouble ye the woman, for she hath wrought a good work on me. Matthew 26:10.

32. Pleasant; cheerful; festive.

We come in a good day. 1 Samuel 25:3.

33. Companionable; social; merry.

It is well known, that Sir Roger had been a good fellow in his youth.

34. Brave; in familiar language. You are a good fellow.

35. In the phrases, the good man, applied to the master of the house, and good woman, applied to the mistress, good sometimes expresses a moderate degree of respect, and sometimes slight contempt. Among the first settlers of New England, it was used as a title instead of Mr.; as Goodman

Good continue . . .

Jones; Goodman Wells.

36. The phrase good will is equivalent to benevolence; but it signifies also an earnest desire, a hearty wish, entire willingness or fervent zeal; as, we entered into the service with a good will; he laid on stripes with a good will.

37. Comely; handsome; well formed; as a good person or shape.

38. Mild; pleasant; expressing benignity or other estimable qualities; as a good countenance.

39. Mild; calm; not irritable or fractious; as a good temper.

40. Kind; friendly; humane; as a good heart or disposition.

GOOD advice, wise and prudent counsel.

GOOD heed, great care; due caution.

In good south, in good truth; in reality.

To make good to perform; to fulfill; as, to make good one's word or promise; that is to make it entire or unbroken.

1. To confirm or establish; to prove; to verify; as, to make good a charge or accusation.

2. To supply deficiency; to make up a defect or loss. I will make good what is wanting.

3. To indemnify; to give an equivalent for damages. If you suffer loss, I will make it good to you.

4. To maintain; to carry into effect; as, to make good a retreat.

To stand good to be firm or valid. His word or promise stands good

To think good to see good is to be pleased or satisfied; to think to be expedient.

If ye think good give me my price. Zechariah 11:12.

As good as, equally; no better than; the same as. We say, one is as good as dead. Hebrews 11:2.

As good as his word, equaling in fulfillment what was promised; performing to the extent.

GOOD, noun That which contributes to diminish or remove pain, or to increase happiness or prosperity; benefit; advantage; opposed to evil or misery. The medicine will do neither good nor harm. It does my heart good to see you so happy.

There are many that say, who will show us any good Psa 4.

1. Welfare; prosperity; advancement of interest or happiness.

He labored for the good of the state.

The good of the whole community can be promoted only by advancing the good of each of the members composing it.

2. Spiritual advantage or improvement; as the good of souls.

3. Earnest; not jest.

The good woman never died after this, till she came to die for good and all.

The phrase, for good and all, signifies, finally; to close the whole business;

Good continue . . .

or the last time.

. Moral works; actions which are just and in conformity to the moral law or divine precepts.

Depart from evil, and do good Psa 34.

. Moral qualities; virtue; righteousness.

find no good in this man.

. The best fruits; richness; abundance.

will give you the good of the land. Gen 45.

GOOD, verb transitive To manure. [Not in use.]

GOOD, adverb As good as well; with equal advantage. Had you not as good go with me? In America we use goods, the Gothic word. Had you not as goods go?

In replies, good signifies well; right; it is satisfactory; I am satisfied. I will be with you to morrow; answer, good very good So we use well, from the root of Latin valeo, to be strong.

Goodness

GOOD'NESS, noun The state of being good; the physical qualities which constitute value, excellence or perfection; as the goodness of timber; the goodness of a soil.

. The moral qualities which constitute christian excellence; moral virtue; religion. The fruit of the Spirit is love, joy, peace, long-suffering, gentleness, goodness faith. Galatians 5:22.

. Kindness; benevolence; benignity of heart; but more generally, acts of kindness; charity; humanity exercised. I shall remember his goodness to me with gratitude.

. Kindness; benevolence of nature; mercy. The Lord God--abundant in goodness and truth. Exodus 34:6.

. Kindness; favor shown; acts of benevolence, compassion or mercy. Jethro rejoiced for all the goodness which Jehovah had done to Israel. Exodus 18:9.

Grace

GRACE, noun [Latin gratia, which is formed on the Celtic; Eng. agree, congruous, and ready. The primary sense of gratus, is free, ready, quick, willing, prompt, from advancing.]

. Favor; good will; kindness; disposition to oblige another; as a grant made as an act of grace Or each, or all, may win a lady's grace

. Appropriately, the free unmerited love and favor of God, the spring and source of all the benefits men receive from him. And if by grace then it is no more of works. Romans 11:5.

. Favorable influence of God; divine influence or the influence of the spirit, in renewing the heart and restraining from sin. My grace is sufficient for

Grace continue . . .

thee. 2 Corinthians 12:9.

4. The application of Christ's righteousness to the sinner. Where sin abounded, grace did much more abound. Romans 5:2.

5. A state of reconciliation to God. Romans 5:2:2.

6. Virtuous or religious affection or disposition, as a liberal disposition, faith, meekness, humility, patience, etc. proceeding from divine influence.

7. Spiritual instruction, improvement and edification. Ephesians 4:29.

8. Apostleship, or the qualifications of an apostle. Ephesians 3:8.

9. Eternal life; final salvation. 1 Peter 1:13.

10. Favor; mercy; pardon. Bow and sue for grace With suppliant knee.

11. Favor conferred. I should therefore esteem it a great favor and grace

12. Privilege. To few great Jupiter imparts this grace

13. That in manner, deportment or language which renders it appropriate and agreeable; suitableness; elegance with appropriate

dignity. We say, a speaker delivers his address with grace; a man performs his part with grace GRACE was in all her steps.

Her purple habit sits with such a grace. On her smooth shoulders.

14. Natural or acquired excellence; any endowment that recommends the possessor to others; as the graces of wit and learning.

15. Beauty; embellishment; in general, whatever adorns and recommends to favor; sometimes, a single beauty. I pass their form and every charming grace.

16. Beauty deified; among pagans, a goddess. The graces were three in number, Aglaia, Thalia, and Euphrosyne, the constant attendants of Venus. The loves delighted, and the graces played.

17. Virtue physical; as the grace of plants. [Not used.]

18. The title of a duke or an archbishop, and formerly of the king of England, meaning your goodness or clemency. His grace the Duke of York. Your gracewill please to accept my thanks.

19. A short prayer before or after meat; a

blessing asked, or thanks rendered.

20. In music, graces signifies turns, trills and shakes introduced for embellishment.

Day in grace in theology, time of probation, when an offer is made to sinners.

Days in grace in commerce, the days immediately following the day when a bill or note becomes due, which days are allowed to the debtor or payor to make payment in. In Great Britain and the United States the days of grace are three, but in other countries more; the usages of merchants being different.

GRACE, verb transitive To adorn; to decorate; to embellish and dignify.

Great Jove and Phoebus graced his noble line.

And hail, ye fair, of every charm possess'd,

Who grace this rising empire of the west.

. To dignify or raise by act of favor; to honor.

He might at his pleasure grace or disgrace whom he would in court.

. To favor; to honor.

. To supply with heavenly grace

Great

GREAT, adjective [Latin crassus.]

. Large in bulk or dimensions; a term of comparison, denoting more magnitude or extension than something else, or beyond what is usual; as a great body; a great house; a great farm.

. Being of extended length or breadth; as a great distance; a great lake.

. Large in number; as a great many; a great multitude.

. Expressing a large, extensive or unusual degree of any thing; as great fear;great love; great strength; great wealth; great power; great influence; greatfolly.

. Long continued; as a great while.

. Important; weighty; as a great argument; a great truth; a great event; a thing of no great consequence; it is no great matter.

. Chief; principal; as the great seal of England.

. Chief; of vast power and excellence; supreme; illustrious; as the great God; the great Creator.

. Vast; extensive; wonderful; admirable.

GREAT are thy works. Jehovah.

10. Possessing large or strong powers of mind; as a great genius.

11. Having made extensive or unusual acquisitions of science or knowledge; as a great philosopher or botanist; a great scholar.

12. Distinguished by rank, office or power; elevated; eminent; as a great lord; the great men of the nation; the great Mogul; Alexander the great

13. Dignified in aspect, mien or manner. Amidst the crowd she walks serenely great

14. Magnanimous; generous; of elevated sentiments; high-minded. He has agreat soul.

15. Rich; sumptuous; magnificent. He disdained not to appear at great tables. A great feast or entertainment.

16. Vast; sublime; as a great conception or idea.

17. Dignified; noble. Nothing can be great which is not right.

18. Swelling; proud; as, he was not disheartened by great looks.

19. Chief; principal; much traveled; as a great road. The ocean is called thegreat highway of nations.

20. Pregnant; teeming; as great with young.

21. Hard; difficult. It is no great matter to live in peace with meek people.

22. Familiar; intimate. [Vulgar.]

Great continue . . .

23. Distinguished by extraordinary events, or unusual importance. Jude 1:6.

24. Denoting a degree of consanguinity, in the ascending or descending line, as great grandfather, the father of a grandfather; great great grandfather, the father of a great grandfather, and so on indefinitely; and great grandson, great great grandson. etc.

25. Superior; preeminent; as great chamberlain; great marshal.

The sense of great is to be understood by the things it is intended to qualify .great pain or wrath is violent pain or wrath; great love is ardent love; great peace is entire peace; a great name is extensive renown; a great evil or sin, is a sin of deep malignity, etc.

GREAT, noun The whole; the gross; the lump or mass; as, a carpenter contracts to build a ship by the great

1. People of rank or distinction. The poor envy the great and the great despise the poor.

Happy

HAP'PY adjective [from hap.]

1. Lucky; fortunate; successful.

Chimists have been more happy in finding experiments, than the causes of them. So we say, a happy thought; a happy expedient.

2. Being in the enjoyment of agreeable sensations from the possession of good; enjoying pleasure from the gratification of appetites or desires. The pleasurable sensations derived from the gratification of sensual appetites render a person temporarily happy; but he only can be esteemed really and permanently happy who enjoys peace of mind in the favor of God. To be in any degree happy we must be free from pain both of body and of mind; to be very happy we must be in the enjoyment of lively sensations of pleasure, either of body or mind.

Happy am I, for the daughters will call me blessed. Genesis 30:13.

He found himself happiest, in communicating happiness to others.

3. Prosperous; having secure possession of good.

Happy is that people whose God is Jehovah. Psalms 144:15.

4. That supplies pleasure; that furnishes enjoyment; agreeable; applied to things; as a happy condition.

5. Dexterous; ready; able. One gentleman is happy at a reply, another excels in a rejoinder.

6. Blessed; enjoying the presence and favor of God, in a future life.

7. Harmonious; living in concord; enjoying the pleasures of friendship; as a happy family.

8. Propitious; favorable.

heal

HEAL, verb transitive [Latin celo; Heb. to be whole or entire, all.]

To cure of a disease or wound and restore to soundness, or to that state of body in which the natural functions are regularly performed; as, to heal the sick.

Speak, and my servant shall be healed. Matthew 8:7.

To cure; to remove or subdue; as, to heal a disease.

To cause to cicatrize; as, to heal a sore or wound.

To restore to soundness; as, to heal a wounded limb.

To restore purity to; to remove feculence or foreign matter.

Thus saith the Lord, I have healed these waters. 2 Kings 2:21.

To remove, as differences or dissension; to reconcile, as parties at variance; as, to heal a breach or difference.

In Scripture, to forgive; to cure moral disease and restore soundness.

I will heal their backsliding. Hosea 14.

To purify from corruptions, redress grievances and restore to prosperity Jeremiah 14:1.

To cover, as a roof with tiles, slate, lead, etc.

HEAL, verb intransitive To grow sound; to return to a sound state; as, the limb heals, or the wound heals; sometimes with up or over; it will heal up or over.

health

HEALTH, noun helth. [from heal.] That state of an animal or living body, in which the parts are sound, well organized and disposed, and in which they all perform freely their natural functions. In this state the animal feels no pain. This word is applied also to plants.

Sound state of the mind; natural vigor of faculties.

Sound state of the mind, in a moral sense; purity; goodness.

There is no health in us.

Salvation or divine favor, or grace which cheers God's people. Psalms 3:5,

Wish of health and happiness; used in drinking. Come, love and health to all; an elliptical phrase, for, I wish health to you.

honor

HON'OR, noun on'or. [Latin honor honos.]

The esteem due or paid to worth; high estimation. A prophet is not without honor except in his own country. Matthew 13:1.

A testimony of esteem; any expression of respect or of high estimation by words or actions; as the honors of war; military honors; funeral honors; civil honors.

Dignity; exalted rank or place; distinction. I have given thee riches and honor 1 Kings 3:1. Thou art clothed with honor and majesty. Psalms 104:1.

doing a good thing, there is both honor and pleasure.

Honor continue . . .

4. Reverence; veneration; or any act by which reverence and submission are expressed, as worship paid to the Supreme Being.

5. Reputation; good name; as, his honor is unsullied.

6. True nobleness of mind; magnanimity; dignified respect for character, springing from probity, principle or moral rectitude; a distinguishing trait in the character of good men.

7. An assumed appearance of nobleness; scorn of meanness, springing from the fear of reproach, without regard to principle; as, shall I violate my trust? Forbid it, honor

8. Any particular virtue much valued; as bravery in men, and chastity in females.

9. Dignity of mien; noble appearance. Godlike erect, with native honor clad.

10. That which honors; he or that which confers dignity; as, the chancellor is an honor to his profession.

11. Privileges of rank or birth; in the plural. Restore me to my honors.

12. Civilities paid.

Then here a slave, or if you will, a lord, To do the honors, and to give the word.

13. That which adorns; ornament; decoration. The sire then shook the honors of his head.

14. A noble kind of seignory or lordship, held of the king in capite.

On or upon my honor words accompanying a declaration which pledge one's honor or reputation for the truth of it. The members of the house of lords in Great Britain are not under oath, but give their opinions on their honor aws of honor among persons of fashion, signify certain rules by which their social intercourse is regulated, and which are founded on a regard to reputation. These laws require a punctilious attention to decorum in external deportment, but admit of the foulest violations of moral duty.

Court of honor a court of chivalry; a court of civil and criminal jurisdiction, having power to redress injuries of honor and to hold pleas respecting matters of arms and deeds of war. HON'OR, verb intransitive on'or. [Latin honoro.]

1. To revere; to respect; to treat with deference and submission, and perform relative duties to. Honor thy father and thy mother. Exodus 20:1.

2. To reverence; to manifest the highest veneration for, in words and actions; to entertain the most exalted thoughts of; to worship; to adore. That all men should honor the Son, even as they honor the Father. John 5:1.

3. To dignify; to raise to distinction or notice; to elevate in rank or station; to exalt. Men are sometimes honored with titles and offices, which they do nc merit. Thus shall it be done to the man whom the king delighteth to honor Esther 6:1.

4. To glorify; to render illustrious.

will be honored upon Pharaoh, and upon all his host. Exodus 14:3.

To treat with due civility and respect in the ordinary intercourse of life. The troops honored the governor with a salute.

In commerce, to accept and pay when due; as, to honor a bill of exchange.

Hope

HOPE, noun [Latin cupio.]

A desire of some good, accompanied with at least a slight expectation of obtaining it, or a belief that it is obtainable. hope differs from wish and desire in this, that it implies some expectation of obtaining the good desired, or the possibility of possessing it. hope therefore always gives pleasure or joy; whereas wish and desire may produce or be accompanied with pain and anxiety. The hypocrite's hope shall perish. Job 8:13.

He wish'ed, but not with hope- Sweet hope! kind cheat! He that lives upon hope will die fasting.

Confidence in a future event; the highest degree of well founded expectation of good; as a hope founded on God's gracious promises; a scriptural sense. A well founded scriptural hope is, in our religion, the source of ineffable happiness.

That which gives hope; he or that which furnishes ground of expectation, or promises desired good. The hope of Israel is the Messiah. The Lord will be the hope of his people. Joel 3:16.

An opinion or belief not amounting to certainty, but grounded on substantial evidence. The christian indulges a hope that his sins are pardoned.

HOPE, verb intransitive

To cherish a desire of food, with some expectation of obtaining it, or a belief that it is obtainable. HOPE for good success. Be sober and hope to the end. 1 Peter 1:3.

HOPE humbly then, with trembling pinions soar.

To place confidence in; to trust in with confident expectation of good. Why art thou cast down, O my soul, and why art thou disquieted within me?hope thou in God. Psalms 43:5.

HOPE, verb transitive To desire with expectation of good, or a belief that it may be obtained. But as a transitive verb, it is seldom used, and the phrases in which it is so used are elliptical, for being understood.

So stands the Thracian herdsman with his spear,

Full in the gap, and hopes the hunted bear.

HOPE, noun A sloping plain between ridges of mountains. [Not in use.]

Humble

HUM'BLE, adjective [Latin humilis.]

1. Low; opposed to high or lofty.

Thy humble nest built on the ground.

2. Low; opposed to lofty or great; mean; not magnificent; as a humble cottage.

A humble roof, and an obscure retreat.

3. Lowly; modest; meek; submissive; opposed to proud, haughty, arrogant or assuming. In an evangelical sense, having a low opinion of one's self, and a deep sense of unworthiness in the sight of God.

God resisteth the proud, but giveth grace to the humble. James 4:1.

Without a humble imitation of the divine author of our blessed religion, we can never hope to be a happy nation.

HUM'BLE, verb transitive To abase; to reduce to a low state. This victory humbled the pride of Rome. The power of Rome was humbled, but not subdued.

1. To crush; to break; to subdue. The battle of Waterloo humbled the power of Buonaparte.

2. To mortify.

3. To make humble or lowly in mind; to abase the pride of; to reduce arrogance and self-dependence; to give a low opinion of one's moral worth; to make meek and submissive to the divine will; the evangelical sense.

Humble yourselves under the mighty hand of God, that he may exalt you. 1 Peter 5:1.

Hezekiah humbled himself for the pride of his heart. 2 Chronicles 32:1.

4. To make to condescend.

He humbles himself to speak to them.

5. To bring down; to lower; to reduce.

The highest mountains may be humbled into valleys.

6. To deprive of chastity. Deuteronomy 21:1.

To humble one's self, to repent; to afflict one's self for sin; to make contrite.

Humility

HUMIL'ITY, noun [Latin humilitas.]

1. In ethics, freedom from pride and arrogance; humbleness of mind; a modest estimate of one's own worth. In theology, humility consists in lowliness of mind; a deep sense of one's own unworthiness in the sight of God, self-abasement, penitence for sin, and submission to the divine will.

Before honor is humility Proverbs 15:33.

Serving the Lord with all humility of mind. Acts 20:19.

2. Act of submission.

With these humilities they satisfied the young king.

Ignorant

I'GNORANT, adjective [Latin ignorans.]

Destitute of knowledge; uninstructed or uninformed; untaught; unenlightened. A man may be ignorant of the law, of any art or science. He may be ignorant of his own rights, or of the rights of others.

Unknown; undiscovered; a poetical use; as ignorant concealment.

Unacquainted with. Ignorant of guilt, I fear not shame.

Unskillfully made or done. [Not legitimate.] Poor ignorant baubles.

I'GNORANT, noun A person untaught or uninformed; one unlettered or unskilled. Did I for this take pains to teach. Our zealous ignorants to preach?

Impossible

IMPOSS'IBLE, adjective [Latin impossibilis; in and possibilis, from possum, to be able.]

That cannot be. It is impossible that two and two should make five, or that a circle and a square make five, or that a circle and a square should be the same thing, or that a thing should be, and not be at the same time.

Impracticable; not feasible; that cannot be done.

With men this is impossible; but with God all things are possible. Matthew 9:26. Without faith it is impossible to please God. Hebrews 11:6.

There are two kinds of impossibilities; physical and moral. That is a physical impossibility, which is contrary to the law of nature. A thing is said to be morally impossible when in itself it is possible, but attended with difficulties or circumstances which give it the appearance of being impossible [See Possible, Practicable and Impracticable.]

Increase

INCRE'ASE, verb intransitive [Latin incresco; in and cresco, to grow.]

To become greater in bulk or quantity; to grow; to augment; as plants. Hence, to become more in number; to advance in value, or in any quality good or bad. Animal and vegetable bodies increase by natural growth; wealth increases by industry; heat increases, as the sun advances towards the meridian; a multitude increases by accession of numbers; knowledge increases with age and study; passion and enmity increase by irritation, and misery increases with vice.

The Lord make you to increase and abound in love one toward another. 1 Thessalonians 3:12.

To become more violent; as, the fever increases; the pain increases; cold, wind or a storm increases.

To become more bright or vivid; as, the light increases.

To swell; to rise. The waters increased and bore up the ark. Genesis 7:17.

To swell; to become louder, as sound.

Increase continue . . .

6. To become of more esteem and authority. He must increase but I must decrease. John 3:30.

7. To enlarge, as the enlightened part of the moon's disk.

INCRE'ASE, verb transitive To augment or make greater in bulk, quantity or amount; as, to increase wealth or treasure; to increase a sum or value.

1. To advance in quality; to add to any quality or affection; as, to increase the strength of moral habits; to increase love, zeal or passion.

2. To extend; to lengthen; as, to increase distance.

3. To extend; to spread; as, to increase fame or renown.

4. To aggravate; as, to increase guilt or trespass.

INCRE'ASE, noun Augmentation; a growing larger; extension.

Of the increase of his government and peace, there shall be no end. Isaiah 9:7.

1. Increment; profit; interest; that which is added to the original stock.

Take thou no interest of him or increase; but fear thy God. Leviticus 25:7.

2. Produce, as of land. Then shall the earth yield her increase Psalms 67:6.

3. Progeny; issue; offspring.

All the increase of thy house shall die in the flower of their age. 1 Samuel 2:33.

4. Generation.

5. The waxing of the moon; the augmentation of the luminous part of the moon, presented to the inhabitants of the earth.

Seeds, hair, nails, hedges and herbs will grow soonest, if set or cut in thein-crease of the moon.

6. Augmentation of strength or violence; as increase of heat, love or other passion; increase of force.

7. Augmentation of degree; as increase of
happiness or misery.

Integrity

INTEG'RITY, noun [Latin integritas, from integer.]

1. Wholeness; entireness; unbroken state. The
constitution of the United States guaranties to each state the integrity of its territories. The contracting parties guarantied the integrity of the empire.

2. The entire, unimpaired state of any thing, particularly of the mind; moral soundness or purity; incorruptness; uprightness; honesty.

integritycomprehends the whole moral character, but has a special reference to uprightness in mutual dealings, transfers of property, and agencies for others.

The moral grandeur of independent integrity is the sublimest thing in nature, before which the pomp of eastern magnificence and the splendo of conquest are odious as well as perishable.

3. Purity; genuine, unadulterated, unimpaired state; as the integrity of language

Joy

JOY, noun
The passion or emotion excited by the acquisition or expectation of good; that excitement of pleasurable feelings which is caused by success, good fortune, the gratification of desire or some good possessed, or by a rational prospect of possessing what we love or desire; gladness; exultation; exhilaration of spirits.

JOY is a delight of the mind, from the consideration of the present or assured approaching possession of a good. Bring heavenly balm to heal my country's wounds, JOY to my soul and transport to my lay.

Gayety; mirth; festivity. The roofs with joy resound.

Happiness; felicity. Her heavenly form beheld, all wished her joy

A glorious and triumphant state. --Who for the joy that was set before him, endured the cross. Hebrews 12:2.

The cause of joy or happiness. For ye are our glory and joy Thessalonians 2:19.

A term of fondness; the cause of you. JOY, verb intransitive To rejoice; to be glad; to exult. I will joy in the God of my salvation. Habakkuk 3:18.

JOY, verb transitive To give joy to; to congratulate; to entertain kindly.

To gladden; to exhilarate. My soul was joyed in vain.

To enjoy; to have or possess with pleasure, or to have pleasure in the possession of. [Little used. See Enjoy.]

Joyful

JOY'FUL, adjective Full of joy; very glad; exulting. My soul shall be joyful in my God. Isaiah 61:10. Rarely, it has of before the cause of joy.
...d for their loss, but joyful of our life.

Knowledge

KNOWL'EDGE, noun nol'lej.
A clear and certain perception of that which exists, or of truth and fact; the perception of the connection and agreement, or disagreement and repugnancy of our ideas. We can have no knowledge of that which does not exist. God has a perfectknowledge of all his works. Human knowledge is very limited, and is mostly gained by observation and experience.

Learning; illumination of mind.

Ignorance is the curse of God, knowledge the wing wherewith we fly to heaven.

Skill; as a knowledge of seamanship.

Acquaintance with any fact or person. I have no knowledge of the man or thing.

Cognizance; notice. Ruth 2:10.

Information; power of knowing.

Knowledge continue . . .
7. Sexual intercourse. But it is usual to prefix carnal; as carnal knowledge
KNOWLEDGE, for acknowledge or avow, is not used.

Love
LOVE, verb transitive luv. [Latin libeo, lubeo. See Lief. The sense is probably
to be prompt, free, willing, from leaning, advancing, or drawing forward.]
1. In a general sense to be pleased with; to regard with affection, on account of some qualities which excite pleasing sensations or desire of gratification. We love a friend, on account of some qualities which give us pleasure in his society. We love a man who has done us a favor; in which case,
gratitude enters into the composition of our affection. We love our parents
and our children, on account of their connection with us, and on account of many qualities which please us. We love to retire to a cool shade
in summer. Welove a warm room in winter. we love to hear an eloquent
advocate. The christian loves his Bible. In short, we love whatever gives us
pleasure and delight, whether animal or intellectual; and if our hearts are
right, we love God above all things, as the sum of all excellence and all
the attributes which can communicate happiness to intelligent beings. In
other words, the christian loves God with the love of complacency in his
attributes, the love of benevolence towards the interest of his kingdom, an
the love of gratitude for favors received.
Thou shalt love the Lord thy God with all thy heart, and with all thy soul, anc
with all thy mind - Thou shalt love thy neighbor as thyself. Matthew 22:37.
2. To have benevolence or good will for. John 3:16.
LOVE, noun
1. An affection of the mind excited by beauty and worth of any kind, or by
the qualities of an object which communicate pleasure, sensual or intellec
tual. It is opposed to hatred. love between the sexes, is a compound affec
tion, consisting of esteem, benevolence, and animal desire. love is excited
by pleasing qualities of any kind, as by kindness, benevolence, charity,
and by the qualities which render social intercourse agreeable. In the latter
case, love is ardent friendship, or a strong attachment springing from good
will and esteem, and the pleasure derived from the company, civilities anc
kindness of others.
Between certain natural relatives, love seems to be in some cases
instinctive. Such is the love of a mother for her child, which manifests itself
toward an infant, before any particular qualities in the child are unfolded.
This affection is apparently as strong in irrational animals as in human
beings. We speak of the love of amusements, the love of books, the love o
money, and the love of whatever contributes to our pleasure or supposed
profit. The love of God is the first duty of man, and this springs from just
views of his attributes or excellencies of character, which afford the highes
delight to the sanctified heart. Esteem and reverence constitute ingredients in

is affection, and a fear of offending him is its inseparable effect.

 Courtship; chiefly in the phrase, to make love that is, to court; to woo;
 solicit union in marriage.

 Patriotism; the attachment one has to his native land; as the love of
ountry.

 Benevolence; good will. God is love 1 John 4:7.

 The object beloved. The lover and the love of human kind.

 A word of endearment.

ust me, love

 Picturesque representation of love. Such was his form as painters,
hen they show their utmost art, on naked loves bestow.

 Lewdness. He is not lolling on a lewd love-bed.

 A thin silk stuff. obsolete LOVE in idleness, a kind of violet. Free of love
 plant of the genus Cercis.

editate

ED'ITATE, verb intransitive [Latin meditor.]

 To dwell on any thing in thought; to contemplate; to study; to turn or
volve any subject in the mind; appropriately but not exclusively used
 pious contemplation, or a consideration of the great truths of religion.
s delight is in the law of the Lord, and in his law doth he meditate day
nd night. Psalms 1:2.

 To intend; to have in contemplation.

neditate to pass the remainder of life in a state of undisturbed repose.

ED'ITATE, verb transitive To plan by revolving in the mind; to contrive;
 intend.

ome affirmed that I meditated a war.

 To think on; to revolve in the mind.

essed is the man that doth meditate good things.

editation

EDITA'TION, noun [Latin meditatio.] Close or continued thought; the
rning or revolving of a subject in the mind; serious contemplation.

t the words of my mouth and the meditations of my heart be acceptable
 thy sight, O Lord, my strength and my Redeemer. Psalms 19:14.

eek

EEK, adjective [Latin mucus; Eng. mucilage; Heb. to melt.]

 Mild of temper; soft; gentle; not easily provoked or irritated; yielding;
ven to forbearance under injuries.

ow the man Moses was very meek above all men. Numbers 12:3.

 Appropriately, humble, in an evangelical sense; submissive to the divine
ll; not proud, self-sufficient or refractory; not peevish and apt to complain

of divine dispensations. Christ says, 'Learn of me, for I am meek and lowly in heart, and ye shall find rest to your souls.' Matthew 11:29. Blessed are the meek for they shall inherit the earth. Matthew 5:5.

Meekness

MEE'KNESS, noun Softness of temper; mildness; gentleness; forbearance under injuries and provocations.

1. In an evangelical sense, humility; resignation; submission to the divine will, without murmuring or peevishness; opposed to pride, arrogance and refractoriness. Galatians 5:23.

I beseech you by the meekness of Christ.

1 Corinthians 10:1.

Meekness is a grace which Jesus alone inculcated, and which no ancient philosopher seems to have understood or recommended.

Mercy

MER'CY, noun [Latin misericordia.]

1. That benevolence, mildness or tenderness of heart which disposes a perso to overlook injuries, or to treat an offender better than he deserves; the disposition that tempers justice, and induces an injured person to forgive trespasses and injuries, and to forbear punishment, or inflict less than law o justice will warrant. In this sense, there is perhaps no word in our language precisely synonymous with mercy That which comes nearest to it is grace. It implies benevolence, tenderness, mildness, pity or compassion, and clemency, but exercised only towards offenders. mercy is a distinguishing attribute of the Supreme Being. The Lord is long-suffering and of great merc forgiving iniquity and transgression, and by no means clearing the guilty. Numbers 14:18.

2. An act or exercise of mercy or favor. It is a mercy that they escaped.

I am not worthy of the least of all thy mercies. Genesis 32:1.

3. Pity; compassion manifested towards a person in distress.

And he said, he that showed mercy on him. Luke 10:37.

4. Clemency and bounty.

Mercy and truth preserve the king; and his throne is upheld by mercy. Proverbs 28:13.

5. Charity, or the duties of charity and benevolence. I will have mercy an not sacrifice. Matthew 9:13.

6. Grace; favor. 1 Corinthians 7:25. Jude 1:2.

7. Eternal life, the fruit of mercy 2 Timothy 1:2.

8. Pardon. I cry thee mercy with all my heart.

9. The act of sparing, or the forbearance of a violent act expected. The prisoner cried for mercy. To be or to lie at the mercy of, to have no means of self-defense, but to be dependent for safety on the mercy or

compassion of another, or in the power of that which is irresistible; as, to be at the mercy of a foe, or of the waves.

Mindful

MINDFUL, adjective Attentive; regarding with care; bearing in mind; needful; observant. I promise to be mindful of your admonitions. What is man, that thou art mindful of him? Psalms 7:1.

Minded

MINDED, adjective Disposed; inclined.

men were minded to live virtuously.

Joseph was minded to put her away privily. Matthew 1:19.

MINDED is much used in composition; as high-minded; low-minded; feeble-minded; sober-minded; double-minded.

Mouth

MOUTH, noun

1. The aperture in the head of an animal, between the lips, by which he utters his voice and receives food. In a more general sense, the mouth consists of the lips, the gums, the insides of the cheeks, the palate, the salival glands, the uvula and tonsils.

2. The opening of a vessel by which it is filled or emptied; as the mouth of a jar or pitcher.

3. The part or channel of a river by which its waters are discharged into the ocean or into a lake. The Mississippi and the Nile discharge their waters by several mouths.

4. The opening of a piece of ordnance at the end, by which the charge issues.

5. The aperture of a vessel in animal bodies, by which fluids or other matter is received or discharged; as the mouth of the lacteals.

6. The opening or entrance of a cave, pit, well or den. Daniel 8:1.

7. The instrument of speaking; as, the story is in every body's mouth

8. A principal speaker; one that utters the common opinion.

Every coffee house has some statesman belonging to it, who is the mouth of the street where he lives.

9. Cry; voice.

The fearful dogs divide,

All spend their mouth aloft, but none abide.

10. In Scripture, words uttered. Job 19:16. Isaiah 49:2. Psalms 73:9.

11. Desires; necessities. Psalms 103:5.

12. Freedom and boldness of speech; force of argument. Luke 21:15.

13. Boasting; vaunting. Judges 9:38.

Mouth continue . . .

14. Testimony. Deuteronomy 17:6.

15. Reproaches; calumnies. Job 5:15.

To make a mouth to distort the mouth;

To make mouths, to make a wry face; hence, to deride or treat with scorn.

1. To pout; to treat disdainfully.

Down in the mouth dejected; mortified.

To have God's law in the mouth to converse much on it and delight in it. Exodus 13:9.

To draw near to God with the mouth to make an external appearance of devotion and worship, while there is no regard to him in the heart. Isaiah 29:13.

A froward mouth contradictions and disobedience. Proverbs 9:1.

A smooth mouth soft and flattering language. Proverbs 5:3.

To stop the mouth to silence or to be silent; to put to shame; to confound. Romans 3:14. lay the hand on the mouth to be struck silent with shame. Micah 7:5.

To set the mouth against the heavens, to speak arrogantly and blasphemously. Psalms 73:9.

MOUTH, verb transitive To utter with a voice affectedly big or swelling; as, to mouth words or language.

Twitch'd by the sleeve, he mouths it more and more.

1. To take into the mouth; to seize with the mouth

2. To chew; to grind, as food; to eat; to devour.

3. To form by the mouth as a bear her cub. [Not used.]

4. To reproach; to insult.

MOUTH, verb intransitive To speak with a full, round, or loud, affected voice; to vociferate; to rant; as a mouthing actor.

I'll bellow out for Rome and for my country,

And mouth at Caesar, till I shake the senate.

Obedience

OBE'DIENCE, noun [Latin obedientia. See Obey.]

Compliance with a command, prohibition or known law and rule of duty prescribed; the performance of what is required or enjoined by authority, or the abstaining from what is prohibited, in compliance with the command or prohibition. To constitute obedience the act or forbearance to act must be in submission to authority; the command must be known to the person, and his compliance must be in consequence of it, or it is not obedience

obedience is not synonymous with obsequiousness; the latter often implying meanness or servility, and obedience being merely a proper submission to authority. That which duty requires implies dignity of conduct rather

Obedience continue . . .

than servility. obediencemay be voluntary or involuntary. Voluntary obedience alone can be acceptable to God.

Government must compel the obedience of individuals; otherwise who will seek its protection or fear its vengeance?

Obedient

OBE'DIENT, adjective [Latin obediens.] Submissive to authority; yielding compliance with commands, orders or injunctions; performing what is required, or abstaining from what is forbid.

The chief his orders gives; the obedient band, with due observance, wait the chief's command.

Obey

OBEY, verb transitive [Latin obedio; Gr.]

1. To comply with the commands, orders or instructions of a superior, or with the requirements of law, moral, political or municipal; to do that which is commanded or required, or to forbear doing that which is prohibited.

Children, obey your parents in the Lord. Ephesians 6:1.

Servants, obey in all things your masters. Colossians 3:20.

He who has learned to obey will know how to command.

2. To submit to the government of; to be ruled by.

All Israel obeyed Song of Solomon 1:1Chron. 29. Daniel 7:27.

3. To submit to the direction or control of. Seamen say, the ship will not obeythe helm.

Let not sin therefore reign in your mortal body, that ye should obey it in the lusts thereof. Romans 6:12. James 3:3.

4. To yield to the impulse, power or operation of; as, to obey stimulus.

Relentless time, destroying power, whom stone and brass obey

Overcome

OVERCOME, verb transitive [See Come.]

1. To conquer; to vanquish; to subdue; as, to overcome enemies in battle.

2. To surmount; to get the better of; as, to overcome difficulties or obstacles.

3. To overflow; to surcharge. [Not used.]

4. To come upon; to invade. [Not used.]

OVERCOME, verb intransitive To gain the superiority; to be victorious. Romans 3:4.

Pleasant

PLEASANT, adjective plez'ant.

1. Pleasing; agreeable; grateful to the mind or to the senses; as a pleasantride; a pleasant voyage; a pleasant view. Light is pleasant to the eye; an orange is pleasant to the taste; harmony is pleasant to the ear; a rose is pleasant to the smell.

How good and how pleasant it is for brethren to dwell together in unity!Psalms 133:1.

2. Cheerful; enlivening; as pleasant society or company.

3. Gay; lively; humorous; sportive; as a pleasant companion.

4. Trifling; adapted rather to mirth than use.

5. Giving pleasure; gratifying.

This word expresses less than delightful, to the mind, and delicious, to the taste.

Pleasantness

PLEASANTNESS, noun plez'antness. State of being pleasant or agreeable; as the pleasantness of a situation.

1. Cheerfulness; gayety; merriment; as the pleasantness of youth.

Please

PLEASE, verb transitive s as z. [Latin placere, placeo.]

1. To excite agreeable sensations or emotions in; to gratify; as, to please the taste; to please the mind.

Their words pleased Hamor, and Shechem, Hamor's son. Genesis 34:18.

Leave such to trifle with more grace than ease,

Whom folly pleases, and whose follies please

2. To satisfy; to content. What next I bring shall please Thy wish exactly to thy heart's desire.

3. To prefer; to have satisfaction in; to like; to choose. Many of our most skilful painters were pleased or recommend this author to me. To be pleased in or with, to approve; to have complacency in. Matthew 3:17.

To please God, is to love his character and law and perform his will, so as to become the object of his approbation.

They that are in the flesh cannot please God. Romans 8:8.

PLEASE, verb intransitive s as z. To like; to choose; to prefer. Spirits, freed from mortal laws, with ease

Assume what sexes and what shapes they please

1. To condescend; to comply; to be pleased; a word of ceremony.

PLEASE you, lords, In sight of both our battles we may meet.

The first words that I learnt were, to express my desire that he would please to give me my liberty. PLEASE expresses less gratification than delight.

Pleasing

PLE'ASING, participle present tense Gratifying; exciting agreeable sensations or emotions in.

PLE'ASING, adjective Giving pleasure or satisfaction; agreeable to the senses or to the mind; as a pleasing prospect; a pleasing reflection; pleasing manners.

1. Gaining approbation. 1 John 3:1. PLE'ASING, noun The act of gratifying.

Poor

POOR, adjective [Latin pauper.]

1. Wholly destitute of property, or not having property sufficient for a comfortable subsistence; needy. It is often synonymous with indigent, and with necessitous, denoting extreme want; it is also applied to persons who are not entirely destitute of property, but are not rich; as a poor man or woman; poor people

2. In law, so destitute of property as to be entitled to maintenance from the public.

3. Destitute of strength, beauty or dignity; barren; mean; jejune; as a poor composition; a poor essay; a poor discourse.

4. Destitute of value, worth or importance; of little use; trifling.
That I have wronged no man, will be a poor plea or apology at the last day.

5. Paltry; mean; of little value; as a poor coat; a poor house.

6. Destitute of fertility; barren; exhausted; as poor land. The ground is become poor

7. Of little worth; unimportant; as in my poor opinion.

8. Unhappy; pitiable.
Vex'd sailors curse the rain
For which poor shepherds pray'd in vain

9. Mean; depressed; low; dejected; destitute of spirit.
A soothsayer made Antonius believe that his genius, which was otherwise brave, was, in the presence of Octavianus, poor and cowardly.

10. Lean; emaciated; as a poor horse. The ox is poor

11. Small, or of a bad quality; as a poor crop; a poor harvest.

12. Uncomfortable; restless; ill. The patient has had a poor night.

13. Destitute of saving grace. Revelation 3:17.

14. In general, wanting good qualities, or the qualities which render a thing valuable, excellent, proper, or sufficient for its purpose; as a poor pen; a poor ship; a poor carriage; poor fruit; poor bread; poor wine, etc.

15. A word of tenderness or pity; dear. POOR, little, pretty, fluttering thing.

16. A word of slight contempt; wretched.
The poor monk never saw many of the decrees and councils he had occasion to use.

17. The poor collectively, used as a noun; those who are destitute of property;

the indigent; the needy; in a legal sense, those who depend on charity or maintenance by the public.

I have observed the more public provisions are made for the poor the less they provide for themselves.

POOR in spirit, in a Scriptural sense, humble; contrite; abased in one's own sight by a sense of guilt. Matthew 5:3.

Possible

POS'SIBLE, adjective [Latin possibilis, from posse. See Power.]
That may be or exist; that may be now, or may happen or come to pass; that may be done; not contrary to the nature of things. It is possible that the Greeks and Turks may now be engaged in battle. It is possible that peace of Europe may continue a century. It is not physically possible that a stream should ascend a mountain, but it is possible that the Supreme Being may suspend a law of nature, that is, his usual course of proceeding. It is notpossible that 2 and 3 should be 7, or that the same action should be morally right and morally wrong. This word when pronounced with a certain emphasis, implies improbability. A thing is possible but very improbable.

Power

POW'ER, noun [The Latin has posse, possum, potes, potentia. The primary sense of the verb is to strain, to exert force.]
1. In a philosophical sense, the faculty of doing or performing any thing; the faculty of moving or of producing a change in something; ability or strength. A man raises his hand by his own power or by power moves another body. The exertion of power proceeds from the will, and in strictness, no being destitute of will or intelligence, can exert power power in man is active or speculative. Active power is that which moves the body; speculative power is that by which we see, judge, remember, or in general, by which we think. Power may exist without exertion. We have power to speak when we are silent. Power has been distinguished also into active and passive, the power of doing or moving, and the power of receiving impressions or of suffering. In strictness, passive power is an absurdity in terms. To say that gold has a powerto be melted, is improper language, yet for want of a more appropriate word,power is often used in a passive sense, and is considered as two-fold; viz.as able to make or able to receive any change.
2. Force; animal strength; as the power of the arm, exerted in lifting, throwing or holding.
3. Force; strength; energy; as the power of the mind, of the imagination, of the fancy. He has not powers of genius adequate to the work.
4. Faculty of the mind, as manifested by a particular mode of operation;

as the power of thinking, comparing and judging; the reasoning powers.

5. Ability, natural or moral. We say, a man has the power of doing good; his property gives him the power of relieving the distressed; or he has the powerto persuade others to do good; or it is not in his power to pay his debts. The moral power of man is also his power of judging or discerning in moral subjects.

6. In mechanics, that which produces motion or force, or which may be applied to produce it. Thus the inclined plane is called a mechanical power as it produces motion, although this in reality depends on gravity. The wheel and axle, and the lever, are mechanical powers, as they may be applied to produce force. These powers are also called forces, and they are of two kinds, movingpower and sustaining power

7. Force. The great power of the screw is of extensive use in compression. Thepower of steam is immense.

8. That quality in any natural body which

produces a change or makes an impression on another body; as the power of medicine; the power of heat; thepower of sound.

9. Force; strength; momentum; as the power of the wind, which propels a ship or overturns a building.

10. Influence; that which may move the mind; as the power of arguments or of persuasion.

11. Command; the right of governing, or actual government; dominion; rule, sway; authority. A large portion of Asia is under the power of the Russian emperor. The power of the British monarch is limited by law. The powers of government are legislative, executive, judicial, and ministerial. Power is no blessing in itself, but when it is employed to protect the innocent. Under this sense may be comprehended civil, political, ecclesiastical, and military power

12. A sovereign, whether emperor, king or

governing prince or the legislature of a state; as the powers of Europe; the great powers; the smaller powers. In this sense, the state or nation governed seems to be included in the wordpower Great Britain is a great naval power

13. One invested with authority; a ruler; a civil magistrate. Romans 13:1.

14. Divinity; a celestial or invisible being or agent supposed to have dominion over some part of creation; as celestial powers; the powers of darkness.

15. That which has physical power; an army; a navy; a host; a military force. Never such a power--Was levied in the body of a land.

16. Legal authority; warrant; as a power of attorney; an agent invested with ample power The envoy has full powers to negotiate a treaty.

17. In arithmetic and algebra, the product arising from the multiplication of

Power continue . . .

a number or quantity into itself; as, a cube is the third power; the biquadrate is the fourth power

18. In Scripture, right; privilege. John 1:12.

1 Corinthians 9:4.

19. Angels, good or bad. Colossians 1:11.

Ephesians 6:10.

20. Violence, force; compulsion. Ezekiel 4:1.

21. Christ is called the power of God, as through him and his gospel, God displays his power and authority in ransoming and saving sinners.

1 Corinthians 1:18.

22. The powers of heaven may denote the

celestial luminaries. Matthew 24:30.

23. Satan is said to have the power of death, as he introduced sin, the cause of death, temporal and eternal, and torments men with the feat of death and future misery.

24. In vulgar language, a large quantity; a great number; as a power of good things. [This is, I believe, obsolete, even among our common people.]

Power of attorney, authority given to a person to act for another.

Prosper

PROS'PER, verb transitive [Latin prospero, from prosperus, from the Gr. to carry to or toward; to bear.] To favor; to render successful.

All things concur to prosper our design.

PROS'PER, verb intransitive To be successful; to succeed.

The Lord made all that he did to prosper in his hand. Genesis 39:3.

He that covereth his sins, shall not prosper Proverbs 28:13.

1. To grow or increase; to thrive; to make gain; as, to prosper in business.

Our agriculture, commerce and manufactures now prosper

Prosperity

PROSPER'ITY, noun [Latin prosperitas.]

Advance or gain in any thing good or

desirable; successful progress in any

business or enterprise; success; attainment of the object desired;

as the prosperity of arts; agricultural or commercial prosperity; national prosperity Our disposition to abuse the blessings of providence renders prosperity dangerous.

The prosperity of fools shall destroy them. Proverbs 1:32.

Prudent

PRU'DENT, adjective Cautious; circumspect; practically wise; careful of the consequences of enterprises, measures or actions; cautious not to act

Prudent continue . . .

when the end is of doubtful utility, or probably impracticable.

The prudent man looketh well to his going. Proverbs 14:8.

A prudent man foreseeth the evil and hideth himself. Proverbs 22:3.

1. Dictated or directed by prudence; as prudent behavior.

2. Foreseeing by instinct; as the prudent crane.

3. Frugal; economical; as a prudent woman; prudent expenditure of money.

4. Wise; intelligent.

Quiet

QUI'ET, adjective [Latin quietus.]

1. Still; being in a state of rest; now moving. Judges 16:2.

2. Still; free from alarm or disturbance; unmolested; as a quiet life.

n his days the land was quiet ten years. 2 Chronicles 14:1.

3. Peaceable; not turbulent; not giving offense; not exciting controversy, disorder or trouble; mild; meek; contented.

The ornament of a meek and quiet spirit. 1 Peter 3:4.

1 Thessalonians 4:11.

4. Calm; not agitated by wind; as a quiet sea or atmosphere.

5. Smooth; unruffled.

6. Undisturbed; unmolested; as the quiet possession or enjoyment of an estate.

7. Not crying; not restless; as a quiet child.

QUI'ET, noun [Latin quies.]

1. Rest; repose; stillness; the state of a thing not in motion.

2. Tranquility; freedom from disturbance or alarm; civil or political repose.

Our country enjoys quiet

3. Peace; security. Judges 18:7.

QUI'ET, verb transitive

1. To stop motion; to still; to reduce to a state of rest; as, to quiet corporeal motion.

2. To calm; to appease; to pacify; to lull; to tranquilize; as, to quiet the soul when agitated; to quiet the passions; to quiet the clamors of a nation; to quietthe disorders of a city or town.

3. To allay; to suppress; as, to quiet pain or grief.

Receive

RECE'IVE, verb transitive [Latin recipio; re and capio, to take.]

1. To take, as a thing offered or sent; to accept. He had the offer of a donation, but he would not receive it.

2. To take as due or as a reward. He received the money on the day it was payable. He received ample compensation.

3. To take or obtain from another in any manner, and either good or evil. Shall we receive good at the hand of God, and shall we not receive evil? Job 2:10.

4. To take, as a thing communicated; as, to receive a wound by a shot; toreceive a disease by contagion.

The idea of a solidity we receive by our touch.

5. To take or obtain intellectually; as, to receive an opinion or notion from others.

6. To embrace.

Receive with meekness the engrafted word. James 1:7.

7. To allow; to hold; to retain; as a custom long received.

8. To admit.

Thou shalt guide me with thy counsel, and

afterward receive me to glory.Psalms 73:24.

9. To welcome; to lodge and entertain; as a guest.

They kindled a fire and received us every one, because of the present rain and because of the cold. Acts 28:2.

10. To admit into membership or fellowship.

Him that is weak in the faith, receive ye.

Romans 14:1.

11. To take in or on; to hold; to contain.

The brazen altar was too little to receive the burnt-offering. 1 Kings 8:64.

12. To be endowed with. Ye shall receive power after that the Holy Spirit has come upon you. Acts 1:8.

13. To take into a place or state.

After the Lord had spoken to them, he was received up into heaven. Mark 16:19.

14. To take or have as something ascribed; as, to receive praise or blame. Revelation 4:11. Revelation 5:12.

15. To bear with or suffer. 2 Corinthians 11:4.

16. To believe in. John 1:11.

17. To accept or admit officially or in an

official character. The minister was received by the emperor or court.

18. To take stolen goods from a thief, knowing them to be stolen.

Redemer

REDEE'MER, noun

1. One who redeems or ransoms.

2. The Savior of the world, JESUS CHRIST. Redeemed

Redeemed

REDEE'MED, participle passive Ransomed; delivered from bondage, distress, penalty, liability, or from the possession of another, by paying an equivalent.

Redeemer

REDEE'MER, noun

1. One who redeems or ransoms.

2. The Savior of the world, JESUS CHRIST.

Rich

RICH, adjective [Latin rego, regnum, Eng. reach, region, from extending.]

1. Wealthy; opulent; possessing a large portion of land, goods or money, or a larger portion than is common to other men or to men of like rank. A farmer may be rich with property which would not make a nobleman rich An annual income of 500 sterling pounds would make a rich vicar, but not a rich bishop. Men more willingly acknowledge others to be richer, than to be wiser than themselves.

Abram was very rich in cattle, in silver and in gold. Genesis 13:2.

2. Splendid; costly; valuable; precious; sumptuous; as a rich dress; a richborder; a rich silk; rich furniture; a rich present.

3. Abundant in materials; yielding great quantities of any thing valuable; as arich mine; rich ore.

4. Abounding in valuable ingredients or qualities; as a rich odor or flavor; richspices.

So we say, a rich description; a discourse rich in ideas.

5. Full of valuable achievements or works.

Each minute shall be rich in some great action.

6. Fertile; fruitful; capable of producing large crops or quantities; as a rich soil; rich land; rich mold.

7. Abundant; large; as a rich crop.

8. Abundant; affording abundance; plentiful.

The gorgeous East with richest hand pours on her sons barbaric pearl and gold.

9. Full of beautiful scenery; as a rich landscape; a rich prospect.

10. Abounding with elegant colors; as a rich picture.

11. Plentifully stocked; as pastures rich in flocks.

12. Strong; vivid; perfect; as a rich color.

13. Having something precious; as a grove of rich trees.

14. Abounding with nutritious qualities; as a rich diet.

15. Highly seasoned; as rich paste; a rich dish of food.

16. Abounding with a variety of delicious food; as a rich table or entertainment.

17. Containing abundance beyond wants; as a rich treasury.

18. In music, full of sweet or harmonious sounds.

Rich continue . . .

19. In Scripture, abounding; highly endowed with spiritual gifts; as rich in faith. James 2:5.

20. Placing confidence in outward prosperity. Matthew 19:23.

21. Self-righteous; abounding, in one's own opinion, with spiritual graces.Revelation 3:17.

RICH in mercy, spoken of God, full of mercy, and ready to bestow good things on sinful men.

Ephesians 2:4. Romans 10:12.

The rich used as a noun, denotes a rich man or person, or more frequently in the plural, rich men or persons.

The rich hath many friends. Proverbs 14:20.

RICH, verb transitive To enrich.

Righteousness

RIGHTEOUSNESS, noun ri'chusness.

1. Purity of heart and rectitude of life; conformity of heart and life to the divine law. righteousness as used in Scripture and theology, in which it is chiefly used, is nearly equivalent to holiness, comprehending holy principles and affections of heart, and conformity of life to the divine law. It includes all we call justice, honesty and virtue, with holy affections; in short, it is true religion.

2. Applied to God, the perfection or holiness of his nature; exact rectitude; faithfulness.

3. The active and passive obedience of Christ, by which the law of God is fulfilled. Daniel 9:7.

4. Justice; equity between man and man. Luke 1:75.

5. The cause of our justification.

The Lord our righteousness Jeremiah 23:6.

Rock

ROCK, noun [Gr., Latin rupes, from the root of rumpo, to break or burst. If this is not the origin of rock I know not to what root to assign it.]

1. A large mass of stony matter, usually compounded of two or more simple minerals, either bedded in the earth or resting on its surface. Sometimes rocks compose the principal part of huge mountains; sometimes hugh rocks lie on the surface of the earth, in detached blocks or masses. Under this term, mineralogists class all mineral substances, coal, gypsum, salt, etc.

2. In Scripture, figuratively, defense; means of safety; protection; strength; asylum. The Lord is my rock 2 Samuel 22:2.

3. Firmness; a firm or immovable foundation. Psalms 28:1. Matthew 7:24. Matthew 16:18.

4. A species of vulture or condor.

5. A fabulous bird in the Eastern tales.

ROCK, noun
A distaff used in spinning; the staff or frame about which flax is arranged, from which the thread is drawn in spinning.

ROCK, verb transitive
1. To move backward and forward, as a body resting on a foundation; as, torock a cradle; to rock a chair; to rock a mountain. It differs from shake, as denoting a slower and more uniform motion, or larger movements. t differs from swing, which expresses a vibratory motion of something suspended. A rising earthquake rock'd the ground.
2. To move backwards and forwards in a cradle, chair, etc.; as, to rock a child to sleep.
3. To lull to quiet. Sleep rock thy brain. [Unusual.]

ROCK, verb intransitive To be moved backwards and forwards; to reel.
The rocking town supplants their footsteps.

Season

SE'ASON. noun se'zn.Season literally signifies that which comes or arrives; and in this general sense, is synonymous with time. Hence,
1. A fit or suitable time; the convenient time; the usual or appointed time; as, the messenger arrived in season; in good season. This fruit is out of season.
2. Any time, as distinguished from others.
The season prime for sweetest scents and airs. Milton.
3. A time of some continuance, but not long.
Thou shalt be blind, not seeing the sun for a season. Acts 13:11.
4. One of the four divisions of the year, spring, summer, autumn, winter.
Theseason is mild; it is cold for the season.
We saw in six days' traveling, the several seasons of the year n their beauty. Addison.
We distinguish the season by prefixing its appropriate name, as the spring-season, summer-seacon, etc.
To be in season, to be in good time, or sufficiently early for the prupose.
To be out of season, to be too late, beyoun the proper time, or beyond the usually appointed time.
From the sense of convenience, is derived the following.
5. That which matures or prepares for the taste; that which gives a relish.
You lack the season of all nature, sleep. Shak. But in this sense, we now use seasoning.

SE'ASON, verb transitive
1. To render palatable, or to give a higher relish to, by the addition or mixture of another substance more pungent or pleasant; as, to season meat with salt; to season any thing with spices. Leviticus 2:13.
2. To render more agreeable, pleasant or delightful; to give relish or zest to

by something that excites, animates or exhilarates.

You season still with sports your serious hours. Dryden.

The proper use of wit is to season conversation. Tillotson.

3. To render more agreeable, or less rigorous and severe; to temper; to moderate; to qualify by admixture. When mercy seasons justice. Shak.

4. To imbue; to tinge or taint. Season their younger years with prudent and pious principles. Taylor.

5. To fit any use by time or habit; to mature; to prepare. Who in want a hollow friend doth try, Directly seasons him an enemy. Shak.

6. To prepare for use by drying or hardening; to take out or suffer to escape the natural juices; as, to season timber.

7. To prepare or mature for a climate; to accustom to and enable to endure; as, to season the body to a particular climate. Long residence in the West Indies, or a fever, may season strangers.

SE'ASON, verb intransitive

1. To become mature; to grow fit for use; to become adapted to a climate, as the human body.

2. To become dry and hard by the escape of natural juices, or by being penetrated with other substances. Timber seasons well under cover in the air, and ship timber seasons in salt water.

3. To betoken; to savor.

Seek

SEEK, verb transitive pret and participle passive sought, pronounced sawt. [L.sequor, to follow; for to seek is to go after, and the primary sense is to advance, to press, to drive forward, as in the L. peto.]

1. To go in searh or quest of; to look for; to search for by going from place to place. The man asked him, saying, what seekest thou? And he said, I seek my brethen. Genesis 37:16.

2. To inquire for; to ask for; to solicit; to endeavor to find or gain by any means. The young lions roar after their prey, and seek their meat from God. Psalms 104:21.

He found no place for repentance, though he sought it carefully with tears.Hebrews 12:1

Others tempting him, sought of him a sign. Luke 11:9.

3.Seek is followed sometimes by out or after. To seek out, properly implies to look for a specific thing among a number. But in general, the use of out andafter with seek, is unnecessary and inelegant. To seek God, his name, or his face, in Scripture, to ask for his favor, direction and assistance. Psalms 83:16. God seeks men, when he fixes his love on them, and by his word and Spirit, and the righteousness of Christ, reclaims and recovers them from their miserable condition as sinners. Ezekiel 34:6. Psa 119. Luke 15:8. To seek after the life, or soul, to attempt by arts or machinations; or to attempt to destroy or ruin. Psalms 35.

To seek peace, or judgement, to endeavor to promote it; or to practice it. Psa 34. Isaiah 1:17.

To seek an altar, temple, or habitation, to frequent it; to restore to it often. 2 Chronicles 1:1. Amos 5:4.

To seek out God's works, to endeavor to understand them. Psa 111.

SEEK, v. i.

1. To make search or inquiry; to endeavor to make discovery.

Seek ye out of the book of the Lord. Isaiah 34:16.

2. To endeavor.

Ask not what pains, nor further seek to know Their process, or the forms of law below. Dryden.

To seek after, to make pursuit; to attempt to find or take. [See No. 3 supra.]

To seek for, to endeavor to find. Knolles.

To seek to, to apply to; to resort to. 1 Kings 10:1.

To seek, at a loss; without knowledge, measures or experience.

Unpractic'd, unprepar'd and still to seek. Milton. [This phrase, I believe, is wholly obsolete.]

Serve

SERVE, verb transitive serv. [Latin servio. This verb is supposed to be from the noun servus, a servant or slave, and this from servo, to keep.]

1. To work for; to bestow the labor of boky and mind in the employment of another.

Jacob loved Rachel and said, I will serve thee seven years for Rachel thy youngest daughters. Genesis 29:15. No man can serve two masters. Matthew 6:24.

2. To act as the minister of; to perform official duties to; as, a minister serveshis prince. Had I served God as diligently as I have served the king, he would not have given me over in my gray hairs. Cardinal Woolsey.

3. To attend at command; to wait on. A goddess among gods, ador'd and serv'd By anbels numberless, thy daily train. Milton.

4. To obey servilely or meanly. be not to wealth a servant.

5. To supply with food; as, to be served in plate.

6. To be subservient or subordinate to.

Bodies bright and greater should not serve The less not bright. Milton.

7. To perform the duties required in; as, the curate served two churches.

8. To obey; to perform duties in the employment of; as, to serve the king or the country in the army or navy.

9. To be sufficient, or to promote; as, to serve one's turn, end or purpose.

10. To help by good offices; as, to serve one's country.

11. To comply with; to submit to. They think herein we serve the time, because thereby we either hold or seek preferment. Hooker.

12. To be sufficient for; to satisfy; to content. One half pint bottle serves them both to dine, And is at once their vinegar and wine. Pope.

13. To be in the place of any thing to one. A sofa serves the Turks for a seat and a couch.

14. To treat; to requite; as, he served me ungratefully; he served me very ill; We say also, he served me a trick, that is he deceived me, or practiced an artifice on me.

15. In Scripture and theology, to obey and worship; to act in conformity to the law of a superior, and treat him with due reverence.

Fear the Lord and serve him in sincerity and truth. As for me and my house, we will serve the lord. Joshua 24:14.

16. In a bad sense, to obey; to yeild compliance or act according to. Serving divers lusts and treasures. Titus 3:1.

17. To worship; to render homage to; as, to serve idols or false gods.

18. To be a slave to; to be in bondage to.

19. To serve one's self of, to use; to make use of; a Gallicism, [se sevir de.] I will serve myself of this concession. Chillingworh.

20. To use; to manage; to apply. The guns are well served.

21. In seamen's language, to wind something round a rope to prevent friction.

To serve up, to prepare and present in a dish; as, to serve up a sirloin of beef in plate; figuratively, to prepare. To serve in, as used by Shakespeare, for to bring in, as meat by an attendant, I have never to be used in America. To serve out, to distribute in portions; as, to serve out provisions to soldiers. To serve a writ, to read it to the defendant; or to leave an attested copy at his usual place of abode.

To serve an attachment, or writ of attachment, to levy it on the or goods by seizure; or to seize.

To serve an execution, to levy it on lands, goods or person by seizure or taking possession. To serve a warrant, to read it, and to seize the person against whom it is issued. In general, to serve a process, is to read it so as to give due notice to the party concerned, or to leave an attested copy with him or his attorney, or at his usual place of abode.

To serve an office, to discharge a public duty. [This phrase, I believe, is not used in America. We say, a man serves in an office, that is, serves the public in an office.]

SERVE, verb intransitive serv.

1. To be a servant or slave.

The Lord shall give thee rest from thy sorrow, and from thy fear, and from the hard bondage wherein thou wast made to serve Isaiah 14:3.

2. To be employed in labor or or other business for another.

3. To be in subjection.

4. To wait; to attend; to perform domestic offices to another.

5. To perform duties, as in the army, navy or in any office. An officer ervesfive years in India, or under a particular commander. The late cretary of the colony, and afterwards state, of Connecticut, was annually appointed, andserved in the office sixty years.

6. To answer; to accomplish the end. She feared that all would not serve. Sidney.

7. To be sufficient for a purpose. This little brand will serve to light your fire. Dryden.

8. To suit; to be convenient. Take this, and use it as occasion serves.

9. To conduce; to be of use. Our victory only served to lead us on to other visionary prospects. Swift.

10. To officiate or minister; to do the honors of; as, to serve at a public dinner.

Soul

SOUL, noun

1. The spiritual, rational and immortal substance in man, which distinguishes him from brutes; that part of man which enables him to think and reason, and which renders him a subject of moral government. The immortality of the soulis a fundamental article of the christian system. Such is the nature of the human soul that it must have a God, an object of supreme affection.

2. The understanding; the intellectual principle. The eyes of our soul then only begin to see, when our bodily eye are closing.

3. Vital principle. Thou son, of this great world both eye and soul

4. Spirit; essence; chief part; as charity, the soul of all the virtues. Emotion is the soul of eloquence.

5. Life; animation principle or part; as, an able commander is the soul of an army.

6. Internal power. There is some soul of goodness in things evil.

7. A human being; a person. There was no a soul present. In Paris there are more than seven hundred thousand souls. London, Westminster, Southwark and the suburbs, are said to contain twelve hundred thousand souls.

8. Animal life. To deliver their soil from death, and to keep them alive in amine. Psalms 33:7.

9. Active power. And heaven would fly before the driving soul

10. Spirit; courage; fire; grandeur of mind. That he wants caution he must needs confess, but not a soul to give our arms success.

11. Generosity; nobleness of mind; a colloquial use.

12. An intelligent being. Every soul in heav'n shall bend the knee.

13. Heart; affection. The soul of Jonathan was knit with the soul of David. I Sam. 18.

14. In Scripture, appetite; as the full soul; the hungry soul Proverbs 27:7. Job 33:18.

Soul continue . . .
15. A familiar compellation of a person, but often expressing some qualities of the mind; as alas, poor soul; he was a good soul
SOUL, verb transitive To endure with a soul [Not in use.]
SOUL, SOWL, verb intransitive To afford suitable sustenance. [Not in use.]

Strength
STRENGTH, noun [See Strong.]
1. That property or quality of an animal body by which it is enabled to move itself or other bodies. We say, a sick man has not strength to walk, or to raise his head or his arm. We say, a man has strength to lift a weight, or to draw it. This quality is called also power and force. But force is also used to denote the effect of strength exerted, or the quantity of motion. strength in this sense, is positive, or the power of producing positive motion or action, and is opposed to weakness.
2. Firmness; solidity or toughness; the quality of bodies by which they sustain the application of force without breaking or yielding. Thus we speak of thestrength of a bone, the strength of a beam, the strength of a wall, the strengthof a rope. In this sense, strength is a passive quality, and is opposed to weakness or frangibility.
3. Power or vigor of any kind.
This act shall crush the strength of Satan.
STRENGTH there must be either of love or war.
4. Power of resisting attacks; fastness; as the strength of a castle or fort.
5. Support; that which supports; that which supplies strength; security.
God is our refuge and strength Psalms 46:1.
6. Power of mind; intellectual force; the power of any faculty; as strength of memory; strength of reason; strength of judgment.
7. Spirit; animation.
Me thinks I feel new strength within me rise.
8. Force of writing; vigor; nervous diction. The strength of words, of style, of expression and the like, consists in the full and forcible exhibition of ideas, by which a sensible or deep impression is made on the mind of a hearer or reader. It is distinguished from softness or sweetness. strength of language enforces an argument, produces conviction, or excites wonder or other strong emotion; softness and sweetness give pleasure.
And praise the easy vigor of a line, where Denhams strength and Wellers sweetness join.
9. Vividness; as strength of colors or coloring.
10. Spirit; the quality of any liquor which has the power of affecting the taste, or of producing sensible effects on other bodies; as the strength of wine or spirit; the strength of an acid.
11. The virtue or spirit of any vegetable, or of its juices or qualities.
12. Legal or moral force; validity; the quality of binding, uniting or securing;

Strength continue . . .

as the strength of social or legal obligations; the strength of law; the strength of public opinion or custom.

13. Vigor; natural force; as the strength of natural affection.

14. That which supports; confidence.

The allies, after a successful summer, are too apt upon the strength of it to neglect preparation for the ensuing campaign.

15. Amount of force, military or naval; an army or navy; number of troops or ships well appointed. What is the strength of the enemy by land, or by sea?

16. Soundness; force; the quality that convinces, persuades or commands assent; as the strength of an argument or of reasoning; the strength of evidence.

17. Vehemence; force proceeding from motion and proportioned to it; as thestrength of wind or a current of water.

18. Degree of brightness or vividness; as the strength of light.

19. Fortification; fortress; as an inaccessible strength [Not in use.]

20. Support; maintenance of power.

What they boded would be a mischief to us, you are providing shall be one of our principal strengths. [Not used.]

STRENGTH, verb intransitive To strengthen. [Not in use.]

Strengthen

STRENGTHEN, verb transitive

1. To make strong or stronger; to add strength to, either physical, legal or moral; as, to strengthen a limb; to strengthen an obligation.

2. To confirm; to establish; as, to strengthen authority.

3. To animate; to encourage; to fix in resolution.

Charge Joshua, and encourage him, and strengthen him. Deuteronomy 3:28.

4. To cause to increase in power or security.

Let noble warwick, Cobham and the rest, with powerful policy strengthen themselves.

STRENGTHEN, verb intransitive To grow strong or stronger.

The disease that shall destroy at length, grows with his growth, and strengthens with his strength.

Grows with his growth, and strengthens with his strength.

Strong

STRONG, adjective [G., Latin The sense of the radical word is to stretch, strain, draw, and probably from the root of stretch and reach.]

1. Having physical active power, or great physical power; having the power of exerting great bodily force; vigorous. A patient is recovering from sickness, but is not yet strong enough to walk. A strong man will lift twice his own weight.

That our oxen may be strong to labor. Psalms 144:14.

Orses the strong to greater strength must yield.

2. Having physical passive power; having ability to bear or endure; firm; solid;

Strong continue . . .

as a constitution strong enough to bear the fatigues of a campaign.

3. Well fortified; able to sustain attacks; not easily subdued or taken; as astrong fortress or town.

4. Having great military or naval force; powerful; as a strong army or fleet; astrong nation; a nation strong at sea.

5. Having great wealth, means or resources; as a strong house or company of merchants.

6. Moving with rapidity; violent; forcible; impetuous; as a strong current of water or wind; the wind was strong from the northeast; we had a strong tide against us.

7. Hale; sound; robust; as a strong constitution.

8. Powerful; forcible; cogent; adapted to make a deep or effectual impression on the mind or imagination; as a strong argument; strong reasons; strong evidence; a strong example or instance. He used strong language.

9. Ardent; eager; zealous; earnestly engaged; as a strong partisan; a strong whig or tory.

Her mother, ever strong against that match--

10. Having virtues of great efficacy; or having a particular quality in a great degree; as a strong powder or tincture; a strong decoction; strong tea; strong coffee.

11. Full of spirit; intoxicating; as strong liquors.

12. Affecting the sight forcibly; as strong colors.

13. Affecting the taste forcibly; as the strong flavor of onions.

14. Affecting the smell powerfully; as a strong scent.

15. Not of easy digestion; solid; as strong meat. Hebrews 5:7.

16. Well established; firm; not easily overthrown or altered; as a custom grown strong by time.

17. Violent; vehement; earnest.

Who in the day of his flesh, when he offered up prayers with strong crying and tears - Hebrews 5:7.

18. Able; furnished with abilities.

I was stronger in prophecy than in criticism.

19. Having great force of mind, of intellect or of any faculty; as a man of strong powers of mind; a man of a strong mind or intellect; a man of strong memory, judgment or imagination.

20. Having great force; comprising much in few words.

Like her sweet voice is thy harmonious song, as high, as sweet, as easy and as strong

21. Bright; glaring; vivid; as a strong light.

22. Powerful to the extent of force named; as an army ten thousand strong.

Teach

TEACH, verb transitive preterit tense and participle passive taught. [Latin doceo; dico, dicto, and both these and the Gr. to show, may be of one family; all implying sending, passing, communicating, or rather leading, drawing.

1. To instruct; to inform; to communicate to another the knowledge of that of which he was before ignorant.

He will teach us of his ways, and we will walk in his paths. Isaiah 2:3.

Lord, teach us to pray, as John also taught his disciples. Luke 11:1.

2. To deliver any doctrine, art, principles or words for instruction. One sect of ancient philosophers taught the doctrines of stoicism, another those of epicureanism.

In vain they worship me, teaching for doctrines the commandments of men.Matthew 15:1.

3. To tell; to give intelligence.

4. To instruct, or to practice the business of an instructor; to use or follow the employment of a preceptor; as, a man teaches school for a livelihood.

5. To show; to exhibit so as to impress on the mind.

If some men teach wicked things, it must be that others may practice them.

6. To accustom; to make familiar.

They have taught their tongue to speak lies. Jeremiah 9:20.

7. To inform or admonish; to give previous notice to.

For he taught his disciples, and said--Mark 9:1.

8. To suggest to the mind.

For the Holy Spirit shall teach you in that same hour what ye ought to say.Luke 12:12.

9. To signify or give notice.

He teacheth with his fingers. Proverbs 6:13.

10. To counsel and direct. Habakkuk 2:19.

TEACH, verb intransitive To practice giving instruction; to perform the business of a preceptor.

The heads thereof judge for reward, and the priests thereof teach for hire.Micah 3:11.

TEACH, noun In sugar works, the last boiler.

Testimony

TEST'IMONY, noun [Latin testimonium.] A solemn declaration or affirmation made for the purpose of establishing or proving some fact. Such affirmation in judicial proceedings, may be verbal or written, but must be under oath. testimony differs from evidence; testimony is the declaration of a witness, and evidence is the effect of that declaration on the mind, or the degree of light which it affords.

1. Affirmation; declaration. These doctrines are supported by the uniform

Testimony continue . . .

testimony of the fathers. The belief of past facts must depend on the evidence of human testimony or the testimony of historians.

2. Open attestation; profession.

Thou for the testimony of truth hast borne
Universal reproach.

3. Witness; evidence; proof of some fact.

Shake off the dust under your feet, for a testimony against them. Mark 6:11

4. In Scripture, the two tables of the law.

Thou shalt put into the ark the testimony which I shall give thee. Exodus 25:16.

5. The book of the law.

He brought forth the king's son--and gave him the testimony 2 Kings 11:12.

6. The gospel, which testifies of Christ and declares the will of God.

1 Corinthians 2:1. 2 Timothy 1:8.

7. The ark. Exodus 16:34.

8. The word of God; the Scriptures.

The testimony of the Lord is sure, making wise the simple Psalms 19:7.

9. The laws or precepts of God. 'I love thy testimonies.' 'I have kept thy testimonies.'

10. That which is equivalent to a declaration; manifestation.

Sacrifices were appointed by God for a testimony of his hatred of sin.

11. Evidence suggested to the mind; as the testimony of conscience. 2 Corinthians 1:12.

12. Attestation; confirmation.

TEST'IMONY, verb transitive To witness. [Not in use.]

Thanks

THANKS, noun generally in the plural. Expression of gratitude; an acknowledgment made to express a sense of favor or kindness received. Gratitude is the feeling or sentiment excited by kindness; thanks are the expression of that sentiment. Luke 6:1.

THANKS be to God, who giveth us the victory. 1 Corinthians 15:57.

THANKS be to God for his unspeakable gift. 2 Corinthians 9:15.

He took bread and gave thanks to God. Acts 27:35.

Trust

TRUST, noun

1. Confidence; a reliance or resting of the mind on the integrity, veracity, justice, friendship or other sound principle of another person.

He that putteth his trust in the Lord shall be safe. Proverbs 29:25.

2. He or that which is the ground of confidence.

O Lord God, thou art my trust from my youth. Psalms 71:1.

Trust continue . . .

3. Charge received in confidence.
Reward them well, if they observe their trust

4. That which is committed to one's care. Never violate a sacred trust

5. Confident opinion of any event.
His trust was with th' Eternal to be deem'd
Equal in strength.

6. Credit given without examination; as, to take opinions on trust

7. Credit on promise of payment, actual or implied; as, to take or purchase goods on trust

8. Something committed to a person's care for use or management, and for which an account must be rendered. Every man's talents and advantages are a trust committed to him by his Maker, and for the use or employment of which he is accountable.

9. Confidence; special reliance on supposed honesty.

10. State of him to whom something is entrusted.
 serve him truly, that will put me in trust

11. Care; management. 1 Timothy 6:17.

12. In law, an estate, devised or granted in confidence that the devisee or grantee shall convey it, or dispose of the profits, at the will of another; an estate held for the use of another.

TRUST, verb transitive To place confidence in; to rely on. We cannot trust those who have deceived us.
He that trusts every one without reserve, will at last be deceived.

1. To believe; to credit.
TRUST me, you look well.

2. To commit to the care of, in confidence. trust your Maker with yourself and all your concerns.

3. To venture confidently.
Fool'd by thee, to trust thee from my side.

4. To give credit to; to sell to upon credit, or in confidence of future payment. The merchants and manufacturers trust their customers annually with goods to the value of millions.
It is happier to be sometimes cheated, than not to trust

TRUST, verb intransitive To be confident of something present or future.
 trust to come to you, and speak face to face. 2 John 1:12.
We trust we have a good conscience. Hebrews 13:18.

1. To be credulous; to be won to confidence.
Well, you may fear too far
Safer than trust too far.

To trust in, to confide in; to place confidence in; to rely on; a use frequent in the Scriptures.
TRUST in the Lord, and do good. Psalms 37:3.
They shall be greatly ashamed that trust in graven images. Isaiah 42:17.
To trust to, to depend on; to have confidence in; to rely on.

323

Trust continue . . .
The men of Israel--trusted to the liars in wait.
Judges 20:36.

Unbelief
UNBELIE'F, noun
1. Incredulity; the withholding of belief; as, unbelief is blind.
2. Infidelity; disbelief of divine revelation.
3. In the New Testament, disbelief of the truth of the gospel, rejection of Christ as the Savior of men, and of the doctrines he taught; distrust of God' promises and faithfulness, etc. Matthew 13:58. Mark 16:14. Hebrews 3:12. Romans 4:20.
4. Weak faith. Mark 9:24.

Understanding
UNDERSTAND'ING, participle present tense
1. Comprehending; apprehending the ideas or sense of another, or of a writing; learning or being informed.
2. adjective Knowing; skillful. He is an understanding man.
UNDERSTAND'ING, noun
1. The faculty of the human mind by which it apprehends the real state of things presented to it, or by which it receives or comprehends the ideas which others express and intend to communicate. The understanding is called also the intellectual faculty. It is the faculty by means of which we obtain a great part of our knowledge. Luke 24:45. Ephesians 1:18.
By understanding I mean that faculty whereby we are enabled to apprehend the objects of knowledge, generals or particulars, absent or present, and to judge of their truth or falsehood, good or evil.
There is a spirit in man, and the inspiration of the Almighty giveth him understanding Job 32:8.
2. Knowledge; exact comprehension.
Right understanding consists in the perception of the visible or probably agreement or disagreement of ideas.
3. Intelligence between two or more persons; agreement of minds; union of sentiments. There is a good understanding between the minister and his people.

Verily
VER'ILY, adverb [from very.]
1. In truth; in fact; certainly.
2. Really; truly; with great confidence. It was verily thought the enterprise would succeed.